A TIME TO WEEP,
A TIME TO SING

A TIME TO WEEP,
A TIME TO SING

Faith Journeys of
Women Scholars of Religion

Edited by Mary Jo Meadow
and Carole A. Rayburn

WINSTON PRESS

Library of Congress Catalog Card Number: 85-50227

ISBN: 0-86683-791-4

Printed in the United States of America

5 4 3 2 1

Winston Press, Inc.
430 Oak Grove
Minneapolis, Minnesota 55403

For Frances Mabel Strupper Wiesner
(1912-1982),
mother of the first editor,
whose own faith journey is now complete.

Contents

Preface

Writing autobiography is, in many ways, both an instructive and paradoxical endeavor. The act of trying to recount our life experiences for others involves us in "recreating" our life. Each time we tell our story, we tell it from our current perspectives, emphasizing those features now highly relevant to us and neglecting—even "forgetting"—those not now salient. When the autobiographical endeavor is topical—as in these tellings of our faith journeys—we share much of our current spiritual perspectives in our selection of the details to which we attend. We build for ourselves and the reader what seems to us a congruent account that makes sense of where we now find ourselves.

We invite you to read our accounts in the same spirit of adventure and discovery with which we wrote them. Of course, they are not necessarily exactly historically accurate, although we tried to make them so. And they overlook what may have been potent formative influences on us in our eagerness to share those that now seem important. If in the future we again write autobiographically, we will undoubtedly choose some different emphases. However, these sharings impose meaning on our lives as we now see them.

The accounts are in no specific order so you should dip in where you wish and move about as you feel inclined. However, a book like this is best digested in small amounts. Perhaps it might most appropriately sit on a bedside table for a brief dip in the evening—or travel in a tote bag for the fifteen- to twenty-minute periods of waiting that come our way. To try to swallow several lives in one sitting is to invite failure to comprehend the pattern of all, as diverse events and ideas confusedly blend with each other.

So we invite you to ponder our lives slowly and meditatively. We hope that our sharings will bring you enjoyment and will help you in whatever spiritual endeavor you are now engaging. May they be truly re-creational for you in the fullest sense of the word. And may your own journey—wherever it is leading you—bear fruit and guide you to what you are seeking!

The editors want to thank our project editor Hermann Weinlick and also Jan Johnson and Pamela Johnson of Winston who helped the project along with advice and support. Finally, we are most grateful to our authors who in these pages have shared their lives and themselves.

Mary Jo Meadow
February 1985

A TIME TO WEEP,
A TIME TO SING

JILL RAITT

Jill Raitt is Professor of Religious Studies and Chairwoman of the Department of Religious Studies at the University of Missouri-Columbia. She served as national secretary of the American Academy of Religion from 1972 to 1975 and then as President in 1980-1981. Her area of scholarly research has been medieval and reformation theology. Her recent books are *Shapers of Religious Traditions in Germany, Switzerland and Poland, 1550-1600* (Yale University Press, 1981) and *The Spirituality of the Middle Ages and Reformation* (Volume 17 of the World Spirituality series) to be published by Crossroad Press in 1985. She has lectured on the subject of women and religion and published two articles on the subject in the *Journal of the American Academy of Religion*: "The Vagina Dentata and the Immaculatus Uterus Divini Fontis" (September 1980, pp. 415-431) and "Strictures and Structures: Relational Theology and a Woman's Contribution to Theological Conversation" (Volume 50, Number 1, 1981, pp. 3-17).

Deserts, Glades, and Precipices

As a rather wild Californian given to crossing whatever lay before me to see what was on the other side, I had the advantage of growing up without a specific religious tradition but with a very definite religious orientation. Whether I was sitting beside the sea near Santa Monica, California, or riding across the upper deserts of Arizona checking fences and cattle on a 40,000-acre ranch, God was never far from my thoughts and pursuits. It was on that ranch that I learned the cowboy's prayer, which I still remember and which in some way continues to sum up my attitude. It says,

O Lord, I've never lived where churches grow.
I love creation better as it stood that day you finished it
    so long ago and looked upon your work and called it
    good.
I've never found you in the light that's filtered down
    through tinted windowpanes,
But you seem near to me tonight in the dim quiet starlight
    of the plains.

The poem continues, but the reader can see my basic attitude. In the heart of a flower, in a star, in the wide sweep of a desert horizon, in the rhythms of the earth and the rhythm of a horse's hooves, I found ample evidence of a creator near enough to engage my whole self. It was also on a ranch in Arizona, at the age of sixteen, that I engaged in arguments with a Roman Catholic who predicted my conversion, which of course I resisted. But my rides to the top of an Arizona "hogback" soon involved my stopping and staring a long time at the reflected lights of Phoenix ninety miles away, with the thought that somewhere in Phoenix was a Catholic church, and within that Catholic church was a tabernacle, and within that tabernacle was a consecrated host from which radiated the strength of the presence of God. Focusing on the heart of a flower, sleeping under the stars, singing to the God of nature now became a concentration on the presence of God in the Eucharist. And true to my adversary's prediction, at the end of my sophomore year at Radcliffe College, I was baptized on Holy Saturday. That night, to compound the intensity of the situation, I was one of the Harvard-Radcliffe Chorale that sang the St. Matthew Passion with Charles Münch conducting the Boston Symphony Orchestra.

Becoming a "Roman" was a matter of literal definition when that following summer I traveled to Rome with a friend to attend a wedding. I got the idea while there that it would be a shame simply to come home again, and so I found a job working in a family, taking care of children. I remained in Rome for nine months studying philosophy and theology at the General House of the Society of Jesus. During those nine months I decided that God was calling me to religious life and specifically to the Society of the Sacred Heart of Jesus. Thereupon, since I was not at all sure that it would be possible for me to live wholly in the company of women for the rest of my life, I transferred from Radcliffe College, where I had been intensely happy, to San Francisco College for Women, which was run by the Religious of the Sacred Heart of Jesus. I found there intellectual women professors, strong, able, and quite different from the stereotypes of women, and especially of nuns, that I had imbibed from the general culture. I began to reverse my notion that most women—I being an exception of course—were involved in trivia and decided that, in fact, I could spend my life in a situation that excluded the company of men. Upon graduation I entered the Society of the Sacred Heart of Jesus and spent the next eleven years in the cloister, first in upper New York State, then in California, followed by two years studying in Rome. Upon my return to California, I found that I had achieved, in a sense, whatever goals had been presented and also discovered that the California government of the Society of the Sacred Heart of Jesus was quite different from that which I had experienced in New York and Rome. I therefore left "religious life" in the summer of 1964 with papal permission and continued my theological education at

Marquette University. When I left the convent, I hoped to marry, but while I enjoyed many friendships with men, some of them quite close, none eventuated in marriage. Although I would still like to share my life with a family of my own, I realize that had I married, my life, which has been rich and full, would have been quite different.

So far, I have not mentioned my father, mother, and brother. What sort of parents would allow a daughter to quit high school to work on a cattle ranch and then, a few years later, see her convert to a "foreign religion" and then allow her to leave a prestigious college in order to spend a year supporting herself in Rome? The answer is simply, "Very trusting parents." Why they were so trusting is a bit of a mystery, since I had not been an ideal child. In fact, my excessive independence was demonstrated at two years of age when I ran away and was brought home in a police car. At twelve, I packed my sleeping bag with dried soup, soap, and a towel and prepared to ride my recently acquired horse over the hills of Eagle Rock to some ranch that I imagined must lie on the other side. Actually, Glendale lay on one side of Eagle Rock and Pasadena on the other, so it was fortunate that instead I went off to Murrieta, California, to a new school founded by the parents of my best friend. There I helped in the kitchen, found colts to break, worked in the watermelon and onion fields, and studied by the light of a kerosene lamp. The school lasted two years and I returned home, which was now on the beach at Malibu La Costa, and to the eleventh grade at Santa Monica High School. It was between the eleventh and twelfth grades that I took off a year to work on the Quarter Circle V Bar Ranch thirty miles from Prescott, Arizona. (The ranch is now Orme School; then it also had a small school, but my interest was in the horses and cattle.) My brother was quite a different sort of person, a football player, a party-goer, and, until he joined the army, an indifferent scholar. Since then, he has done well as an engineer, raising his four sons in California's San Fernando valley.

I attribute to my peregrinations my excellent relations with my parents as a teenager. Since I was home only for two of my teen years, I appreciated home as others, who experienced it as something stifling, may not. My mother and I developed a relationship that has outlasted her death October 1, 1975. She is still much missed nine years later. I remember as a child going downtown with her on the big red streetcar, and ever after we enjoyed shopping together. When my father died in 1972, my mother and I combined households. We were good friends as well as mother and daughter, and I was determined that her last years would be as happy as I could make them. The house I bought in Durham, N.C., when we moved there in 1973 was decorated and furnished for her. She loved to watch the birds in the woods behind the house, and when I was away, she had the constant and faithful companionship of her big golden dog, Biff, and my bright-eyed intelligent German shepherd, Rapunzel. Both of us loved animals, even though my mother was very much of a city person. How can I communicate the strength and depth of my love for my mother? Perhaps by telling you that I was infuriated by the book *My Mother, My Self.* I am equally angered by the constant Freudian blaming of the mother. I simply find it all untrue of my mother and myself.

But let us return to my life after the convent. In 1965, with an M.A. and very good courses from Bernard Cooke behind us, four of us Catholics migrated from Marquette University to the University of Chicago, where we were among the first Roman Catholics to enter the Divinity School. It was an exciting, invaluable four years, and my devotion to the Divinity School, to friends I met there, to its faculty, and to its method of education remains a focal point in my life.

In 1969, with all but the conclusion of my dissertation completed, I took a job at the University of California-Riverside as the foundation stone in a new program of religious studies. Jeffrey Russell and Ed Gaustad were my mentors, and excellent ones they were. The program thrived, we added two more faculty and had classes of 100-200 students, and I found there a spirit of collegiality that remained, with the collegiality at Chicago, a model for academic life. There was only one difficulty at Riverside: In my four years there, I taught twenty-two different courses in order to meet the needs of our growing program and its majors. I felt spread far too thin, and that, together with the smog and ever present destructive motorcyclists, made an invitation from the Divinity School at Duke University very appealing. From 1973 to 1981 I was an associate professor at Duke University, where I could more narrowly concentrate my academic effort in medieval and reformation studies.

At Duke I became aware of what it can mean to be a woman in academia. The women students in the Divinity School, who were at that time 25% of the student body, asked for a course on "women, religion and theology," which I taught in the fall of 1973 and continued to teach nearly every year. Teaching this course was an education that rocked the depths of my being. I had been unaware of what had been done to women in patriarchal religion. Until then, I had escaped from the effects that women usually suffer. My career had been uniformly successful. At Duke I not only taught the course, "Women, Religion and Theology" but began to experience what other women experience. I was the first and only woman on the Divinity School faculty of thirty men for the full eight years. It was an education that does not bear repeating. During those difficult years, I found some support from good friends on the faculty, the women students, and, toward the end, men students. What gave me most strength and support, however, was the university-wide Women's Network. This effective group, small at first, succeeded in regularizing uniform policies for promotion and tenure that, insofar as they were observed, benefited both women and men on the faculty. The Network also provided a voice for nontenured women who feared that their protests against unfair, or even unethical, behavior would endanger their tenure procedure. My own tenure was granted in 1977 after three years of opposition from a small, powerful clique, the like of which I had never before encountered and hope never to meet again. Among the adjectives I frequently applied to it were "irrational" and "unbelievable." The Provost reviewed my dossier, asked for letters from all the tenured faculty of the Divinity School, and apparently also found the opposition's case unbelievable.

In June of 1975, seven months after my fight for tenure began at Duke, I discovered a lump in my breast. The Breast Cancer Detection Clinic at Duke diagnosed it as benign, and I went away greatly relieved. In August of that year, my mother and I moved to Cambridge, Massachusetts, where I was to spend a year as an NEH Fellow and a Fellow of the Radcliffe Institute (now called the Bunting Institute). Mom and I had a small apartment across the street from the Radcliffe Quadrangle, and I plunged into my work, rapidly picking up "Harvard fever," a maniacal dedication to study from 8:00 A.M. to 10:00 or 11:00 P.M. I reserved all day on Saturdays to be with Mom, who was then eighty years old. We had two wonderful outings, the last to Concord, before she suffered a stroke and died three days later on October 1, 1975. New and old friends in Cambridge supported me during those extremely difficult weeks. In December, I returned to Durham, N.C., to see how the student in my house was doing, to visit my two dogs, and to bring home Mom's ashes. I also returned to the clinic and was told again that the lump was benign and that I need not return for twelve months.

Back in Cambridge and back on the Harvard fever schedule, I contracted flu that I could not shake. The young doctor who examined me found the lump and expressed concern. I reassured him that Duke had it under observation, but he insisted I see a surgeon. The upshot of this sad tale is that a biopsy proved positive and was followed by a modified radical mastectomy in April. I returned to Durham in May and began two long years of chemotherapy. My research came to a halt, but in January of 1976 I began teaching full time in spite of the weariness and periods of nausea resulting from the poisons one ingests on such a regimen. The happy side of this story is that the chemotherapy worked in spite of metastasis to the lymph nodes and I am here to write about it! Another happy side of the "Cambridge story" is that in spite of the death of my mother and the discovery of cancer, it was a happy year. Why? Because of the wide network of friends that developed at the Institute, at Leverett House where I was an Associate of the Senior Common Room, and in the Jesuit Community. The transition from a situation of almost no support to one of unquestioning acceptance and appreciation provided freedom and respect. One can bear a great deal in such an atmosphere.

The Radcliffe Institute was then under the direction of Patricia Graham. I remember the exhilaration I felt when I walked daily into a building filled with women scholars, writers, and artists. Each of us knew, most for the first time, what men experience all their lives, namely a professional environment in which one's own sex predominates. The experience was freeing and inspiring. I wish every professional woman could share it. Every week, one of the fellows presented her work, in either lecture or concert form. We also enjoyed the "hot lunch program" that provided a delicious foreign meal to all the fellows as well as one or two women students sent from each department at Harvard-Radcliffe. This program allowed postdoctoral scholars the opportunity to share their experience and knowledge with students preparing for similar careers. The close relations and nonhierarchical nature of the Institute became visible (and edible!) in the concern and marvelous basket of fruit, wine and cheeses from Radcliffe's president, Matina Horner, and from Pat Graham, which awaited me on my return from the hospital.

In 1972 I was elected as National Secretary of the American Academy of Religion, a position I held until 1975. Then in 1978 I was elected as Vice-President and in December of 1981 finished my presidential year. This was followed by two years further service on the Executive Committee as an Associate Director. My association with the American Academy of Religion was an enriching one. I not only grew in self-confidence in dealing with the officers and affairs of the Academy but acquired a wide understanding of the people and the problems that the study of religion involves in the United States. I also found there the collegiality and acceptance that I had enjoyed at Chicago and Riverside.

For me 1981 was a banner year. I not only served as President of the AAR but was awarded two fellowships, one from the National Endowment for the Humanities, complemented by another from the National Center for the Humanities in Research Triangle Park, North Carolina. In the same year, I was named Alumna of the Year by the Divinity School of the University of Chicago. Adding to these riches, the University of Missouri at Columbia invited me to found a Department of Religious Studies. The opportunity to leave Duke University in order to accept the challenge of building a new department seemed even more attractive than the long-coveted invitation to spend a year in that scholar's paradise, the National Humanities Center. On the Fourth of July, 1981, in a torrential thunderstorm, I arrived at my new home. At the University of Missouri I found again the collegiality that is so important to an academic career. Support for our new department is widespread within the College of Arts and Science, and we have had, with one exception, excellent support from the administration. Our program is small but strong, and we hope our efforts will be of general use to religious studies departments when in 1986 we publish the results of a three-year seminar that we are presently conducting with our own faculty on the study of religion in a public institution. Our seminar is supported by a generous grant from the National Endowment for the Humanities.

At Missouri I am once again not aware personally of discrimination against women, but there are pockets of it on the campus. The year 1985 is not the millennium anywhere! A deeper problem remains, however: How one can espouse Christianity, a deeply patriarchal religion, and claim one's identity as a woman? I addressed this problem in my presidential address for the American Academy of Religion. I cannot say that I have come far beyond the dilemma I posed there. I am still in love with symbolism and tradition, yet deeply affected and angered by continuing patriarchal attitudes within the Roman Catholic Church and indeed within the structures of other highly sacramental Christian churches. I remain a Roman Catholic, but there is no service that I attend during which I am not keenly aware, through the liturgy, through the scripture readings, of continuing indoctrination and discrimination against women, even though, as in most Newman Centers, the clergy are enlightened and understanding. The challenge this presents can be dealt with only by living in the question until the answer begins to show itself.

A source of deep satisfaction to me now is my farm. Horses remain a joy to me, and in 1975 I was given a beautiful half-thoroughbred, half-quarter horse mare named Kathy's Thunder, or K.T. for short. K.T. had been raced for a year as a two-year-old and so was not pleasant riding for the people who owned her. I had begun exercising her in Riverside in 1972, and in 1975 her owners sent her to me. When I moved to Missouri, I looked for ten acres so that I could have K.T. at home. I bought forty-one acres, which K.T. really owns! The farm needed new fences, renovated pastures, stalls built into the barn, and other improvements. It had good out-buildings, rolling land, and an acre pond ten feet deep stocked with fish. I acquired the equivalent of a second Ph.D. as I learned what I needed to know to make the place a good operating farm. Now it has pastures that yield 2,000 bales of hay every summer and on which graze five Hereford cows, a bull, and seven horses: K.T., three part-Arabians, and two stunning purebred Arabians who bear the responsibility of making the farm profitable in these days of depressed prices for farm products and inflated prices for farm machinery and services. The seventh horse, a thoroughbred mare, belongs to Pam McClure, a student who lives in an apartment near the barn and helps with the chores. Pam is a horse-loving radical feminist poet and Religious Studies major recently elected president of the Associated Women Students at UMC. She keeps me alert to women students' problems and hopes.

My ideal vacation is not two weeks in the Bahamas, but two weeks of uninterrupted farm work (made easier by the recent acquisition of a secondhand tractor), training my horses, building fences, haying, and working in a huge vegetable garden. My freezer contains vegetables and apples and beef produced on the farm last year. Relaxation in summer is diving into the pond, racing with my swimming bloodhound, Callisto, and floating in the sun-warmed water, looking at the big white clouds or lying on the dock and watching the cattle and horses in the fields. Two cats keep the mice out of the hay bales and round out the animal population at "Inversnaid

Pastures," named for the poem by Gerard Manley Hopkins. In a sense, my life has returned full circle, enriched by the joys and pains of choices wise and unwise, the society of good friends, and the constant challenge to ride over the next mountain and wonder at new horizons.

ELLEN M. UMANSKY

Ellen M. Umansky is Assistant Professor of Religion at Emory University and the author of *Lily Montagu and the Advancement of Liberal Judaism: From Vision to Vocation*, published by the Edwin Mellen Press. She is currently working on a source book of Lily Montagu's sermons, letters, and addresses, also to be published by Edwin Mellen, and a social history of the Society of Jewish Science, a twentieth-century American Jewish movement, still in existence today.

Reclaiming the Covenant:
A Jewish Feminist's Search for Meaning

Up until high school, being Jewish was something I took for granted. I didn't think about it much. We lived in a Jewish neighborhood, had Jewish friends, belonged to a Reform Temple, liked "Jewish" food, and celebrated Jewish holidays with the rest of our family. My sister Amy and I spent one morning each weekend in religious school. We were confirmed at sixteen and post-confirmed after the twelfth grade. For seven years we went to a summer camp that was as offhandedly Jewish as we were. Its Jewishness consisted of brief worship services on Saturday mornings and a camp population that was almost entirely, if not exclusively, Jewish.

It wasn't that we knew only Jews. Going to public school, Amy and I had a few non-Jewish friends. But to us, at least, it was they who were atypical, part of—in our worldview—the "minority population." My father often spoke of the prejudice he had encountered in his youth: quotas that made it difficult for him to enter medical school, pressures that led many of our relatives to Americanize (i.e., shorten) their last name. Yet that was their world, not mine. Theirs was a world of anti-Semitism, a world that allowed the Holocaust to happen; mine was a world in which the state of Israel was already a reality, and with it the conviction that a Holocaust would never happen again. The world that my parents held out to me was one of unlimited opportunity. If I worked hard enough, they told me, I could go to any college I desired and, should I want a career to "fall back on," could enter the profession of my choosing. I could do all of this, they said, without having to hide my Jewish identity. Indeed, I was encouraged to feel proud of being a Jew.

As a child, I never tired of the stories my grandfather used to tell me: his family fleeing from Russia, the dangerous boat trip to America, the move from New Orleans to New York, boxing to earn some money, fighting his way up from poverty, the successes and failures of his life. Most of all, I loved the songs and imaginary stories he taught me. They spoke of Eastern European Jewish immigrants trying to "make it" in America—poor but proud, clever, and determined to succeed. My grandmother told fewer stories. Yet it was from her, I think, that I first felt the beauty of Judaism. She and my grandfather (my father's parents) lived with us, just as my parents and older sister had lived with them for the thirteen years before Amy and I were born. I remember coming home from school late Friday afternoons, walking into the house and finding the Shabbos candles already lit, casting a soft and sacred glow.

My grandmother and mother always made us a special dinner on Friday nights: chopped liver, chicken soup, pot roast or roasted chicken. It was the one night, too, that we ate bread—fresh challah from the neighborhood bakery. There was something special about Friday nights. As I think back on it now, I'm not sure what that special quality was. Perhaps it had something to do with the creation of sacred time and sacred space. Though we ate in the kitchen, as we always did during the weekdays, the lit Shabbos candles and the special cloth on the table transported us to another kitchen, a "Jewish" kitchen, where bacon and pork chops weren't served (as they were in my home though never on Friday nights), where words like "kreplach" and "knaidlach" rolled off the tongue, and where meat and milk were never mixed together (one might eat a cheeseburger in my house but never on Friday evenings). Moreover, the vast quantity of food we consumed helped to create a feeling of sacred time. On other nights of the week we often ate quickly, but to get through our Friday night meal took time and effort (stopping frequently to rest and begin eating anew). Thus, for the hour or two that we sat around the kitchen table, we forgot about homework and television and talking on the phone to our friends. Friday night dinner became our Sabbath celebration. It helped us unselfconsciously to affirm—all of us—the fact that we were Jews.

There were other things we did as a family that also affirmed our Jewishness. We went to Rosh Hashanah and Yom Kippur services together, gave each other gifts at Chanukah, had two large Passover Seders conducted by my father, and attended weddings and Bar Mitzvahs of relatives and family friends. When my grandfather died, we sat *shiva* for a week, with ten men saying *kaddish* for him in our living room. I remember thinking it strange that my father felt it necessary to get on the phone in order "round up" extra men for the brief worship service. At the time, the word *minyan*— prayer quorum—was foreign to me. As a Reform Jew, I had learned that public worship could begin as soon as one person arrived, male or female, and that the prayer of one Jew was as important as the prayers of a thousand. Thus, I couldn't understand either why we needed ten people or why all of those people needed to be men. We had plenty of women in our family. Why was it, I wondered, that the participation of my mother, grandmother, and aunts somehow didn't count?

None of us, however, questioned my father's actions. Perhaps my aunts were too grief stricken to notice; more likely, they had simply reverted to the kind of Judaism in which they had been raised. Traditionally, they knew, only men said *kaddish*. Women could grieve, but only men could pray. Perhaps I would have articulated my own feeling of strangeness concerning my father's behavior had I been able to separate in my mind the notion of spiritual quest from that of Jewish self-identity. To me, however, being a Jew simply meant being part of a particular historical and religious community to which I, my parents, and ancestors belonged. It was my responsibility to understand Judaism's teachings and to follow them, not to question why we believed certain things but to accept those beliefs as my own. Spiritual quests were for Abraham and Moses. The covenant of which I was a part was a covenant that *they* had made. The ground rules had already been set. They had defined what it meant to be a Jew. It was my task to embody this definition.

While Judaism may not have been something I thought about a great deal, I always knew that it was part of *who I was* and I never hesitated to fight against those who I thought were trying to deny me my Jewish heritage. In school, I flatly refused to sing Christmas carols that contained the words "Christ," "Bethlehem," or "Jesus." We had a Christmas tree at home but to me, at least, it represented an American, not Christian, celebration of peace and the "brotherhood of man." Christians celebrated Christmas by going to church and placing a star at the top of the tree. Though as Jews we did neither, we could still partake, I felt, in a more universal "Christmas spirit." We might even participte in ecumenical services, expressing human hopes and fears. Yet while I remained unopposed to the idea of Jews and Christians worshiping together, I felt distinctly uncomfortable with the notion of our voicing identical prayers.

I remember one particularly memorable event in the sixth grade that helped to crystallize these feelings. Our teacher (who wasn't Jewish) insisted that the class recite a short prayer after the pledge of allegiance each morning. She went on to teach us a prayer which I thought sounded un-Jewish. It wasn't a prayer *I* had ever learned and was one that the non-Jews in the class—I think there were three out of a class of twenty-seven—seemed to know already. I raised my hand and informed my teacher that I was Jewish and would not recite a Christian prayer. She tried to argue that the prayer was not explicitly Christian, but I was adamant. If we *had* to pray in school (and she insisted we did), I would say the *Shema* ("Hear O Israel, the Lord Our God, the Lord is One") but nothing else. To her dismay, I convinced the other Jewish students in the class to recite the prayer with me. Her compromise, which I took as a personal victory, was that we all pray silently instead.

As I think back on this incident, I can't help but wonder why I, of all my classmates, chose to challenge my teacher. Would I have been as bold had I been the only Jew in the class? Was it perhaps growing up in the suburbs of New York (a city where people spoke in accents that I considered to be Jewish) that gave me a confidence, a self-assurance about being Jewish that I might not otherwise have possessed? I have no way of answering these questions. But as I got older and left New York, occasionally finding myself in situations where I was the only Jew present, I remained as much a "defender of the faith" as I had been at age eleven.

Yet what did the words "Jewish faith" mean? To me, I think, they meant the teachings of Reform Judaism. In religious school, we learned that there were three branches of Judaism in America: Orthodox, Conservative, and Reform. Each had its own separate understanding of what it meant to be a Jew. While I never exactly had the feeling that our understanding was superior, I did see Reform as the most modern and therefore most relevant (or least obsolete) form of Jewish life.

Not knowing any Orthodox Jews, I thought of Orthodoxy in only the most abstract way. To be an Orthodox Jew, I believed, meant attempting to live one's Judaism as it had been lived in the past, holding on to observances that might or might not have personal meaning, and praying in a language that one might or might not undertand. I did attend an Orthodox Bar Mitzvah once (though neither the boy nor his family considered themselves to be Orthodox Jews). It was the first time I'd been to a synagogue where men and women sat separately. I found the service boring and the separation from my male relatives somewhat silly. Since for me much of my Jewish identity stemmed from a sense of identification with my family, all of whom were Jewish, I wondered why we should not join our voices together in prayer. I didn't know then that we were seated separately so as not to distract the men, nor did I know that our voices were *not supposed* to be joined together. If I thought about it at all, I assumed it was a coincidence that no women were called up to the Torah and that only men sat on the *bimah*—the pulpit—facing the congregation. If someone had told me that Orthodox men recited a prayer thanking God for not having created them as women, I would have been shocked and thoroughly confused. This was not Judaism as I knew it. Nor was it Judaism as I thought it should be.

I had far greater admiration for Conservative Judaism. I was impressed by the number of times a week my Conservative friends went to religious school (indicating, to me, a great sense of dedication) and by how much more Hebrew they knew than I. Men and women sat together during the synagogue service, many of the prayers were in English (and therefore intelligible to me), and my female friends had Bat Mitzvahs paralleling, it seemed to me, the Bar Matzvahs of their brothers. True, my girlfriends' Bat Matzvahs were on Friday night, not on Saturday, and true, they did not read from the Torah as did my male friends. But I never thought to ask why Bat and Bar Mitzvah occurred on different days of the week. Nor did I even notice that my girlfriends did not read from the Torah but from a separate Haftorah portion in a printed Hebrew Bible.

What impressed me most, I think, was how much more conscious of their Judaism my Conservative friends seemed to be than I—especially those who insisted on keeping kosher. I remember one party at my house. I was no more than twelve years old. My mother served Italian food, including all of my favorites: spaghetti, meatballs, and pizza. As she went around serving the food, I heard one of my friends (a Conservative Jew) explain to my mother that she had to choose. She could eat *either* the spaghetti and meatballs *or* the pizza but not both, since one dish had meat and one had cheese and she could not mix meat and dairy products together. With great strength of purpose, I thought, she chose one of the two dishes, although I don't remember which. The meatballs, of course, weren't kosher to begin with: While we often bought kosher meat, we did not have separate "meat" and "milk" cooking utensils. Yet at the time, I didn't realize this. Even if I had, I'm not sure it would have made any difference. It wasn't the strictness of my friend's observance that impressed me. It was the fact that she was willing, in whatever way, to make a sacrifice for her Judaism and that she made this sacrifice not with anger or regret but with great dignity and love for the Jewish people.

On the other hand, however, I'm sure I was secretly glad that "my" Judaism did not demand such a sacrifice from me.

I had learned in religious school that eating cheeseburgers, shrimp, and bacon had nothing whatsoever to do with Judaism *as we understood it.* Judaism, we learned, was not a religion of ritual observance but of internal belief and external moral action. During the ten years in which I attended religious school, I was taught ideas that I now can identify as part of the ideology of American Reform Judaism. Although to my knowledge my religious school teachers never used the word "mission," I learned that it was my responsibility as a Jew to follow the ethical teachings of the prophets and to be a witness to the reality of God. At my Confirmation ceremony, I made a pledge of allegiance "to the Torah of Israel and to the Faith for which it stands—one God, Father of all men, exalted through Righteousness, Brotherhood, and Peace." I vowed dutifully to obey the Ten Commandments and to "hallow my life, in the name of the Eternal God, to the religion of Israel" and with the rest of my class formally entered into the covenant established between the Jewish people and their God.

As a member of that covenant, I struggled to find meaning in both private and public prayer. If I had indeed entered into a covenant with God, I wanted to be sure *who* He was and *what* He demanded. In religious school, we learned that God is the "highest and the best that we know and can say," a Being who reveals Himself in nature, in history, and as the "still small voice" of conscience within us. I remember once, in high school, questioning God's reality. As an experiment, I tried *not* to pray, telling myself, in John Lennon's words, that God was merely a "concept by which we measure our pain." Yet over and over again I found myself turning to the Divine, asking Him for strength, guidance, comfort, and protection. I wasn't sure whether God existed as I/we imagined Him to be. In college, I became convinced (through the influence of Immanuel Kant) that God-as-He-really-is would *always* be inaccessible to me. But from the age of sixteen on, my *belief* in God became stronger. I believed that the Divine, though universal, had entered into a special relationship with the Jewish people and that I was obligated—in behavior and thought—to prove myself worthy of that relationship. Without realizing it (and despite my earlier belief that spiritual quests were for Abraham and Moses), I had begun my own spiritual journey.

In part, this exploration of what God demanded from me stemmed from the seriousness with which I took my Confirmation vows. Yet of equal importance were the arguments that I had with my father concerning the separateness of the Jewish people. During my Confirmation year I began dating a non-Jewish boy. He wasn't the first non-Jew I'd ever dated, but he was the first I'd ever dated seriously. My father insisted that I end the relationship. The primary reason he gave was religious. He could never accept my marrying a non-Jew (and threatened to disown me should I do so) and therefore felt it hypocritical to support a mixed dating relationship as long as it didn't lead to marriage. It was better, he reasoned, for me not to date non-Jewish boys at all, thus removing any possibility of my marrying a non-Jew in the future.

My father never tried to justify his demand. He didn't feel he had to. To be a Jew, for him, was to be separate, by circumstance and by choice, and he expected me, if not to understand, at least to respect his opinion. God never entered into our discussions. I don't know whether or not my father even believed in the reality of God. When he spoke of Judaism he spoke of the Jewish people. Mostly, he spoke of Jewishness—ethnicity—and the fact that we were not *just like other Americans,* that somehow we were different. Yet when I thought about how we lived—eating non-kosher food, spending Saturday afternoons at the movies, celebrating Christmas —I wasn't exactly sure what was different about us. Somehow, celebrating an occasional Jewish holiday together and attending religious school once a week didn't seem sufficient. Couldn't I continue to celebrate Jewish holidays even if I married a non-Jew? Couldn't I still choose to raise my children as Jewish? I constantly badgered my father with these and other questions. Yet at the same time, I intuitively knew that he was right.

I defied his demands because I didn't want to break up with my boyfriend. To myself, however, I began thinking of ways in which I could make concrete this feeling of being different. It wasn't that I wanted to shut myself off from the non-Jewish world. I had no intention of ending the non-Jewish friendships that I had already formed, nor did I want to avoid non-Jews in the future. But I wanted my non-Jewish friends (and boyfriends) to accept me *because* of who I was and not in spite of it. I didn't want them to take my being Jewish for granted (as I had) because I found it inevitably—and conveniently—led them to forget that I was a Jew. The anti-Semitic jokes they often told in front of me, their snide comments about Jews and money, infuriated me. Even when my Jewishess came up in conversation, it was usually in the form of a backhanded compliment. I was supposed to be flattered that they saw me as "different" from most Jews. Their understanding of this difference was that I wasn't cheap or gaudy or narrow-minded (like my father!). I tried to counter their charges. Yet the irrationality of their anti-Semitic attacks and the fact that even to my boyfriend I was not like most Jews but an "exception" led me to feel that, if anything, it was non-Jews I differed from, not other Jews.

I began to feel that it was my responsibility to make this difference clear. I couldn't expect non-Jews to understand what for me was little more than an intuitive feeling. Thus, very slowly, I began to think of ways in which I could visibly live my life *as a Jew.* I announced to my mother that I would no longer eat pork chops. I also made it clear that I would not celebrate Christmas (and would not accept any family gifts wrapped in Christmas paper). My resolve to make my life more Jewish, however, ended there. By the end of eleventh grade, I was dating a Jewish boy, had a whole new set of Jewish friends, and—while I still wouldn't eat pork chops or celebrate Christmas—began once again to take my Jewishness for granted.

My complacency, however, was irrevocably shattered once I entered college. As a freshman at Wellesley (and one of only a handful of Jews in my dorm), I found that it was I who was atypical, part of the "minority population." Moreover, I discovered that not all non-Jews even wanted to see me as the exception. Some (including one of my professors) were incapable of viewing me as anything other than an unredeemed, obstinate, and ignorant Jew. How, my professor asked me, could I not understand the meaning of the word "salvation"? Why, a few of my dormmates wanted to know, did I refuse to accept that which was (religiously) true? Did I *want* to go to hell? Didn't I understand *who Jesus was*? How could I believe in a God of anger when their God was a God of love? A few members of Campus Crusade for Christ even tried to convert my parents on one of their visits to Wellesley. Handing my father a few pamphlets, they spoke of Jesus' love for the sinner and assured him that if he and my mother opened their hearts to Christ, they too could receive the gift of salvation.

Not all Wellesley students, of course, were anti-Semites. But the considerable anti-Semitism that I encountered led me to study the New Testament and the history of early Christianity in an attempt to understand why my being Jewish was so important to those that continued to challenge my religious upbringing. Why did they feel the need to redeem me? Of what truths, exactly, was I ignorant? And why was their understanding of the "Jewish God" so unlike anything I had ever been taught to believe?

My religion courses at Wellesley—which came to include every course offered in Old and New Testaments—opened an entirely new world to me. I came to understand the differences between Judaism and Christianity more clearly, learned what it meant to view Judaism through Christian eyes, and began to realize why a Christian understanding of Judaism was so antithetical to my own. These courses made me feel more Jewish than I had ever felt before. I vigorously argued with my Old Testament professor when he insisted that the Suffering Servant passages in Isaiah referred to Jesus, and I tried to make him understand why the very title of our course—"Old Testament" as opposed to "Hebrew Bible"—gave the course a specific bias that I did not share. In New Testament classes, I constantly found myself on the defensive. Forced by other students to explain why I did not

believe in either original sin, personal salvation, or the resurrection, I found myself thinking, in a way I never had before,
about what it meant to be Jewish.

By the time I left Wellesley, I was determined to pursue my
study of religion further. While I had enthusiastically
embraced philosophy as an undergraduate major, the study of
religion had become an obsession. In learning more about the
Bible and the history of Christianity (I would have taken
history of Judaism courses, but none was offered at Wellesley
then), I felt that I was learning more about myself and those
around me. Most exciting was the thought that what I was
learning would bring me closer to other people. While the
insights I'd discovered in my philosophy courses seemed of
little interest to people I met outside of the academic world,
the study of religion seemed to illuminate for me how millions
of people, over thousands of years, of different races, classes,
and genders, had attempted to give their lives meaning. I
honestly don't think I began graduate school to ask my *own*
questions. Yet as my study grew—and deepened—the questions I began to ask most often were those I came to recognize
as my own.

Unsure about whether I wanted to enter a Ph.D. program
(and ignorant of the fact that women had recently been
admitted to Hebrew Union College, the Reform rabbinical
seminary), I decided to enter a two-year master's program at
Yale Divinity School. During my first year at Yale, I continued to explore the relationship between Judaism and Christianity, becoming particularly fascinated with the
development of anti-Semitism in the early church. By the
second year, however, my studies had shifted focus. Having
begun to understand Hebrew and taking a variety of courses
at the Divinity School, the Graduate School, and Yale College,
not in Old Testament but *Hebrew Bible*, Jewish history,
rabbinic literature, and the history of Jewish ethics, I felt my
intellectual and emotional selves begin to merge and for the
first time began to see myself not simply as Jewish but as
"religious."

My earlier vow to remain faithful to God's covenant with
Israel took on new meaning as I began to understand the

uniqueness of that covenant within the Ancient Near East. The development of Israelite religion from polytheism to henotheism to monotheism gave me a new and richer insight into the teachings of the Hebrew prophets. For the first time, I began to recognize the importance of ritual observance and ways in which the rabbis of the Talmud had succeeded in making Judaism an all-encompassing way of life. Perhaps most importantly, my study of Jewish ethics convinced me that even modern problems could be examined from a Jewish perspective. It wasn't enough, as I had imagined, simply to be a "good person." Through my courses at Yale, and later Columbia, I began to explore ways in which I could become a "good Jew."

When I moved into my first apartment, in the spring of 1973, I decided to observe *kashrut* (the Jewish dietary laws). A few years later, I joined the New York Havurah, an alternative Jewish group, with whom I celebrated Shabbat, holidays, and *simchas* (joyous occasions). I especially looked forward to monthly retreats, when we spent two days away from the city together. Most memorable were late-into-the-night discussions on being Jewish, our feelings towards prayer, the significance of observance, and the political situation in the Middle East. I'd been in Israel during the spring of 1972 and again, to study Hebrew, during the summer of 1974, but it was only within the Havurah that I felt "safe enough" to discuss both the pride and disappointments I felt during my trips to Israel. The Havurah became the first Jewish community of which I truly felt a member. While as a group we were far from homogeneous, all of us, it seemed to me, were engaged in a common struggle. All of us were trying to live our lives in personally and *Jewishly* meaningful ways.

Yet at the same time I was struggling to redefine my Jewish identity, I found myself engaged in another struggle relating to my identity as a woman. The feminist movement, whose impact I'd first felt at Wellesley, slowly but radically began to reshape how I saw the world and how I viewed myself. I began to question my father's assumption that for a woman a career was only something to "fall back on." As a college freshman, I saw my intelligence as a future source of frustration. I tried to convince myself that somehow I would learn to stifle my questions, put aside my abilities, and remain content with the life that a future Prince Charming would carve out for me. Four years later, having found a number of important role models in my female professors, two consciousness-raising groups that set scores of "clicks" going off in my head, and a boyfriend (later to become my husband) who encouraged me to carve out a life of my own, I began to explore *my* needs and expectations.

Consequently, many of the papers I wrote in graduate school focused on women's role in Judaism. These papers combined my academic interest in Jewish history, my personal interest in discovering a new sense of Jewish self-identity, and a growing feminist awareness that I would not be able to create this identity until I understood what it meant to be *a woman and a Jew*. What I discovered was that throughout most of Jewish history, the religious life of women was centered around the home. Women were seen primarily as wives and mothers. In theory, these roles were equal to those assumed by men, but in reality they reduced women to a subordinate if not inferior position.

Comparative essays that I wrote on the position of women in ancient Israelite, Mesopotamian, and Egyptian societies forced me to recognize that in many significant respects, women's lives were more restricted within Israelite society than in the other ancient Near Eastern cultures out of which Judaism emerged. The misogynism of the rabbis, made clear in legal and nonlegal material, the development of a liturgy exclusively focusing on male images of the Divine, and the exemption of women from important religious obligations, including study and communal prayer, led me to conclude, with great reluctance, that perhaps women were more peripheral to Jewish life than I had wanted to believe. The more I read, the more I came to identify Judaism as a religion created by and for men. My own doctoral research on nineteenth- and twentieth-century Jewish women seemed to verify the sense of alienation and exclusion that I had begun to feel. Many of the modern Jewish women about whose lives I read had undergone a struggle that seemed to echo my own.

They too had sought to find a place for themselves within Judaism without sacrificing either self-fulfillment or personal growth. Yet many, like myself, had found themselves confronted with a seemingly insoluble dilemma.

Modernity helped create for Jewish women a new set of expectations, based on notions of individualism and freedom. New social, economic, and educational opportunities, contrasting sharply with the more limited opportunities available to them in traditional Jewish society, led many Jewish women to embrace the modern world as their own. Though many, like their male counterparts, attempted to establish a "fully modern" identity that was "fully Jewish" as well, the critical reevaluation of Judaism thrust upon them by the modern world led many to question whether as women they ever had been—or could be—fully Jewish. Not surprisingly, many Jewish women began to view Judaism with far greater ambivalence than did their male counterparts. Some, like Lily Montagu—the woman whose life became the subject of my dissertation—overcame these feelings through the redefinition of women's religious role, while others either left Judaism or readjusted their expectations. Many, however, continued to struggle, frequently forced to choose between their own needs and those of a community from which they often were excluded.

Within the last few years, my own struggle to reclaim the Jewish covenant as a bond between God and *all* of the Jewish people—male and female—has been both challenging and frustrating. At times, I have almost abandoned my struggle. The continued exclusion of women from positions of secular and religious leadership within the Jewish community, the extent to which women's spirituality—past and present—is still ignored, the lack of formal ceremonies celebrating important life-cycle events of women, and the liturgical description of God as "God of our Fathers" (but not our mothers) make me angry and sad. At first, I directed my anger towards Judaism itself, ready to write it off as hopelessly patriarchal. But more recently, I've come to redirect my anger. It's not Judaism itself that angers me but those who seem to have forgotten that Judaism has never been monolithic and that in every period of Jewish history Judaism has developed and grown.

Those who argue that liturgy cannot be changed have lost sight of Judaism as a living religion. How meaningful today are images of God as King, Lord, and Shepherd? And why, if both men and women have been created in God's image, should we not address the Divine as Father *and* Mother, Master and Mistress of Heaven? Martin Buber envisioned Judaism as arising out of a We-Thou dialogue between the Jewish people and God. I'm beginning to suspect, however, that my forefathers did most of the talking. Consequently, Judaism as we now know it was largely fashioned by generations of men who decided what *they* wanted Judaism to be.

Yet even the rabbis of the Talmud admitted that the covenant established at Sinai was given to men *and women*. Perhaps my foremothers were content to live out their membership vicariously, through the rituals and prayers of their fathers, husbands, and sons. Vicarious membership, however, will no longer do. As a feminist, I have begun to reclaim my voice; as a Jew, I am ready to activate my membership within the covenant and to reopen the dialogue with *our* God.

As I think about my spiritual journey, I realize that my search for meaning may never end. What I've learned in the seventeen years since I took my Confirmation vows is that the ground rules are *not* preestablished, that it is my obligation as a Jew to help create a Judaism that is meaningful for my generation. Three thousand years ago, Moses stood at Mt. Sinai and received the Ten Commandments from God. When he came down the mountain and saw the Israelites worshiping a golden calf, he broke the tablets in anger. Perhaps he did so not only to warn us against idolatry but also to make it clear that not even God's words are irrevocably carved in stone.

RITA M. GROSS

Rita M. Gross is Associate Professor of Comparative Studies in Religion at the University of Wisconsin—Eau Claire. She was awarded a Ph.D. in the History of Religions from the University of Chicago for the dissertation *Exclusion and Participation: The Role of Women in Aboriginal Australian Religion,* and is co-editor of *Unspoken Worlds: Women's Religious Lives in Non-Western Cultures.* She has been chairperson of the Women and Religion section of the American Academy of Religion and has published widely in feminist scholarship and theology. Currently she is working on a book on Buddhism and feminism. A student of Vajracarya the Venerable Chogyam Trungpa, Rinpoche, she is also coordinator of the Dharma Study Group of Eau Claire, Wisconsin. She also is active in national and international formats for Buddhist-Christian dialogue.

Three Strikes and You're Out:
An Autobiography at Mid-Life

Autobiography invites contemplation. What is the subject of the autobiography? How did it get to this point? What should be included and what excluded in one's story? How will the autobiography read to its author in five, ten, or twenty years? Do such personal, idiosyncratic features matter? How does one avoid fixating on one's self while telling one's story? How does one appreciate one's life without clinging to one's existence? The exercise of formal autobiography brings up profound questions and provides an opportunity for careful and disciplined reflection.

No autobiography is complete. One cannot recall all the events of life; one could not even commit all recalled events to paper. One chooses from myriad recollections the ones that seem best to "explain" the genesis of the person who one now thinks one is. What I now think I am is ephemeral. Five years earlier, five years hence, the everflowing stream of one's life is different and different events seem important. Furthermore, some decisive events are too raw and too tender to be committed to the medium of a typeset, public book. Therefore an autobiography is self-edited.

Today I am a Buddhist feminist scholar. Obviously, that has not always been my identity. In telling a version of the story of how I became a Buddhist feminist scholar, I will focus more on intellectual and spiritual factors and less on interpersonal and relational factors. I do this both because I feel idiosyncratic and lonely in my vision-quest and because I do not wish to discuss some decisive relational elements of my experience in this context.

I

Log Cabin to Midway:
Excommunication to Conversion

I was the only child of an immigrant and a first-generation U.S. citizen. I grew up in a small log cabin on a marginal, impoverished dairy farm in northern Wisconsin. For four years I attended a one-room country school with about thirty students in the eight grades. Then there were four years of parochial school in a Wisconsin Synod (perhaps the most conservative American Lutheran denomination) Lutheran Day School and then four years of public high school. These were followed by four years as an on-campus student at a nonresidential urban university, the University of Wisconsin in Milwaukee. At the end of these years, I found myself accepted to the History of Religions program at the University of Chicago as a Woodrow Wilson Fellow. I had also been excommunicated, shortly after my mother's death, from the Lutheran Church—Wisconsin Synod, and I was on the brink of conversion to Judaism. I had also had some thoughts, years before the current women's movement, that I later discovered were feminism; these had been met with scepticism, bewilderment, or disapproval.

These years, 1943 to 1965, seem now to oscillate between two themes, neither of which ever predominated over the other. On the one hand, the sensuous richness of the natural world of country farm, animals, spirituality, and mental curiosity was a ground of never-ceasing wonder and joy. On the other, the cultural world of parents, school, and institutional religion provided the texture of struggle. The dark, joyful eyes of my dog, the feel of my horse between my legs, the sensation of drawing milk from cows' teats, the whispering sad voice of pine trees, and the power of working with heavy farm machinery were probably the major factors of those years. Now I remember most that natural world with all its incredible richness, and I am grateful for that foundation. However, at the time, the cultural world of school, church, and family and my frustrations with all three seemed to predominate.

There is no better place than in the country, no better way than with animal friends and hard work. I remember struggling to awake at 4:30 A.M., saddling my horse quickly, and cantering across fields so dew-drenched that we (my horse and I) left trails through the dew.

The dog ran alongside and as my horse's feet rang on the concrete barn floor, all the calves I fed began to bellow in anticipation. After pressing my forehead into the flanks of ten cows while extracting their milk, we three (my horse, my dog, myself) took the cows back to pasture; meanwhile I contemplated the values of socialism and free enterprise. Later in the day, I might cut many acres of hay or load and unload several tons of hay, or both, and then milk the damn cows again in the evening, with tight, aching muscles. Sometimes I got time to play the piano or to read. My first serious theological reading occurred sometime in high school. I read what I now know was a Jungian Biblical interpretation while taking refuge under the haywagon during rainstorms; I was profoundly influenced by the book. I also completed a major college term paper on Reinhold Niebuhr during storm breaks under the haywagons.

In contrast was the world of school and church. I loved both and wanted so much to please and excel in both. Now I feel that both institutions seriously failed me.

"School" can perhaps be best summed up through the narrative of my experiences with the library. In primary school, though I read several years above my grade level, the teacher of my one-room school insisted that I be allowed to read only at or below my grade level. Furthermore, the county librarians in my home town refused to allow me to check books out from the county library "because the family property is a few yards over the county line and your parents don't pay taxes in our county." Later, when we bought property on their side of the county line and paid taxes, they insisted that wasn't enough; our residence had not moved the yards over the county line. The librarians threatened that my grade school friends, who checked out books for me on their library cards, would lose their own library privileges. The education provided was not much above the quality of library access. Though there were some exceptionally capable or caring teachers, the four school systems I attended all had serious deficiencies in both the intellectual and emotional training provided. During these years, my interests and inclinations began to diverge more and more from those of my parents, especially my mother's vision of my life plan. She dreamed of having me settle on the farm, while I dreamed of intellectual and spiritual adventure in law, foreign service, or education. This divergence in dreams probably is best summed up by a harried and frustrated outburst to me: "Why don't you throw that book into the corner and do something useful! Do you think you're going to make a living reading books?" Nevertheless, though my parents could not appreciate or approve of my life choices, they did not try to forbid me from pursuing those choices.

Religion always seemed to me to be the only arena that really asked or answered life questions, and for a while I tried hard to remain within the confines of the very dogmatic and narrow-minded Wisconsin Synod of the Lutheran Church. Though there were struggles in high school, real conflict developed in college. The issue already then was the issue that later propelled me into the comparative study of religion and has remained a major concern during my entire life, both professional and personal: religious pluralism. I never accepted the Lutheran version of the notion that there is no salvation outside the church. The misdemeanor that brought things to a head was my college participation in the "wrong kind" of Lutheran church choir. While being reprimanded for this disobedience, I suggested that actually all religions were striving for the same goal, using different methods. (I had not yet studied Hinduism.) This opinion was erroneous and heretical, I was told. The confrontation was traumatic, but I was growing away from the church through my philosophy major and my study of Hebrew language and civilization. At my mother's funeral, I was the target of an anti-Semitic and anti-

intellectual sermon; a few months later, I was excommunicated for heresy and consigned to hell, in the opinion of the
church.

Even through all this conflict, the deepest trauma of my
religious upbringing remained repressed and resurfaced only
years later. As a young child, probably preschool, I found for
myself affirmation of my gender. God, I realized, was male,
and I wondered where that left me. Jesus was, too, I reflected,
but the angels were clearly women. Their femininity com-
forted and affirmed me for years. During confirmation class,
when the subordination of women was linked to the gender of
God, I questioned that link and the consequent subordination
of women, since the angels were women. I was informed that,
despite their looks, the angels too were men and that male
supremacy held on all levels.

II

Affirming Womanhood:
Graduate School and Becoming a Teacher

By 1976 I had earned a Ph.D. in the History of Religions from
an ambivalent University of Chicago, been married and
divorced, experienced the death of my lover, and survived a
traumatic first teaching position. I had also spent many
years exploring Judaism as personal religious pursuit and
discovering, expressing, and refining my feminism. In 1975 I
began Buddhist meditation and in 1976 I spent a memorable
summer in India. I was also on the brink of receiving tenure
at the University of Wisconsin—Eau Claire. Feminism,
Judaism, and professional training and development dominate those difficult years. I marvel that I survived them.

Though I had excelled in college, the transition to graduate
school at the University of Chicago was an immense leap. I
was not really prepared for the heady intellectualism of the
University of Chicago; furthermore, I was now in a man's
world—one of a minority of women graduate students in the
Divinity School. Graduate School was probably the most
critical and formative period of my life. The University of

Chicago both tortured me and nurtured me. I left with the second History of Religions Ph.D. granted to a woman by the University of Chicago, and the first dissertation in women's studies in religion to be approved by any major graduate school in religion. Being a woman and a feminist at that institution during those years was not easy. Perhaps it could not have been easy, but the university made it unnecessarily difficult. On the other hand, the education I received at the University of Chicago made me a competent scholar and thinker and prepared me well for the profession I love, teaching world religions.

Two stories of graduate school suffice. I remember clearly the first time (1966) I heard of the Vajrayana, in a class taught by Mircea Eliade. The classroom full of students was incredibly quiet as we listened to his enthusiasm. As he left the room, I said, "If I ever practice an Eastern religion, that's it"—thinking it impossible that I ever would.

In my second year (1966), completely frustrated and angry about the treatment of women in Western culture, I decided to write some of my required papers on women in other cultures, to find out if "things were as bad everywhere." I wrote a massive paper on "The Role of Women in Australian and Melanesian Religions," which Mircea Eliade praised very highly. He then expounded on the importance of the topic and the lack of literature and suggested, "Of course, you'll write your dissertation on this topic." My immediate reaction, despite my feminism and my frustration: "No! I want to do my dissertation on something important." Consciousness raising happens slowly. Of course, I did end up writing my dissertation on *Exclusion and Participation: The Role of Women in Aboriginal Australian Religion.* My criticisms about the androcentric character of the history of religions methodology were not always appreciated by the faculty, but I did eventually win out.

Those were also the Jewish years, particularly while I was in Chicago. I converted to Judaism early in 1966 and almost immediately began to discover and rebel against its traditional male dominance, as my feminism and my new religious identity collided. The University of Chicago Hillel Foundation was probably the warmest and most congenial community to which I have ever belonged. Our Saturday services were traditional, sexually egalitarian, intelligent, and friendly. There I launched some of my first feminist suggestions and experienced the fulfillment of seeing an institution change, in part because of my initiative.

People sometimes ask why I converted to Judaism. It was a careful choice. I spent several years simultaneously attending church and synagogue and explored variants of Christianity. I think my choice for Judaism turned on its combination of warm community and respect for learning and intelligence, which I did not find anywhere else. Theologically, my childhood and adolescent piety had been theocentric rather than Christocentric, and I experienced no conflict over giving up any attachment to Jesus. I also liked the nondogmatic and almost nontheological way that God was discussed and the rich liturgy. One then wonders why I am no longer an actively practicing Jew. It is not because of feminism, for my Jewish-Christian leanings are more to the reformist than to the revolutionary side. But, after I left Chicago, I experienced a great problem—the lack of a Jewish community to which I could really belong. I am drawn to religious practice and experience too much to be merely a nominal Jew. Furthermore, I was discovering meditation, which drew me beyond Judaism. In any case, I do not consider myself an ex-Jew, even though I am now active in practicing and teaching Buddhism. I could not renounce a tradition and a community that nurtured me so well in crucial times.

Some account of the beginnings of feminist awakening, early clashes with antifeminist institutions, and successes in presenting feminism has already been given. Actually, I was already quite aware of and angry about sexism by the time I graduated from college, but at that time (pre-1965) I had neither a language nor a community with which to express or explore those insights and feelings. Sometime in those years I also experienced a profound breakthrough when I realized I was angry, not for *being* a woman, but because of the treatment meted out to women. I realized that the frustrations and limitations I experienced were due to discrimination and stereotyping directed at me, not due to something intrinsically wrong with my femaleness. Femaleness is good, in its intrinsic nature! In Buddhist terms, this kind of liberating insight regarding one's basic goodness and one's ability to work with one's situation is fundamental to any further development. I did not then have the language to call this an experience of *maitri*—friendliness toward one's self—but that lack of language did not diminish the experience.

Through my involvement with Judaism and scholarship, I developed and refined all these insights and feelings greatly and entered the professional world of teaching in 1971 with feminism as a leading component of my personal identity and my professional stance. In 1971 I attended the Alverno College Conference for women theologians, the first ever. That same year, I attended the American Academy of Religion meetings at which the Women's Caucus was formed and Chris Downing's nomination for President of the AAR came out of the Caucus. In 1972 I presented my first AAR paper and from 1975 to 1980 I chaired the Women and Religion section of the AAR. I edited two books during those years. One of them, *Unspoken Worlds: Women's Religious Lives in Non-Western Cultures,* is important. I also did considerable feminist theology, specifically on Hindu goddesses as a resource for Western religions—much to the consternation of some more conventional historians of religion. The work on Hindu goddesses opened my memory to the incidents of my childhood regarding the angels. Sometimes when I worked with these Hindu materials, I felt that I was in touch with something deep and primordial, and I often felt that the greatest need was to keep "myself" out of the way so that these goddesses and their myths and symbols could come through.

This period of my life ended with a summer-long trip to India—my only foreign travel. I felt at home in India, as if touching the energy stream of former lives. So many evenings sitting at the dinner table with my hosts—a guru and his wife —I felt uncannily at ease. The day I left we revisited several temples, including the Kali temple that I loved so much there. The priest garlanded me with a garland that he took off the temple icon and explained in Hindu to my companion that the garland was all he had to offer the goddess. I listened in wonder as my companion translated for me. It was not the only such experience I had. Pictures taken that day of me eating off a leaf plate with a group of Indian friends show me fitting in to the extent that people sometimes say, "Oh! You're in that picture too! Only your glasses look out of place."

III

I Take Refuge in the Buddha; I Take Refuge in the Dharma; I Take Refuge in the Sangha

In 1977 I received tenure, bought my house (which suits me wonderfully), and went to Boulder, Colorado, to teach at Naropa Institute for the summer. There I fell in love. So I took refuge in the Buddha, the Dharma, and the Sangha, despite earlier commitments to myself not to convert again and years of scepticism regarding the guru phenomenon. This was a turn in the life plan that was not planned or expected! But I suppose one's consummate love affair does not happen as planned or expected.

Of course I had known a great deal about Buddhism for a long time, since I had studied and taught it for years, even though it was not an early favorite of mine. Early on I felt more drawn to Hinduism, though I did not feel it was my personal spiritual path, even when my Indian guru-host urged me to become his disciple. The one exception to my early leanings toward Hinduism occurred while I was preparing a chapter that never made it into my dissertation. I read everything I could on Tantrism, including almost everything then available on Tibetan religion. Uncannily I somehow was hooked by the stories of Naropa, Marpa, and Mila Respa; they stayed with me while the other Tibetan stories of Padmasambhava and Tsong-ka-pas, as well as most of the Hindu tantra, I hardly remembered. What does it mean that these figures are the early lineage holders of the Kagyr Buddhists—the Tibetan Buddhist group to which I now belong? Now their names come up every time I recite the lineage supplication of the morning liturgy! "Coincidence" means much more in Buddhism than random happenstance. Things coincide because they have an affinity—a Karmic connection.

Probably my first strong personal inclination toward Buddhism occurred in 1973. After two difficult years at New College in Sarasota, Florida, I had just moved to Eau Claire. I had just visited my lover, who had an inoperable brain tumor, for what I knew would be the last time. Alone in a new town, one classic fall day I walked toward my office to teach my Buddhism class. The coemergence of my misery and the beauty of the world snapped something in my mind. "The Four Noble Truths are true!" I exclaimed. In particular I saw how much my suffering was caused by my desire for things to be different. I began then to try to tame my desire and appreciate my situation—even when it seemed miserable. Later I learned to articulate that nonjudgmental appreciation for the totality of one's situation and one's mind as another experience of *maitri* or self-acceptance. Almost as soon as I began to have intuitive feeling for the truth of basic Buddhist *dharma,* I began following an intuition that is not typical of many academic scholars of religion. Many academics are impressed by the soundness of the Four Noble Truths, but don't act on them in a personal way; this theoretical, nonexperiental approach is applied especially to the Fourth Truth, the Truth of the Eightfold Path, and most especially to those aspects of path concerning meditation practice. At that point I really knew nothing about meditation practice, despite my Ph.D. in History of Religions from the University of Chicago—an interesting comment on the academic approach and its blind spots. I realized that both academically and personally I needed to find out about meditation practice—not so easy a task in Eau Claire. A little over a year later, I began to do *zazen* (basic Zen practice) simply to begin some practice, even though I knew I wanted to practice Tibetan Vajrayana Buddhism eventually. In 1976 I received instruction in mindfulness-awareness practice, which is the first and most basic step in practicing Buddhism as taught by my guru, Chogyam Trungpa, Rinpoche, a Tibetan meditation master in the Kagyu lineage. Meditation practice was the missing ingredient in my previous training—both academic and religious. It is hard to explain why one would sit still, seemingly doing nothing but in a disciplined manner, for hours on end, especially since it can be rather difficult. But that practice is basically what Buddhism offered that had not been offered by anything else I had tried. I felt and still feel that it makes a tremendous difference, though it is very difficult and perhaps not advisable to try to say why or how it makes such a difference.

The decisive factor in my becoming a Buddhist, however, was not my love of practice or my affinity for the teachings. One can be profoundly influenced by these without formally becoming a Buddhist. Meeting my teacher, when I met Trungpa Ripoche's dharma-heir the Vajra Regent Osel Tendzin, was the point of no return that made taking refuge inevitable. Meeting one's guru is a classic, definitive experience in Vajrayana Buddhism—probably the single most important moment in life. At the time, I did not know what was happening and am glad now that I was so unguarded. I had gone to Boulder for the first time (1977) convinced that I would remain a non-Buddhist meditator. After all, converting again seemed a bit much! Three strikes, I thought, and you're out. Furthermore, I didn't trust gurus and did not want to get mixed up with one. I didn't even know there was a Vajra Regent or who he was. Dressed up in one of my saris —after all, I was teaching Hinduism at a Buddhist school—I went to a faculty reception that the Regent attended. Initially I was quite annoyed about the fuss people were making over him. Then, inexplicably I began to feel something I had never felt before. I also began to feel that I wanted to talk with him, though I couldn't imagine why or what I would say. Besides, I don't stand in long lines waiting for short conversation with strangers. But that night I did. Not much later I realized this person was the only person I had ever met who knew something I needed to know and could not learn by myself. I also found everything about Naropa Institute and the strong large Buddhist center in Boulder exciting, provocative, and familiar. Even more than in India, I felt that *here* my mind and the world were one, that what happened "outside" and what happened "inside" were not at odds. So the summer did not end as planned. I took refuge in the Buddha, the Dharma, and the Sangha.

Immediately my life began to change drastically. My connection with Buddhism became the dominant influence in my life. The Buddhist communities in Boulder and in Chicago became important social reference points, and I have gone to both places innumerable times, both as student and as teacher. For the most part, my closest friends now are in those two communities. I also began immediately to start a meditation group in Eau Claire. In November 1977 the first meditation workshop in Eau Claire occurred. One of the people who began practice at that time is still practicing in Eau Claire. Over the years many people in Eau Claire have been introduced to meditation practice, and a great deal of my energy has gone into this group. My teaching style began to change immediately and my academic writing more gradually. Writing and teaching are now more grounded in experience, more concerned with basic existential situations, and less complex and theoretical.

In 1980 I attended Vajrahhatu Seminary, a milestone in one's Buddhist path. At the end of this three-month study and practice intensive, most students receive Vajrayana transmission and begin *ngundro* practice—the Vajrayana preliminaries. Seminary was one of the most important and wonderful things I have ever done. Magically, many of the strands of my life came together while I was there. *Unspoken Worlds* was released just as it began; while there, I completed "Steps Toward Feminine Imagery of Deity in Jewish Theology"; I also made the arrangements to go to the first conference on "Buddhism and Christianity in Encounter" to speak on "Buddhism and Feminism," the topic that has become my major concern.

That conference in Hawaii (1980) was a significant turning point. I had been practicing meditation for four years and had changed a lot. I could no longer just talk like an academic even when I tried. Some people were teasing me, and others were horrified that I sounded like a Buddhist. Buddhist-Christian dialogue was a new enterprise for me, and "Buddhism and Feminism" a new topic. This was my first time speaking to an academic audience from the point of view of a Buddhist practitioner. Furthermore, I began my *ngundro* practice two days before the conference started. The presentation was one of the best I have ever done. Though some academic types looked puzzled and left, Aitken Roshi grinned from ear to ear. I knew I had survived another transition and felt immense gratitude for the path and my teachers.

At that point I really practiced intensely, completing my *ngundro*—100,000 prostrations, 100,000 repetitions of the Vajrasattva mantra, 100,000 mandala-offerings, and 1,000,000 guru-yoga recitations—in a year, which is, relatively speaking, rather quickly. Finally (1981) I arrived at Vajrayana practice—the *sadhana* of Vajrayogini. After another period of intensive practive, I completed my first million recitations and did the fire Puja—an elaborate profound ten-day meditation ritual—to purify the practice (October, 1984). Vajrayogini is a *yidam* (Sanskrit *ishta*) or "personal deity," a nontheistic deity whose practice (the liturgy and the formless meditation) is assigned to the student by the guru to develop the student further. The practice of the Vajrayogini *sadhana* (assigned spiritual practice) is probably infinite in its potential; for me several implications stand out. First is the subtlety of nontheistic "deity practice." Despite the seeming paradox of a "nontheistic deity," working with deity as a projection that reveals and corrects our tendencies is, to me, much more profound than regarding deity as transcendent other. When I became Buddhist, I did not agonize over belief in God, which is so difficult for so many pre-Buddhists. Instead I acknowledged that I had never been much of a theist and was relieved to stop referring to God as an external reference point. A second outstanding facet of Vajrayogini practice for me revolves around

-43-

Vajrayogini's female gender. Here is the missing link in all my work on Hindu goddesses and female God-language in Judaism—an authentic living transmission that I personally could practice regarding the female principle. No longer was I confined to books, art work, and my imagination! In addition, I may soon be initiated into similar practices regarding the masculine principle—an intriguing proposition.

In the three years since Vajrayogini began to dominate my life, another new turn has developed. I have become increasingly involved in Buddhist-Christian dialogue. With only one publication to date in that area, the concern is still quite undeveloped, but I have been invited to join the Buddhist-Christian Theological Encounter Group and expect to become more heavily involved in this area. This development brings me full circle in many ways. Appreciation for the plurality of religions has been as dominant a thread in my life as feminism and spiritual path have been. My early theology of world religions led to my excommunication. Once I decided on the study of religion as my vocation, the cross-cultural comparative study of religion seemed the only relevant approach to me. Presenting various traditions with empathy is the major focus of my teaching. I am glad finally to have some peaceful contact with Christianity, to learn again from it; I seem to be becoming ever more theological and to straddle the line between phenomenological and normative concern with religion; I also, somewhat to my surprise, have a non-feminist (but non-not-feminist) interest for the first time in many years. All in all, the ironies amuse and tickle me.

People often are curious about what happened to my feminism under the impact of so much meditation practice and ask why I would give my energy and support to a religion that does have some problems with sexism, rather than to feminist *wicca*. To be sure, before I took refuge, I investigated the branch of Buddhism I was joining; I did not need a third trip through a sexist religion. I have asked all my teachers about Buddhism, feminism, and sexism and have been consistently encouraged. The advantages of learning from a lineage of unbroken transmission are so great that I am not attracted to the broken lineage of *wicca* and certainly not to separatism or to female supremacy, which I do not think have much potential for easing our human problems and difficulties. But unquestionably my feminism, like the rest of my intellectual and spiritual life, has changed greatly under the impact of meditation practice. I have written a great deal about this transformation. Briefly, ideology and anger as a fixed reference point cannot survive genuine practice; they melt, releasing their intelligence and energy. However, when ideology and anger do dissolve, releasing energy and intelligence, "feminist" concerns remain. I have frequently been a spokesperson for feminism to Buddhists and have not always been initially acclaimed for that activity, though I receive positive mail from concerned Buddhists around the world. My current project is a book on Buddhism and feminism. I feel that the *tendril*—the auspicious coincidence—of Buddhism and feminism in the West is potentially the most promising encounter for both outlooks. Their conjuction would illumine and transform our current dilemmas, whether personal or global. Probably I will spend the rest of my life on this concern.

I also feel that practice has completely soaked through my intellectual and academic life. By now I think I have spent as much time doing meditation practice as I put into getting my degrees. I feel that the practice has done at least as much as my academic training and experience to make me the teacher and scholar I now am.

Together the academic perspective and meditation practice make a perfect, complete whole. It amazes and saddens me that they are so rarely joined. Warmth, communication, clarity, helping others—all the basic virtues and joys of human existence—depend so much on both. Nevertheless I often stress the side of meditation practice these days, because it is the underutilized and underappreciated consort of the pair. Somehow, meditation uncovers existing clarity and warmth. On the other hand, I don't want to sound too romantic. Meditation practice, especially Vajrayana practice, is difficult and brings into unavoidable awareness many things that one might not choose to go through. When things become more vivid, everything becomes more vivid, not just the "good parts." It is difficult to develop unbiased appreciation regarding the "good parts" and the struggles; yet because we learn so much from both, we need to experience both deeply. So perhaps all that I have learned is to hear intuition and to jump in—as much as possible.

CHRISTINE DOWNING

Christine Downing received her B.A. in English Literature from Swarthmore College in 1948 and her Ph.D. in Theology and Culture from Drew University in 1966. She taught in the Department of Religion at Douglass College of Rutgers University from 1963 to 1974 and then went to San Diego State University to assume the chair of the Department of Religious Studies. Since coming to San Diego she has also served on the Core Faculty of the California School of Professional Psychology. In 1982 she received an M.A. in Counseling from United States International University and a Diploma in Gestalt Therapy from the San Diego Gestalt Institute; she has a small private psychotherapy practice. Her many publications include *Face to Face to Face, A Poetics of the Psyche, The Goddess: Mythological Images of the Feminine,* and two forthcoming books, *Journey through Menopause* and *Sisters.*

"Dear Chris. . . . Love, Christine"

Dear Chris,

I had a fantasy once, a year or so ago, in which we met and you embraced me, saying, "I'd like to grow up to be just like you." I wonder if you'd say that if you really knew, really knew me, really knew all that has been part of my becoming the fifty-two-year-old woman now writing this letter.

I think of you often: twenty-eight, mother of five young children, about to begin graduate school. It's difficult to remember now all the ways that being twenty-eight then, almost twenty-five years ago, was different—perhaps especially for middle-class women—from being twenty-eight today. I have a daughter who is now almost as old as you; how different her life is from yours. I wonder if you and she would even know how to be friends.

Despite your ambitious and complex expectations for yourself, it would not have occurred to you to name yourself a feminist; the label had no contemporary currency. Despite your intense involvements with women while in college, the designation lesbian would have seemed utterly irrelevant to your experience. Though you saw your marrying as an undergraduate and immediately beginning having a family as a conscious and personal choice (and as interestingly contrary to some of your adolescent dreams), it was certainly congruent with your time's conventions. Though I do remember how even then you understood "wife" and "mother" as roles you had happily undertaken to play, not as self-definitions. When at twenty-eight you felt ready to move beyond these roles, you certainly seemed imbued with much native confidence that whatever you might choose to do would be possible—you would have the requisite inner resources, and the world would respond welcomingly to your overtures.

My daughter, whom you knew only as an infant, has grown into a radiant, self-assured young woman, more clearly focused in her scholarly interests than you and with a more consciously developed sense of self. Though she values serious, committed relationships (she lived with her lover all through college) and longs for a truly mutual, multidimensional, permanent liaison, she has a well-defined sense of personal boundaries. I cannot imagine her being swallowed up in any relationship; it seems evident that she has given priority to her dedication to her chosen discipline. When she finishes her doctoral degree in a year or so, she will already be a well-published, well-known figure in her field. Yet I sense her to have a much more tempered sense of her own limitations and of the outward possibilities likely to be available to her than you did, and a definite awareness of how those bounds are in part gender-related. It *is* a different time.

Still, you are alike in many ways—in your life-affirming energy, contagious enthusiasm, self-confident physical presence, intellectual acumen. Surprisingly, she would probably be more likely than you to appreciate these similarities, because she is more accustomed to turn to women for intimate friendship and to expect to find them her intellectual peers. I'm quite sure she would be interested in knowing how I'd tell my story to you.

It does make a difference to whom one tells one's story. I vividly remember how aware I became almost a decade ago, when I moved to California, to a strange city where I knew no one, that to the new people I met I *was* my stories. I seemingly had utter freedom to select, to omit, to change, to invent —yet actually each other person demanded a particular truth of me. Sandor Ferenczi once wrote a one-page paper about the significance of the choice of the particular other with whom one shares a particular dream. I tell you my dream because I believe it in some way to be about you; you listen because you believe it to be about me.

Thus I choose you for this telling of my story because I feel it to be about you. I choose you, the twenty-eight-year-old, rather than some earlier or later incarnation because I sense you to be at a juncture where you are deciding to become me or to become someone else. The possibility of your choosing some other, radically different life may exist more truly at this moment than at any preceding or subsequent time. I choose you because you'll be interested in the struggles, not just the successes; the inner aspect, not just the outwardly visible part; the personal dimension, not just the narrowly professional component. I choose you because you'll expect a particular kind of honesty, the kind I see you as having shared with our friend, Pat. What you'd be interested in, no *curriculum vitae* would communicate.

The name "Chris" so well conveys your particular kind of androgynous energy. Recently I have begun to prefer to be called "Christine," feeling myself ready now to accept the more feminine and somehow more whole connotations of the name I was given at birth but have never before been willing to claim. I'm not sure just when Chris became Christine; this letter is in part an exploration of that transition. I don't expect to find *a* particular moment when the change occurs— so for much that happens in the years that intervene between your decision to return to school and my writing of this letter, it may be more appropriate to say "we" than "you" *or* "I."

I wonder if I can imagine you any more clearly than you can imagine me. Oh, it's fairly easy, of course, for me to get the outward facts straight; but the inner meaning, the values, assumptions, questions, fears are more evasive. You are, at twenty-eight, about to celebrate the first birthday of your fifth child, your first daughter. You have just moved into a large, rambling house out in the country. It is all quite different from the life you'd once imagined for yourself, a life that would have had you at twenty-eight already an established writer of fiction, a sophisticated woman of the world with several fascinating lovers, maybe almost ready to choose one with whom to settle down. But the life you've actually chosen is genuinely fulfilling—the sexuality, the childbearing, the close friendships with other young women absorbed in the same challenges give you access to a discovery and validation of your feminine embodiment that you feel you might all too easily have missed.

But marriage isn't all you'd once hoped; there are intellectual interests and spiritual searchings that you find it impossible to share with husband, children, or the neighboring women. Quite early on and very painfully you recognized there was a part of you that felt radically unnurtured—until you met Pat, and luckily that was pretty soon, before your second child was born. Together you two read Jung, you began recording your dreams and working on them with one another's help. You began to write poetry and fiction; she returned to her sculpture. The two of you read the same books and discussed them passionately. You found language and courage to communicate to one another your uncertainties, ambivalences, restlessness, vulnerability, deep but elusive longings. Both of you believed that your searching wasn't simply a psychological matter; that it required some outward expression.

By the time you gave birth to your fifth child, you knew that you were on the verge of a new phase of life, though you had no picture of what that meant. During that first year of your daughter's life, you did some editing and research for a New York psychologist, you had a brief but intense affair. Both left you knowing, "That's not quite it, though I still don't know what is."

Was it just this year that you first read Buber's *Between Man and Man?* I remember that you had been encouraged to read *I and Thou* often before and had tried; but somehow had never gotten very far. This time you received what Buber had to say—that "all real living is meeting," that "I become I in order to say Thou"—as a long-awaited complementation to Jung's emphasis on individuation, on the self. To bring these two perspectives together, experientially if not theoretically, seized you as a life task—though, again, what that might mean concretely remained a mystery.

I remember so vividly the evening you and Pat went to hear Esther Harding, the author of *Woman's Mysteries,* speak. You forgot so quickly the details of what she said, but the impression she made on you was ineradicable. You knew: "Here is a *woman,* not a nurturing mother nor a sexual playmate but a woman who clearly has her center in herself. She is as strong, as intelligent, as direct as the old-maid headmistress of my youth, her face as life-marked as the women in Grant Wood's portraits. But she conveys a gaiety, a wisdom of soul, an unquenched curiosity I have never marked in those other figures." Afterwards in Pat's kitchen, sipping coffee, you discovered that somehow in Harding's presence that evening you had each come to a radical decision. "I am going into therapy," she said; "I want to become an analyst." "I am going to graduate school; I want to write and maybe teach, but first there is so much I want to learn," you replied.

It was already midsummer, but you applied to the only school within easy commuting distance of your home. You didn't have a definite sense of a particular field of study you wanted to pursue. You'd been a literature major as an undergraduate but now wanted to include philosophy, theology, psychology—all the different ways in which we humans have tried to articulate what it means to be a human self. The catalogue of that single possible school suggested one could do that under the rubric "Religion and Culture." You had no idea that there may not have been any other school anywhere that offered such an interdisciplinary doctoral program. You had no idea that one didn't do graduate work in religious studies without first getting a seminary degree. You had no idea that women studied religious education, that only men studied theology. You really had so little idea of how lucky you'd been or of what you were getting into . . . .

How I bless you for the naiveté and courage! How I'd like you to know what happened after that, how you became me!

As you began graduate school you certainly had very little in the way of defined long-range goals; perhaps we never have had. You were there, really, as part of a personal search, not out of professional ambition or economic need. You were there because you wanted a more directed course of study than the stacks of a suburban library could provide, because you wanted people to talk to about what you were reading and thinking, because you wanted respect-worthy criticism of your writing. You longed for contact with people competent to tell you where you were on target and where off, where what you had to say was a commonplace and where original.

It was your good fortune to find just the community of scholars for which you yearned—brilliant, dedicated teachers and bright, emotionally sensitive, warmly affectionate fellow students. The excitement of being in such a world was almost more than you could bear. The alternation between spending a morning studying Hölderlin in a way that called upon all your poetic and intuitive capacities and being required the same afternoon in a class on Barth to think more logically, more rigorously, more quickly than ever before was almost enough to make one schizophrenic.

Luckily you went to school only one day a week. Though you had lots of studying to do in between, that was blessedly balanced by the hours devoted to sorting laundry, making bread, praising crayoned drawings, settling quarrels, reading bedtime stories. Only your oldest had yet started school and, of course, there was no daycare then. But your mother lived nearby; she was very proud of what you were doing and happy to play grandmother once a week. Your husband, too, seemed generously delighted in your new life and very willing to take on household chores and childrearing tasks. By the standards of today the division of family tasks was still very gender-determined, but I well understand how readily you assumed that it was *your* responsibility to do the foodshopping and to plan the meals, to oversee the cleaning and manage the family budget. You understood him to be helping you with *your* tasks.

This remained true later in that period when "you" gradually became "me," when we were both in some sense present. In our first years of teaching it was so important to us to coach a softball team and to teach Sunday school, to play Den Mother and P.T.A. president—as though it were all right to be not just a suburban housewife only if we didn't shirk the housewife's obligations. It was important to us to be known as a gourmet cook and expert seamstress, and as someone who juggled all this well. Now I'm a little embarrassed at how long it took before we questioned the social expectations you took for granted—maybe just because it all seemed to work so easily for us. Even now I see our husband as having been quite remarkable in this easy acceptance of our new endeavors—and later of our financial independence, our having more recognition in our field than he had in his, even our love affairs.

Recently there has been much discussion of the role that mentors have played in the education of successful professional women. We certainly recognized that several of our professors took a special interest in us. We felt they appreciated and encouraged our intellectual gifts and regarded us as a vibrant, attractive young woman. But I don't believe you saw any one of them as having provided decisive direction or support—nor, in retrospect, do I. Indeed, I would say that our most important instructor was really Sigmund Freud (no more popular then among my Jungian cohorts than now among my feminist ones). Lou Salomé once wrote of Freud that his was the father-face of her life (though they didn't meet until both were over fifty); for us his has been the teacher-face. We have read and reread, listened and talked back, and still learn more at each encounter . . . . Though no course on Freud was included in the curriculum, we knew we could no longer rest content with knowing only Jung's version of Freud and so persuaded one of our teachers to serve as tutor. We read through the entire corpus and much of the secondary literature as well; he read with us, book after book, and we met with him one evening each week to discuss and argue. (I remember also how week after week one of the other students sat in his car outside the professor's study window to protect us from being raped—his fantasy, not ours.)

I remember you had feared you might feel like "grandmother" beause of starting graduate school so long after college; instead, because of years spent in seminary, in parishes, or earning money for further schooling, most of the other students were about your age. You were the only woman and reveled in that. The half dozen or so whom we came to know well all seemed half in love with us and yet also willing to include us as "one of the guys." They were not threatened by our brains or our ambition, or even by all those babies. They

were a remarkable group of young men, able to show vulnerability, tenderness, confusion, hurt not only to us but to one
another. We and they were all at least somewhat Jungian and
would have agreed that you were given (and took) an
"anima" role. They welcomed our female presence as a support to their attempt to discover and cultivate their own
"femininity." Long after they were dispersed all over the
country, these men constituted our "kraas"—the community
to which we would most spontaneously turn to share joy,
anxiety, failure, the community to whom our writing was
really addressed.

We had no female role models or colleagues and didn't even
know enough to miss them.

You had wanted to go back to school in part as preparation
for writing about the Buber-Jung dialogue. In the event we
wrote our dissertation on Buber, our closest friend wrote his
on Jung. We wanted very much to escape the constrictions of
the traditional dissertation, to write with life and grace, to
include not only our intellectual but also our emotional and
existential response to Buber's writing. We were interested
primarily in the interrelationship of form and content: how
what Buber had to say forced him out of abstract, discursive
theologizing toward poetry, folktale, drama. Our aim was not
so much to prove a thesis as to explore the unfolding of a
lifework.

Getting it written took longer than we'd expected. At first
we had been wholeheartedly enthusiastic about being back in
school, but after two years that eagerness had, to our great
confusion, disappeared. I remember our being scheduled for a
class presentation and finding we had nothing to say and
couldn't bear any longer to be just a good reader, scholar,
critic. We took a year off, officially to begin work on our
dissertation. By then we had passed the qualifying exams
with distinction, had been elected a Kent Fellow, and had
received some recognition from distinguished scholars in our
field, but weren't sure any more of how any of this connected
with us. Our closest friend had taken a teaching position a
thousand miles away; we missed him terribly. We wondered
whether we wouldn't really rather just be a wife and mother

"like everyone else." It was our youngest child's last year before kindergarten, and we wanted to spend it with her. I write about it lightly, but it was not an easy time for us.

In the late spring of that year we received a phone call asking if we'd be interested in a teaching appointment at the women's college of the state university. It was an ideal opportunity, *the* ideal opportunity—a good school only a half hour away from our home. We realized how much we'd missed *talking* during our year out of school, how much we longed for colleague and students to talk with about what we were reading and thinking. That recognition led us to accept the job, even though we'd not finished the dissertation, even though we'd planned not even to consider teaching until our daughter was in first grade.

The first year of teaching was exhausting—and exhilarating. Students told us later they had never had a teacher as nervous as we were in our first few lectures. Material that we had expected would easily fill a week of classes (and should have) was used up in fifteen minutes; we found we no longer knew how to talk except in the technical theological language that had so bewildered us during our first weeks in graduate school; we wanted discussion and had no idea how to elicit it. We had been assigned courses we were entirely unprepared to teach. We were up till long past midnight every night and lost ten pounds that first semester. But we loved it; we felt that, though we had never consciously decided to become a teacher, we had found our true vocation.

It was a small department; the chair, who'd been there for years, was the only other full-time member. But this was the early sixties, when religion departments were beginning to attract students who in another era would have majored in psychology, philosophy, sociology, literature—and we were ambitious and popular. The department grew quickly; an additional full-time person was added almost every year for the next six or seven. The curriculum also expanded, and we were soon able to teach courses which reflected our interdisciplinary interests: religion and literature, religion and psychology, myth and ritual. We felt the department was one we and the chair had created together. He made it evident how fond he'd become of us (though we never talked about that directly and had no inkling of what that would one day engender).

You had done your graduate work in theology simply because that had made it possible for you to pursue your multidisciplinary interests. Naturally this led to a teaching assignment in a religion department, though we always felt a little uncomfortable there. We were at ease with what the actual teaching required but not with the public identification as a theologian, which seemed a misleading representation. We were never as pious nor as Christian as the label seemed to connote. Nevertheless these were years in which we tried to perform as a scholar in the theological field. We wrote on the exodus metaphor as constitutive for Hebraic faith, on literary amplifications of the Christ figure—always stressing the iconoclastic elements within the biblical tradition. We had no awareness that our claustrophobic response to the tradition might be rooted in its patriarchal androcentrism. Our critique was directed rather against its monotheistic, historicistic, and anthropocentric biases. I don't believe that reading what we published then would lead one to guess the author was female. Nor would we have wanted it otherwise. We would have seen no reason for our content, our style, or our conclusions to be different from what a male scholar might produce.

Our consciousness at that time was defined by what I would call a heterosexual fantasy. We were happy that, though physically located on the campus of the women's college, ours was the only religion department in the university, so that our classes attracted as many men as women. We still felt comfortable with the Jungian notion that there are specifically feminine attributes and attitudes and specifically masculine ones, and that the task of individuation for both women and men is to bring the contrasexual archetype to consciousness. Our ideal—for self and for the men with whom we were involved—was androgyny.

We felt our professional life was well balanced by the very different challenges and rewards of life at home with husband and children, and by our love affairs—which we understood as complementary to our marriage and unlikely to threaten it.

Our life seemed stable and satisfying. But then it all fell apart. And so did the sense of a seamless continuity that has made it possible to speak so easily of "our" life. From this point onward it becomes necessary to use "I" rather than "we."

I fell in love more deeply than we had ever expected; my lover's wife learned of our affair and was shattered. I in turn had a serious breakdown as I came to terms with how badly I had wounded this other woman. I came very close to killing myself. I think that at this point what happened to me becomes something you might have deliberately chosen to avoid, could you have foreseen it. Though in some strange way perhaps you did foresee; I remember so clearly how often in your teens and early twenties you spoke, only half in jest, of your expectation that you would die before you were thirty-seven. In some ways you did. Strangely (not too strangely?) this breakdown occurred the year we'd been awarded an inter-disciplinary fellowship which freed us from our teaching obligations. We had planned to go to Germany with our children and write a book. I did go to Germany and took our children, too, but did no writing—I spent most of that year in the underworld, not at all sure I would emerge. Sometime, perhaps at the beginning of spring, I began to heal . . . .

It seems appropriate that I had gone to my motherland to recover and that recovery led to a loosening of the father-identification that had for so long bound me. When I returned to teaching in the fall of 1968, I felt as though I was entering an entirely new world. My reestablished stability still felt very precarious; I felt fragile. I had no more career ambitions, hoped only to survive; teaching was a way of staying in the world of others. It was years before I wrote again or thought of myself as someone who had anything to say. (I got tenure during this time but on the basis of work we'd completed, though not necessarily published, earlier.) I returned to a world in which my new vulnerability was somehow appropriate. During the spring of 1968 while I was in Europe, student-led uprisings in Berlin and Paris were major events. I came home to discover that in America, too, students had begun to demand political responsibility and moral relevance from their universities and their professors. They wanted participation in shaping the curriculum; they wanted more experiential modes of teaching. They saw connections between the oppression of blacks and the oppressive war in Vietnam and their oppression as students. My female students were newly aware as well of their oppression as women, not only in concrete socioeconomic terms but by assumptions deeply ingrained in literature, philosophy, theology, language itself. They were also beginning to realize how this entered into their denigrating perceptions of themselves and of other women. My students were feminists; many were discovering they were also lesbians—that really valuing and loving themselves as women meant loving women. My students became my teachers—and in a sense my healers also, as they presented me with challenges that reawakened my life-energy.

Our adolescent children, involved by then in the peace movement, in rock music, in psychedelic drugs, were also teachers—as were the younger women I began to know who were just entering my field, women who looked to the women of my generation as role models but who really initiated *us* into the challenges of creating a genuinely feminist theology.

By the time of Cambodia and Kent State, I was visible on campus as one of the more radical faculty. I was not really aware of how alienated I had become from the department chair nor of the degree to which (in a time when university funding was suddenly tighter and when younger colleagues were no longer assured that each would in turn get tenure) the cooperative collegiality of our department had evaporated. The next fall a new instructor joined the department; he and I became close. We two and one other young man in our department were actively involved with the "radical faculty caucus." Our intimacy and our politics—to this day I don't know which was the weightier—were very upsetting to the chair to whom I'd once been so close. It took him several years, but he managed to get rid of all three of us—one of the men was not rehired when his probationary instructorship came to an end, the other was refused tenure. I had tenure and could have stayed, but preferred not to. Though all this was less shattering than the breakdown seven years earlier, I was again having to acknowledge how my own naiveté and recklessness had created havoc in the lives of others. I was also aware that in some definitive way a life phase was over and that leaving this university was a way of marking that transition.

In my personal life, also, it was time to move on. Our children were grown; I wanted to explore who I was apart from the roles of wife, mother, or even lover. I wanted to discover what it would be like to live alone, at least for a time. I was lucky enough to receive an invitation to come as visiting professor to a California university, and when I found I liked being there, arranged to stay on as chair of the department. My first year coincided with my term as the first woman president of the American Academy of Religion. This office came to me almost accidentally when (thanks to the efforts of the women's caucus) it was time for *a* woman to have this position, but my term became a kind of omen of the new blossoming that occurred when I moved here.

More than ever before, I felt I had come into my full power —as teacher, writer, woman—that I was doing exactly what I'd been born to do. I loved my teaching, not so much what I did in the university religion department but rather what I did in my role as adjunct instructor in a graduate clinical psychology program. I felt I had found my subject, my students, my voice. I was teaching Freud in a way that allowed me to pass on to others the gift I most valued from those years in graduate school. I was teaching future therapists about *therapeia*, about serving the wounded and vulnerable souls of their patients. I was teaching in a way that took advantage of all that I had learned through reading, friendship, failure, and joy.

I began to write in a way that brought together my personal experience and searching with my scholarly gifts and expertise—I now write because I *had* to. I wrote in order to make sense of my own life, and because I had something to say I believed would truly matter to others, though it wouldn't be "theology," wouldn't be published in the prestigious professional journals, wouldn't further my career. I began by writing about the Greek goddesses, then about sisters, then about menopause as rite of passage . . . .

More had shifted during that breakdown period than I immediately recognized. Chris became Christine. The androgynous understanding of self, according to which some of my attributes seemed feminine, others masculine, no longer fit. I now knew myself as feminine through and through, as much in my courage and intellectual capacity as in my gifts of empathy and intuition. I found my network had changed, that I now sent my drafts not to the men with whom I'd gone to graduate school but to women: former students and feminist colleagues all over the country, academicians, therapists, poets.

I've been here nine years now; have just resigned as chair of the department and am once again on one of those leaves of absence from the academy that seem to become turning points. I have just finished my twentieth year of teaching. I've just completed menopause. I'm aware that if my life lasts as long as my mother's already has, I'm just beginning the second half of my adult life. It's strange, Chris, but in some ways I feel myself just as much on the threshold of a new beginning as you were at twenty-eight. I've gone back to school and gotten a graduate degree in counseling. I still want to teach—but less—and to be able to focus on teaching the things I really know and care about. I think I want to balance it more with the one-to-one work of therapy. Maybe it is time now to take on for myself that other half of Esther Harding's legacy, the half your friend Pat took on by choosing therapy when you chose teaching. Our lifelong fascination with the tension between Buber's stress on deep person-with-person interaction and Jung's emphasis on the search for self pulls me now to work with individuals in a way that teaching doesn't allow. Though I'm unsure. I know I'm not yet able to bring all that I know and am to this medium—as I can to teaching and writing. Of course, this is part of the attraction —to learn how to do something I don't know how to do. I've also been considering trying my hand at writing fiction. I know I want more time for quiet solitude and for reflective writing. I want to live with the woman I love. The commitment to women becomes more and more central as the years unfold.

I think I've written you all this in part because I want your blessing on what I've made and will make of our life—but also because I want to thank you for your gift to me of hope and courage.

Love,
Christine

BARBARA HARGROVE

Barbara Hargrove is Professor of the Sociology of Religion at the Iliff School of Theology, where she has taught for the past five years. She attended Colorado State University for two years, then dropped out of school and served as a farm housewife for some seventeen years, returning to CSU when the youngest of her four children started first grade.

She received her B.S. in Social Science from CSU in 1961, her M.A. in Sociology in 1963, and her Ph.D. in Sociology in 1968, from the same institution. She has taught sociology at Hollins College in Virginia, the University of North Florida in Jacksonville, and the Divinity School of Yale University. She also spent one year at the University of California at Berkeley, doing research into new religious movements.

She is the author of several books: two texts in the sociology of religion, *Religion for a Dislocated Generation, Reaching Youth: Heirs to the Whirlwind,* and *Women of the Cloth,* a study of women in parish clergy positions in nine Protestant denominations. She has edited the book *Religion and the Sociology of Knowledge* and written a number of articles for professional and popular journals. She is a member of Wellshire Presbyterian Church in Denver and has served on a number of denominational and ecumenical committees and working groups.

Free to Be Me

My interest in scholarship and religion traces back farther than I can remember. I grew up in a very small town, among people who encouraged me to take joy in learning, and where the one local church shared with the consolidated school the status of center of community identity and action. The school and the church were my worlds.

My parents lived a life of simple piety and hard work, struggling to make ends meet during the Great Depression. Their religion was simple and straightforward. Dad, often working overtime seven days a week on the farm, made it to church whenever he could, and served on the board of trustees —served, indeed, putting in many hardly-spare hours working to keep the building in repair and enough money in the till to pay the part-time preachers who served us after the town fell on hard times and had to let its full-time pastor go. One of my earliest church-related memories is of the community auction that was held to get enough money to pay off the minister so that he could leave.

My mother served as substitute pianist for the church, so I spent many hours on the front pew, trying to see pictures in the grain of the wood of the pulpit, but listening nonetheless to the sermons and learning the hymns—mostly "good old gospel songs"—by heart. The messages there, and in the Sunday school, were of a type I learned later to call fundamentalist; at that time and place they were the only thing labeled "Christian." The group of people who dominated the church, which my parents never fully fit into, held their religion in the form of a narrow and rigid moralism. My own appropriation of it denied the dogmatism but accepted the intensity of their teachings. The result was a personal religiosity that knew no limits, and as I moved toward adolescence, it became caught up in the romanticism I was learning from the many books I read.

Reading was one of my primary occupations. I was something of a rebel in many of my activities, so that books became the one approved way that I could live a life of my own. I rebelled against my mother's urgings that I play nice things with nice girls, preferring to be an unwanted tagalong to my older brother and his friends or to play with children of families not defined as quite so "nice." I rebelled against helping with the housework, followed Dad to the fields and the barn, helped with my brother's paper route, delivered milk around town, spent long hours herding cattle down roadsides or sheep in pastures without good enough fences for them to be left untended. And always I read books—anything I could get my hands on in a town without a library. I lived in a world peopled by fictional characters, walked to the rhythm of the poetry of an earlier, more metered day.

One of the most available books, of course, was the Bible. And while I never caught up with the pious accomplishments of my brother, who had read the Bible from cover to cover, I think, before he started high school, I was as compulsive in my reading of Scripture as anything else. I carried a little book of the Psalms in my pocket while herding the cattle and sheep and found the shepherd images there something I could relate to.

In fact, it was Bible reading that sparked my deepest and most long-lasting rebellion. When I was in junior high school our Sunday school class had a couple lessons taken from Galatians—a dangerous book for a rebellious adolescent who read the whole thing instead of the assigned few verses! What narrow moralisms can stand up to such ringing statements as, "For freedom Christ has set us free; stand fast therefore, and do not submit again to a yoke of slavery!" I saw the book as my Magna Charta in relation to those whom I considered my oppressors and who yet had taught me that the Bible was the very word of God and was to be taken literally and with utmost seriousness. No matter how much I am confronted with evidence that St. Paul was a male chauvinist, I count him as my liberator. From that time on, I was convinced that it was my Christian duty to behave as a free person.

It is hard to say what that conviction might have done for my relation to organized religion if my only point of reference had remained that local church. Fortunately, by the time I was fifteen the church had begun to help its youth attend what was then known as the Presbytery's Summer Youth Conference, a week in the mountains that included a series of morning classes, along with afternoon hiking and the like, evening vespers, and all those familiar elements of church camp. My first year, our evening devotions in the dorm were led by a pastor's wife who made great use of candlelight and Kahlil Gibran—a giant leap from the plain and dour fundamentalism of our local church. In those evenings and in her class on "Youth at Worship" I discovered what worship could mean. I adored the woman who gave this gift. She may have been the first woman I ever wanted to emulate. But then, I adored everyone there and everything about Summer Conference. Here were people who believed as I did, who gave me permission to have a religion of joy, freedom, intellectual rigor, and action in the world. I loved them all.

Some of them became my classmates in college, letting that experience seem to some degree an extension of Summer Conference. I entered college with the same joy with which I had returned each year to Conference and with the same expectations of learning and loving. I also went with the hope of freedom and became involved in a social life denied me in our small-town high school. Colorado State College of Agriculture and Mechanical Arts (now Colorado State University) at that time had a student body predominantly male (nearly eight boys for every girl), and I tended to major in boys.

All that was soon to change, for in December of my first year Pearl Harbor brought World War II to our doorstep. My college class was affected perhaps more than any other. Nearly all my male classmates were taken by the military, either through the draft or by enlisting, long before they could finish their college programs.

Like many others in those days, I carried my major in the opposite sex to its logical conclusion, trading in my plans for a B.S. for a Mrs. in the middle of my sophomore year. I dropped out of college at the end of that year to follow my husband around through his military training. I may have rebelled against many of the expected female roles when I was growing up, but my marriage celebrated my having found a man who made me glad to be a woman. It took me many years to discover that his way with women was unusual. Howard could not tolerate hierarchical relationships, no matter where he might stand in them. Our marriage was a full partnership; I had my share of the freedom and of the responsibility. When he came home from his tour of duty we bought a small farm near that small town of my childhood and built up a dairy farm together, raised four children together, and worked in the church together.

Here my rebellion continued. After the war, when returning veterans and high agricultural prices brought prosperity back to the town, the church was once again able to hire a full-time minister, and we finally got a young man and his wife who brought with them echoes of the religious style of my beloved Summer Conference. A new contingent of "young marrieds" and some older supporters formed around this new minister and challenged the older leadership of the church. The result was one of those bitter battles that can happen only in small towns around institutions that have become an important part of persons' identities. Families were divided, friends alienated from one another, businesses threatened. In the end, a number of the Old Guard left, and we were left with the task of rebuilding the church in an image we felt more appropriate for the times. In a roundabout way, it was out of that experience that I became interested in the sociology of religion. I was only one of several mothers in the congregation who, when our youngest children started school, went back to college. In some of those college courses I came to think through the significance of the battle in the church and its relationship to other things that had been going on around me.

At the time of our church battle, a similar one had gone on in a nearby small town in a church with which we had once shared a pastor. They, too, had gotten a new young preacher who had brought new ways to the church. But their Old Guard had won out, and the young pastor was sent on his way. Sometime later, both communities were subject to a new state program of school reorganization that would eventually lead to the closing of their high schools. I believe our town was the only rural district that voted in favor of reorganization. People from the other town, the one that had held out against religious change, organized near-mobs of people to protest the workings of the committee, and were dragged kicking and screaming into the new configuration. My sociology courses came alive as I reflected on that experience. In our community, while dealing with religious values, we had already made up our minds to become actors in the increasingly urban world around us; in the other community, they had held out in the church against what was going to be inevitable in public life, and it had affected the ways in which they could respond to the change.

Of course, this was not the only factor influencing their response. They had a winning football team, while ours never seemed to climb out of the cellar. But my continuing interest in religion and our deep involvement in the conflict in the church made this the salient point for me. So when I was offered a teaching assistantship to go on to graduate school, I jumped at the chance to continue studies and to point them in the direction of assessing social change and its relation to the institution of religion. The assistantship allowed me to remain a student without eating into funds that would soon be needed to send the children to college, and I was enjoying my studies so much that there was little doubt that I would keep on. In fact, I was having such a good time at it that during winter quarter, when he was relatively free, my husband began to take some graduate courses. There were evenings when all six of us were busy doing homework—a new kind of family togetherness!

I was nearing my Master's degree when my husband, just turned forty, suffered a fatal heart attack. The shock was great, but with a career of my own already begun and enough insurance and Social Security money to keep the family afloat, I completed that degree, continued working as a part-time teacher and researcher, and as soon as the department received approval for a doctoral program in sociology, enrolled in it. I wanted to study religion and social change.

In all of this I had encountered few problems related to being a woman. As an older woman and one happily married, I probably encountered less harrassment all the way through than some of my younger colleagues. In actuality, there were not many women who were graduate school colleagues until late in my time there, and I was happily oblivious to any problems they may have had. When I consulted faculty about the advisability of getting three degrees from the same little-known institution, I was told that as a woman I might have difficulty getting into some doctoral programs where they didn't know me. The thought had never crossed my mind.

When I first began to look for a job outside CSU, I found a problem. I had finished all the classwork for a Ph.D. and had begun work on my dissertation when I went to a nearby college to apply for a position being vacated by a young man I knew. They offered me a salary I knew to be the same as what he had been offered when he first went there with no more than a Master's degree. I felt angry, felt that they were taking advantage of someone who was a captive housewife, not free to move to get a more lucrative position. My anger gave me courage to do what I had previously been too timid to attempt—to call and check up on a position I had applied for at Hollins College in Virginia. I was convinced that they would not be interested in me at that kind of elite liberal arts college—the kind I'd always dreamed of attending but had never even seen. But they had not written to say I was out of consideration. So I called. I was asked to fly out for an interview and was hired. It was the first of many times when I found my sex to be a positive advantage; at that women's college they wanted more women faculty.

The next fall, leaving my eldest on the farm with his wife and baby, packing off my older daughter to a college in

California that none of us had ever seen, I loaded up the two youngest, who were high school sophomores, two dogs, and all our worldly possessions and set out on a teaching career in Virginia. It was quite an experience. Hollins was and is a women's college, and I had never been near a sex-segregated school before. It was a private college, and all my experience had been with public education. It was a Southern college in a Southern town, and our Western ways were subject to a good bit of strain. It was for us a strange place full of strangers, after a life nearly all spent in one small, very familiar town.

Anthropologist Victor Turner has made a good case for the importance of religion in providing, with its rituals, its interpretations, and its communal support, a way for persons to function in periods of "liminality," when things are changing and the ground on which one stands is getting shaky. Time after time the religious community has done that for me. The church's Summer Conference gave me me a focus and a community as I moved out of my small-town childhood into the broader world of youth. The community of the local church held my world—and my family—together when my husband died. And now a small group in a church in Roanoke allowed me to put down new roots in this fresh soil and take hold. Called into being by a Sunday sermon challenging parishioners to become a reconciling force in the world, this small group met weekly, studied such works as Bonhoeffer's *Life Together,* and developed a deep and intense fellowship. This fellowship broadened when we expanded the membership to make it an interracial dialogue group related to several others in the community. Some members of that group were also colleagues in the Roanoke Valley Council on Human Relations and also in an ad hoc group known as the Concerned Citizens of the Roanoke Valley, which worked on some specific sources of interracial tension. In other words, my involvement in that small church group offered personal support at a time when I needed it and also gave me avenues into public involvement. Is it any wonder that I feel a kinship with recent movements of Basic Christian Communities, or write of churches as mediating structures? Admittedly, I also learned about the divisive potential of such groups, as ours became a focus of discontent in that congregation.

While all that was going on in my life, things were changing at home. My children graduated from high school and went off to college. I rented their rooms to college students and, it seemed, held a perpetual open house that came to be known as "Mama-San's Boarding House." Before I knew it, something like the counterculture of those times had arrived on my doorstep. Students and dropouts came to visit, classmates of my children dropped in when in town, former Sunday school students roaming the country in search of themselves conducted that search from my couch for a week or two at a time.

I taught a course on sex roles, where I suspect I learned at least as much from my students as I taught them, both about their current worlds and those of the Southern women who expected them to join their ranks when they returned from college. In many ways my involvement with women's issues was similar to my work on racial issues—dealing with injustices I saw but which had never touched me deeply—or so I thought. Only as time went on and I found myself developing a deep respect for many of my students, a respect that formerly I had given only to men, did I realize how caught up I had been in the kind of self-hated generated among minorities by a system in which they are disparaged. This realization was a giant step on the road to understanding the meaning of sisterhood.

My primary interests, however, came out in my sociology of religion courses and in my growing awareness of countercultural religion. The man who had served as my major professor during my Master's degree work had been asked to serve as editor of a new series of sociology texts, and he challenged me to write one on the sociology of religion. I managed to get the job done in the midst of all the other things going on, but I was beginning to hunger for a chance to do some research on religion in the counterculture. I heard of a project being developed by two professors at Berkeley,

Charles Glock and Robert Bellah. So with much trepidation I contacted Glock, was encouraged by him to seek out grant money, received a grant from the National Endowment for the Humanities, and spent a year in Berkeley as part of a team researching the "new religious consciousness."

It was a marvelous year. I lived just off Telegraph Avenue, between the People's Park of legend and the one that was to come to be known as Ho Chi Minh Park. The counterculture I found, however, was no longer in its bright years of "flower power" but was beginning to develop its darker side of drug burnout, political extremism, withdrawal, and the like. (It was after I left that one of the secretaries who worked on our project disappeared, only to show up later as a member of the Symbionese Liberation Army, one of Patty Hearst's captors. But that kind of mood was beginning to build.) Some of the religious groups seemed to be the only holdouts of hope and joy—if indeed they were.

The project had roots both in the University and in the Graduate Theological Union, so I also became involved in seminars and socials at the GTU. One seminar, led by Claire Benedics Fisher, was concerned with feminist approaches to the study of religion. I found it—and the people in it—fascinating. This was my first real introduction into the feminist movement in theological education, or even in the church in general.

The year at Berkeley taught me something else, something that I occasionally feel quite cynical about: the importance of sponsorship in the academic game. Since my alma mater had not really offered courses in the sociology of religion, I had for several years deepened my knowledge of my chosen field by attending annual meetings of the Society for the Scientific Study of Religion and the Religious Research Association. I faithfully attended sections, listened carefully, asked questions, and went on, unnoticed. But the fall after I had worked on the religious consciousness project, our team gave a presentation at the meetings. I was identified with the "big names," and from then on I was called upon by name and known. Within a couple of years I was on the Council of the SSSR, then on the Board of the RRA, and eventually its president. I am not convinced that I learned all that much at Berkeley, but it certainly did make a difference in my professional status. I wonder if it should have.

When it came time to return from Berkeley, I succumbed to my desire for adventure and change and went, not back to Hollins, but to a brand new university, the University of North Florida in Jacksonville. A good friend, who with his wife had been in that small group in Roanoke, had gone to Jacksonville at the time I went to Berkeley. Now he convinced me that I should apply for the position of Chairman (a term later changed) of the Department of Sociology and Social Welfare. Once again my sex was a positive rather than a negative factor, since they were embarrassed to have no women chairing departments in the College of Arts and Sciences. With Jim's sponsorship I got the job.

I learned a number of things in Jacksonville. The first was that I did not like the climate. I discovered also that I could deal with the administrative machinery of a university and make a department run. I also found that I didn't really like to do it, that teaching and writing nourish me in ways that administration does not. Another thing that I discovered—or rediscovered—is that the church can be a quick avenue into community involvement. I joined an "old First Church" downtown and found myself involved in a number of aspects of urban ministry. I also came to serve on the board of a new campus ministry that served not only our university but also the junior college and private Jacksonville University. I also renewed my contact with traditional church women's groups, which I have come to respect more, the more I know of them.

I did not find it too hard, however, to pull up stakes when Yale Divinity School surprised me by offering me a position as Associate Professor of the Sociology of Religion. I had been sure when I interviewed there that they were simply going through the motions of interviewing a woman so that they could say they had tried, before hiring some man whom they really wanted. So much for my cynicism that time!

It was, to say the least, an interesting change to move from perhaps the newest university in the country to one of the oldest. I reveled in the New England autumn, in concerts and plays and the library. I enjoyed my new students and my colleagues. Over time one gets to know more of the negative side of faculty politics, but in comparison with the sociology departments I had known, Yale Divinity School was the most humane teaching environment I had ever experienced.

I was particularly pleased with the other women on the faculty and staff. At UNF I had had only one woman colleague in the department, at Hollins, no other full-time women in the department, and only one other in the division. At YDS there were enough of us to meet with some regularity, partly for political reasons, but also for the sheer sociability of it. We were concerned about women students, women in ministry, and, of course, issues involving the hiring and firing of women faculty and staff. But we tended not to be as strident about it as some faculty women's caucuses seem to be, and rightly or wrongly I liked that. Few of us seemed to have hidden agendas against the male sex in general; the battle was systemic more than personal.

But there were battles, battles that extended through the school and out into church and society. While I was at Yale the Episcopal Church finally gave halfhearted recognition to the ordination of women. Some of our students and graduates were at the convention; the rest of us held our own celebration when they flashed us the news. Another time, we attended the bittersweet ordination of a graduate and colleague who had to leave her Missouri Synod for a sister Lutheran denomination in order to be ordained to the ministry to which she felt she had been called. We worked diligently on the language issue, ever making the point that people believe what they hear and are affected by it. We worked to have women considered in faculty searches, for special lectureships, and the like. And we enjoyed one another's company and support.

Once again I found the church and its agencies an avenue into involvement in the community at large, and put down at least some roots in New Haven while serving on the board of an urban ministry known as Christian Community Action. I also was able to continue my interest in new religious movements as we dealt with the many competing forces of the new religions and the anti-cult movement that swirled around us at the Divinity School.

My classes at Yale were small. The faculty had decided that sociology should be a part of the curriculum, but they had not revised the curriculum in such a way as to push students toward the subject. One may ask whether it was easier for them to hire a woman to teach peripheral courses, rather than courses in central disciplines. That I cannot answer. I know I was accorded all the respect I could desire, perhaps at least partly because so few of the faculty knew much about my field. They had to trust their search process to have brought them someone who knew what she was doing, and, in general, I think they did. I had had enough experience in administration, however, to know that my courses could not be defined administratively as paying their way; and when talk began of budgetary troubles, the administration refused to honor the tenure track nature of my position. I knew that tenure, had it been granted, could have been tenuous.

Instead of fighting their decision, I walked through another door that happened to open to me at that point. My contract would have allowed me to stay one more year at Yale, but when I got a letter from the Iliff School of Theology in Denver asking me to recommend a sociologist for their faculty, I suggested myself. I liked what I saw when I visited the place for an interview. Iliff was in as much of an upswing as Yale was, apparently, in a downswing. Apparently they liked me as well. I was hired and moved to Denver that summer.

Only after I moved did I realize how much I felt as if I were coming home, ending a twelve-year exile. I had not felt like an exile in all those places I had been, but now, back in Colorado, I felt at home in ways not experienced in my wanderings. I remembered my impressions at age nineteen, riding home from the Midwest where I had followed my husband, watching the landscape go by, seeing it lose its lushness and become more barren, but also more open, more raw, somehow younger. Now I was struck again by the vigor of the Rocky Mountain West, the boom-town feeling of hazard and opportunity.

Iliff seemed—and seems—a part of that. As the only mainline seminary between Iowa and the West Coast, it serves a vast and diverse region. Located in the midst of one of the few remaining developing areas of the nation, it seems to have the opportunity to put its imprint on a culture still in the making. With young and active leadership, it has been expanding its faculty, its student body, its program, its facilities. Many of the women at Iliff—many more than at Yale when I was there—are second-career students, seeking theological education after spending a number of years in another profession, including that of homemaker. I feel particularly close to these women whose histories are often similar to my own. I enjoy the balance that our full-time three women faculty can bring, representing, as we sometimes say, three generations of feminists. I have come to appreciate the fact that I probably had more freedom growing up in the thirties and forties than Jean did in the fifties. And Sheila brings the perspective of the sixties to round off the trio. We recognize and celebrate those differences, suspecting that the combination offers a range rare in theological education.

Iliff has also had a long history of making sociology a central part of the curriculum, so I find my teaching affirmed. Our doctoral program is giving me an opportunity to work with more students at that level than ever before. Once again, church-related agencies have given me opportunity to put down roots in the city and the state as I work with urban ministry projects, the Colorado Council of Churches, and some programs for rural ministry as well. More of my family is nearby, and for the first time since I left Colorado in 1967 I have a grandchild in the same city. I am at home—at least for the time being.

In summary, my journey has not been one beset by many obstacles and difficult battles because I am a woman. Rather, it has been a matter of walking through doors that have been opened for me, often by those who have confronted those obstacles and battles before me. I feel I would not be true to the legacy of those sisters who fought at the barricades if I did not go on into the pathways they opened for me, but I will always remember and own their struggles as my own. I am the product of lucky timing, having gotten my degree just a bit ahead of the great onrush of women who finally believed they had the chance, and just after the primary battles had been won. I count myself a feminist, and seek to do what I can to continue the struggle to make our society an open and free place for all persons to gain their full stature and make their full contribution to human life.

I also count myself a Christian, having found in the Christian Church, its teachings, and its community opportunities, encouragement, and the vision to begin to understand what full human stature and mature contributions to human life can mean. My scholarship and my public involvement are to me both expressions of my Christian vocation. My gender has provided me with a perspective only now coming to be appreciated in the society. It is a good time for me to be alive and to be where I am.

In the movie *Chariots of Fire,* the young evangelical runner says something that continues to give me goose bumps. I may not quote quite accurately, but it was something like this: "I know that God made me to do something with my life, and that's why I'm going to China as a missionary. But God also made me fast, and when I run well I can feel his [*sic*] pleasure." That seems to suit me, somehow. I thank God and those who went before me that the pathways were cleared and the doors opened for me to pursue a vocation that seems so right as almost to partake of a cosmic pleasure.

MARY LYTHGOE BRADFORD

Mary Lythgoe Bradford is a free-lance contractor for government agencies and private companies where she edits, writes, and teaches communications courses. She also writes a regular column for *Exponent II*, is working on a collection of her own personal essays, and serves as advisor to the present editors of *Dialogue*. Her articles, poetry, and book reviews appear regularly in magazines and newspapers. She is beginning work on a biography of Esther Peterson, the consumer activist, and on a writing guidebook. She resides with her husband in Arlington, Virginia.

"They Also Serve . . ."
(Who Only Sit and Write)

The Mormon religion is an undeniable part of my being. A descendant of Utah pioneers, I was the first child of parents who never questioned the faith but merely accepted its precepts as facts of life. One of these is the right of every member to certain blessings, among them healing and health. My parents believed that I was actually an incarnation of that blessing, a kind of "miracle baby." At three weeks, I contracted pneumonia. According to the family legend, the doctor had given up, and I was turning blue when the bishop of our ward (congregation), known throughout the neighborhood for the "gift of healing," appeared at our door. He and my father anointed my head with oil, placed their hands upon my head, said a prayer, and restored me to life.

Growing up as a miracle baby was both an advantage and a burden. The miraculous healing meant great expectations for me. I believed that I had been spared for a purpose, and as I grew older, I connected this purpose with writing and publishing. I have a memory of myself at age seven or so in my "Let's Pretend" mood. I am holding one of the stories I was forever writing and reading to anyone who would listen. I have shaped it into a scroll, tied a ribbon around it, and am pretending to hand it over to a New York publisher. The publisher accepts with alacrity, of course.

As an adolescent, and after I learned a bit more about the process of writing, I formed an ambition to write "for the church." This meant volunteering for any writing job that presented itself, from the ward newsletter to the ward play. Though I was disappointed that the articles and poetry I sent to church magazines and newspapers were not always accepted, I was actually proud of my rejection slips, because they made me feel professional. My output was welcomed by local church members, however, and as I grew older, I was able to place more of my poems and articles.

Because of constant encouragement by teachers, family, and friends, I entered the University of Utah in the early fifties with high hopes. This state university, in fact, offered a group of dedicated, mostly male mentors and teachers who seemed determined to help. With the woman's movement just a smudge on the horizon, the university and the Mormon church's Institute of Religion across the street gave both girls and boys every chance to excel. Or so it seemed to me. Dr. Lowell L. Bennion, sociologist, philosopher, and religionist, ran the Institute, which included classes taught by him and two other gifted teachers on everything from world religions to courtship and marriage. I took all of the classes, graduating from the Institute after I had finished my assigned project: the revision and editing of two of Bennion's books. These books were very popular throughout the church, especially with young people seeking to combine their religion with their secular studies. This was my first creative editing experience.

Lowell Bennion, whom we lovingly called "Brother B.," became the very model of my religion, the one who clearly practiced what he preached, a humane, Christian version of the Mormon faith—development through service and study. Through his "work parties" and various service projects in the larger community, we students were taught to seek out the less fortunate and to forget our own troubles. At the same time, he was always available to listen to our troubles. He challenged us through reading, discussion, lecture, and prayer. Even now the still small voice of my conscience often speaks in his voice. He was both nurturing and challenging, in the same way my father was. I never thought to call these traits male or female: They were simply human with a touch of the divine.

I spent seven years at the University, emerging with an M.A. in English and three years experience as a teacher of freshman English. I cherish my rosy memories of that time when "boys and girls together" studied in a kind of charmed, preactivist glow.

Because writing was never really portrayed as a viable goal, I chose to become an English teacher. In spite of the many opportunities given me to write and to edit, only teaching, nursing, and stenography seemed possible for a girl. Since professors of English were usually required to write, I decided that the academic track was the one for me. I departed therefore for the "Lord's University," Brigham Young at Provo, Utah, and my first full-time job as instructor of English.

It was rewarding to be paid for a task I found so enjoyable that I would gladly have volunteered for it. Freshman Mormon students were easy to teach because of the cultural icons we shared. And the salary, which seemed exhorbitant at the time, would support me in my plans for a Ph.D., preferably at Stanford, sometime in the future.

But as my religion had taught me to reverence intelligence, placing it next to godliness in the scriptures, it had also taught me to look for a suitable mate. In my early twenties, I had aspired to serve a foreign mission for the church but had been refused on the grounds that I was young and attractive enough to be married instead. This was my introduction to sexism in the church.

It so happened that Charles Bradford, a young economics instructor and friend from the University of Utah, was a suitable choice. After a brief courtship, we planned a late summer wedding.

It was then that I was summmoned to the office of my department head for questioning. Why hadn't I informed him of my marriage *before* signing my contract for the next year? When I looked puzzled, he informed me that university policy required married women instructors to switch to half-time or to give up teaching entirely. Since I had already signed, he would content himself with consigning me to an office full of graduate students. If I couldn't give up my contract, I could at least give up my privacy!

That was the second consciousness-raising "click" in my sheltered life. Perhaps this made it easier to follow my husband to Washington, D.C., where he could both work for a senator and finish his own Ph.D. I have often wondered why I was so quick to give up my own plans. I can't really blame my gentle and open-minded husband. I am sure he would have supported me if I had applied at one of the many universities in the area instead of getting on as clerk-typist at the Library of Congress. It was part of the culture of the time. A master's degree for a woman was rare in my circles, and, though I was praised for it, most people expected me to settle down with children and live happily ever after. So I accepted a stopgap position while waiting for our first child. (It is amusing to recall that my supervisor, who recognized my M.A. by giving me research assignments in the main reading room, was very understanding when I kept skipping work with morning sickness. Instead of giving me the sack, he advised me to "keep the tummy full.")

I entered wifehood and motherhood in the bosom of new-found friends in Washington and in our ward in Arlington, Virginia, where I was asked to teach literature to the women's auxiliary of the church—the Relief Society. Soon thereafter I experienced my third feminist "click." The choir leader in the ward, charged with the Christmas cantata for Sunday services, asked me to give a short sermon as part of the program. After which she informed me of the bishop's instructions: I was not to discuss "doctrine." If women were to be allowed to speak from the pulpit at all, it had to be on safe, "literary" subjects.

This was my first hint that a married woman might be a threat in the pulpit. Mormonism is a lay church, so most members can expect to be asked to speak. Since public speaking was one of my hobbies, I was always willing. I recall myself at fifteen lambasting the ward for what I perceived as unchristian backbiting and gossip among the members. At another time I emotionally expressed my thanks to God for the miracle of my mother's recovery from pneumonia. Public thanks was expected. As a young girl and later as a young woman, I was often grateful for the many mercies in my life.

Under the influence of Brother B., I had learned that all should serve according to their talents. I had been given ample opportunity in college to show off as a speaker, a teacher, and as a presider over meetings. My attitude toward the male "priesthood holders" therefore could be best summed up in the line from one of the hymns, "as the dew from heaven distilling": The priesthood helps all to develop their talents. The men may bring priesthood power into the room, but men and women share equally in its blessings. Priesthood, therefore, had been presented to me not so much as a political force as a call to serve. My father, a gentle, hardworking man, had used the priesthood to restore the family to health, to pray with us, and to cry with us in our travail. He had served as a missionary, but according to him he had never spoken or prayed in public. My mother, too, was backward about public display. They both had lived their religion more quietly than did any of their four children. I was already married before I fully realized that some Mormons were interpreting the priesthood as male privilege to which no woman, no matter how spiritual, could aspire. But Mormon scripture gives this advice to the church: "No power or influence can or ought to be maintained by virture of the priesthood, only by persuasion, by long-suffering, by gentleness and meekness, and by love unfeigned; by kindness, and pure knowledge, which shall greatly enlarge the soul without hypocrisy, and without guile" (*Doctrine and Covenants* 121:31-42). Any other behavior meant "amen to the priesthood of that man"! Meaning *finis*! Brother B. had never been interested in the trappings of power. He describes it this way: "I don't have any interest in being exalted. I'd like to be in the presence of Christ, be a co-worker, but I believe that he who would save his life shall lose it, and he that would lose his life shall find it" (Lowell L. Bennion, "Saint for All Seasons," Interview in *Sunstone* magazine, X:2, 18, No. 2, p. 18).

Well, I survived the "literary speech" and lived to give doctrinal speeches. For the next ten years I stayed home, more or less, teaching church classes and tutoring Mormon students. When our third and last child was safely in school, I fell into an illness that my doctor diagnosed with these words:

"Mrs. Bradford, when will you get back to your teaching? There is no illness like that of unused talent."

As if on cue, a member of the ward who happened to be a top executive in a government agency appeared with an offer of a job—consulting and teaching in his office. This miraculously coincided with the founding of an independent journal, the first of its kind: *Dialogue: A Journal of Mormon Thought.* The editors, graduate students at Stanford and former disciples of Brother B. and the Institute program, asked me to join their editorial board. Voila! The job and the journal lifted my depression.

In the first issue the editors announced that "a new generation of Mormons has arisen" who are "curious and well-trained and committed to church activity" and who wish to bring "their faith into dialogue with human experience as a whole and to foster artistic and scholarly achievement based on their cultural heritage." (Wesley Johnson and Eugene England, *Dialogue,* Spring 1966, pp. 4-5.)

I was one of these young Mormons. I wanted to be part of the plan for improving the writing of the church. Much in-house writing was disappointing. I felt the need for challenging fiction and poetry and for meaty historical and doctrinal studies. I had no idea then that ten years later I would become the journal's first woman editor when women's issues were paramount, during the excommunication of Sonia Johnson. When Robert Rees, who succeeded England and Johnson, passed the torch to me, he emphasized that "it was time for a woman" to take over, but with one piece of advice: "Remember that your title is 'editor,' not 'mother.'" He sensed that I would have difficulty separating roles, with everything being sandwiched between family responsibilities. *Dialogue* did become a kind of cottage industry because of its office in the commodious basement of our home in Arlington, Virginia, where talented volunteers, including my own children, gathered to edit, write, type, and talk. I fed them with one hand, managed them with the other. The result was almost seven years of high-quality publishing in a remarkable degree of harmony. Now when I gaze at the shelf we produced, twenty-one issues in all, I feel that I did fulfill my childhood ambition, to write and publish for the people who mean the most to me—Mormons.

Another of my favorite scriptures admonishes us to be "anxiously engaged in a good cause" and to "bring to pass much righteousness of our own free will" (*Doctrine and Covenants* 58:27). I came to believe that my contributions were to keep the journal alive during difficult economic times and to publish on women's themes.

I had begun to study women's history, especially Mormon pioneer history, in the early seventies. In 1973 I had assisted in the editing of *Dialogue*'s first women's issue. Edified by a group of Boston Mormon women, it led to the founding of *Exponent II,* a newspaper for Mormon women, now ten years old. This group also published *Mormon Sisters,* a landmark volume of historical essays that they dedicated to Leonard Arrington, the first church historian to open the archives freely to women scholars. These women and other trained women historians began excavating the accomplishments of those pioneer women who at great risk settled in Utah and educated themselves as teachers, writers, suffragists, and artists while rearing large, sometimes polygamous families. The consciousness-raising "click" I experienced through this period was uplifting and motivating.

A few of these descendants of Mormon pioneers formed an organization called Mormons for ERA (MERA) as a protest against the church's anti-ERA campaign. They expected me to join them, hinting that *Dialogue* should officially support their cause. I felt that personal activism on my part was inappropriate, since as editor I was representing not myself alone but the subscribers and the board of editors as well. Looking back, I see that I would not have joined anyway. I am not a joiner, a sign-carrier, nor a protestor at heart.

In 1978 *Dialogue* was preparing a "tutorial" on the ERA by a woman lawyer who favored it but was laying out arguments pro and con in a reasonable way.

The year before I had been asked to become a "spokesperson" by one of the bishops in the area. I had replied that I was not interested in becoming a spokesperson, either for or against. "I just want to get my magazine out," I told him. I went on to say that I believed the very respectable history of the accomplishments of Mormon pioneer women combined with the present accomplishments of Mormon women should speak for themselves. Women, I said, can be trusted to think for themselves and to make up their own minds.

From then on, I was increasingly buttonholed at parties and meetings by angry, worried, or curious women and men who wanted to discuss the ERA. When the Relief Society was organized by the church to protest the ERA in Richmond, I told my diary: "Think what could be done if the women of the church could be mobilized so quickly for seven weeks of really important work!"

I still had little idea of the hysteria that could be generated by this issue, hysteria that would lead to Sonia's excommunication with its attendant media coverage. I resented being told that I should fight against it for no stronger reason that it would "not ennoble women." (This from the letter sent out from the First Presidency.) Nobility is a judgment reserved for posterity. On the other hand, I was less than enthusiastic about banner-tows over the temple grounds. Some things are sacred!

The atmosphere grew increasingly charged. Writers and reporters began calling me for quotations and background information. One of my statements was garbled enough in a local article that my stake president asked me to clarify. A television network wanted to interview me about my relationship with Sonia, an acquaintance of some years. When I offered to be interviewed about *Dialogue* instead, they lost interest. A short *Dialogue* interview aired in Salt Lake City sparked rumors that I had finally been recruited by ERA forces. Arguments heightened. Anti-ERA petitions appeared in Mormon chapels. My husband, who was then bishop of our ward, refused them, but the ward that shared our building did not. Seeing the petition on Sunday morning, my teenage daughter scandalized people by scrawling across it "This is sacrilegious!" Rumors and rumors of rumors were rife.

Sonia Johnson had seemed at first not much different from most Relief Society women I had known—outspoken, sincere, modest in many ways, yet eloquent and fiery when crossed.

Bishop Willis, portrayed in the press as a tough FBI agent, was also a friend whose parents hailed from Dad's hometown. I felt sorry for them both. I could see how things had escalated until they were both trapped. I interviewed them both and researched the issues, trying to pick my way through the sticky labyrinth. Rumors reached *Dialogue* that if we dared publish anything the least bit sympathetic to Sonia, our own membership would be up for grabs. I polled our board, met with the staff and decided to publish an honest appraisal of Sonia and the events leading up to her excommunication. I decided to run an interview with Sonia with an introductory article about her life. The issue included a well-researched piece on the excommunication process and another on the church's diminished public image. After it came out, mail was evenly divided between letters calling us to repentance for publishing such a sympathetic work on an apostate and others complimenting us for our balance. We lost some subscriptions and picked up others. It was rumored that Sonia was unhappy with it, but several members of MERA renewed their subscriptions. We heard from no church authorities.

Though I still felt buffeted, I grew increasingly certain that I could make my best contributions to womankind by publishing the best of Mormon women writers and articles about them. It was clear that I could be both a seeker of truth and a reflector of the times in which I live. I wanted to chronicle these times and my own evolution. I found myself in a still center of a whirlwind where I felt a kind of peace as part of a network of reasonable, kindly people who were researching and publishing the best of Mormonism.

I and my *Dialogue* staff went on to design another women's issue: the 1982 anniversary issue. It celebrated the kaleidoscopic accomplishments of Mormon women on many artistic and academic levels. Contributions included articles and essays on women and the priesthood, the ERA, divorce, abortion, death. Its writers were scholars, poets, fiction writers, artists, dancers, and photographers. After interviewing 100 Mormon women for her photographic essay "In Context," Robin Hammond reported "beneath our Mormon facades, we differ and agree in a multitude of ways."

At the same time, *Dialogue* sponsored a personal essay contest, the brainchild of Marion Mangum of Olympus Publishing in Utah, who also wanted to make a contribution to the discussion. The result was a book, *Mormon Women Speak*, edited by me and published by her. These were honest pieces by a variety of both professional and amateur writers, dealing with some of the most pressing issues in their lives. It was well-received by a wide spectrum of women and men, resulting in a second printing and a sequel, still in preparation.

"Each of us carries a drive toward wholeness, each of us struggles with outer and inner reconciliations. Each is in the process of becoming truly human." This line from one of the essays, "An Underground Journey Toward Repentance" by Helen Stark, sums up my own feelings.

About this time, I accepted an invitation to speak on a panel at a meeting of the American Psychological Association on how religious women use their faith to cope with conflicts. I was given ten minutes to talk about how "committed Mormon women cope." When the *Journal of Pastoral Counseling* published the proceedings, I expanded mine into a brief article addressing the "articulate and outstanding" Mormon woman who elects to remain in the church. I pointed out that Mormon women find the strength to cope with increasing conflicts both in and out of the church through emphasis on some indigenous Mormon traits: belief in the values of education and skill training, belief in the importance of family, and a natural penchant for networking. These mechanisms develop confidence to work for needed change in the church and in the larger society. I urged greater understanding of Mormon women as individuals with differing problems that belie the popular stereotype of sheeplike, obedient housewives waiting for their marching orders.

While preparing this article, I realized that I have become an activist almost by default. I have learned to clarify my positions gradually, not by flagrant protest but by quiet resolve. I have elected to remain in the church of my childhood and to work for change within it. Through my travels, in which I have talked with women around the church, and through my publishing ventures, I have developed a faith in the church's ability to change. Organizational change is slow, to be sure, and I don't expect to see women given the priesthood in my lifetime. But then I hadn't expected to see it given to the Blacks either, although I believed it had to happen sometime. Reforms could be made now by calling couples to church jobs currently held by men alone, by placing women on all governing boards of the church and by excising sexism from the lesson manuals and the rituals of the church.

When I feel especially discouraged, I remember that the three "clicks" that raised my consciousness twenty-five years ago have been silenced. BYU no longer requires women to give up their contracts for marriage; women are encouraged to serve missions, indeed, my daughter is serving in the Philippines; and women routinely speak on doctrinal issues every Sunday throughout the church. They don't speak about the ERA, of course, and I understand why many are impatient about that. I respect their impatience. I think the barnstorming does much to make it safe for brainstorming. There are shades and grades of activism, and there is a place for those who only sit and write. I hope to keep writing the truth as I see it. I am encouraged by the fact that my church raised millions of dollars for Ethiopian relief. I hope it will pay attention to the increasing fragility of this beautiful planet which Mormon doctrine says will one day be glorified in heaven as the Celestial Kingdom.

I admit that because my early role models were nurturing men, I find it impossible to believe that all men are to be mistrusted and that all male leaders—the patriarchy—should be stripped of authority. I do believe that it will be better for all when they learn to share that authority. I am still willing to work with the many men who have helped me grow and with the increasingly large number of women who are actively engaged in the good cause of improving life for themselves and others. In fact, the traditions in which I was reared support the ideals of eternal progression.

In a review of *Mormon Women Speak,* Richard Cummings asserts that the book "offers a refreshingly believable middle ground between the male-oriented preachiness of the collection of sermons by church authorities . . . and the negativism of Sonia Johnson." For better or for worse, I seem to be occupying that middle ground. If this sounds less than courageous, I have to say that I have accepted the fact that the church is part of my body, and I am part of the church body. I feel that the church belongs as much to me as to anyone.

I don't claim that I fully understand either myself or other Mormon women, but my journey continues! It is an exciting one!

FELICITAS D. GOODMAN

After her retirement (1979) from Denison University, where she taught linguistics and anthropology, Felicitas Goodman founded Cuyamungue Institute, where with a loosely organized group of co-workers she continues researching the religious altered state of consciousness within the framework of summer workshops. She is the author of *Speaking in Tongues: A Cross-Cultural Study of Glossolalia,* 1972, and *The Exorcism of Anneliese Michel,* 1981; and with Jeannette H. Henney and Esther Pressel, of *Trance, Healing, and Hallucination: Three Field Studies in Religious Experience,* 1974. She has published a considerable number of articles on religious behavior, most recently "States of Consciousness: A Study of Soundtracks" (*J. Mind and Behavior,* 1981, 2:209-219); "The Shaman's Spirit Journey: An Experimental Investigation" (Paper for the Symposium on Shamanism, XIth International Congress of Anthropological and Ethnological Sciences, Vancouver, 1983); and "Body Posture and the Religious Altered State of Consciousness" (*J. Humanistic Psychology,* in press).

Learning the Daybreak Song

Intellectually, there is little we cannot comprehend. But the innermost fabric of our being remains hidden from us, although it is woven of only a few strands, given to us early in life. Searching to understand ourselves, we seem compelled to weave that cloth over and over again in vain illusion that the true pattern will emerge at last. I will make no apologies for this reweaving. What is, is.

I was born a German child in Hungary, to parents situated in some empty land between agnosticism and atheism. They had me baptized a Lutheran, as they had been before me. Growing into conscious childhood in Nagyvárad, a small Hungarian border town in Rumania, I had Orthodox Jewish playmates and went to a convent school of the Ursuline order. The sisters insisted on my attending the Lutheran church services, and from time to time a neighbor took me to the austere, whitewashed Calvinist meetinghouse. There was a Greek Catholic girl among us, and Relli, my father's secretary who sometimes watched us children, was Greek Orthodox.

As could be expected in such a variegated world, we argued religion at an age when my grandchildren had barely outgrown "Electric Company." "How do you keep from losing your name without a baptism to stick it on?" I asked my Jewish girl friend, while being told by a Catholic benchmate at the convent, "I don't think you Lutherans are even Christians. You don't worship the Virgin Mary, and do you actually celebrate Christmas?"

Matters became less innocent as we grew older. From the adults, we heard cruel jokes about beating up on Jews because they had crucified Christ. One of the *maters* in school pilloried me in history class as a Lutheran; Luther, she said, had no understanding of the Bible and was dead wrong in his dispute with the Pope. During the May novenas, there were prayers for heretics such as I was. And beloved Relli kept emphasizing that her religion was the best, and I should consider converting to the Greek Orthodox faith. In fact, everybody seemed to be convinced that theirs was the only and true path. "They even killed people over religion," I complained to my mother. By that time, I had read about the brutal missionizing of Hungarian shamans by their Catholic kings, about autos-da-fé and wars of religion. She saw the pain. "You know," she said, "there is even a story about two factions in Byzantium who killed each other for the sake of the letter *i*. That was all that distinguished their religious convictions. Don't get involved in disputations over dogma. Study them instead." She would have made a good anthropologist.

My mother never went to church. "Religion depresses me," she would say. "Listen to the sermons. Most of them are set up along similar lines. First they make people feel as unhappy and as low as they possibly can. Then they promise them salvation. Of course, the pain of the human condition is real enough, and I don't need to be reminded of it. But their salvation that I am supposed to abase myself for is abstract, distant, a jumble of formulas. When I try to grasp it, it dissolves. Better I go for a walk to the forest."

Actually, undetected even by my perceptive mother, I had by then discovered such a "forest" of my own, a realm of religion where there were no disputes, only the pulsing of the blood of life. . . . On Saturday mornings as I walked to school, there were Jewish boys and their fathers, talking and laughing and streaming toward the large synagogue on Teleky Street. They wore small, round hats, their *péjess* locks dangled before their ears, and they carried their ritual garb in striped bags. There was something bright and sunny about the scene that gladdened the heart. . . . I watched the mother of my best girl friend bury a kitchen knife in the ground, muttering a prayer and scolding us at the same time for having used a "milk" knife to cut meat that she now had to purify. The aura of ritual danger hung palpably about her. . . . The *mater* who had shamed me over Luther was kneeling in front of the altar in the glittering convent chapel one day, her arms outstretched, so transported that she did not hear us giggling nervously behind her. To me, her arms were wings. . . . One evening, I came by the ancient St. Ladislaus church by the Körös river when the mass was letting out. As I stepped up to the door to hear the organ play, a wizened old woman walked by me. She crossed herself and hummed the hymn that was still being sung inside, all the while smiling toothlessly. Filaments of light clung to her patched winter scarf and glowed about her shoulders. . . . And then there were the candles on our Christmas tree. If you concentrated just right on their flickering light and inhaled the fragrance of the branches, you were rewarded with a sweetness beyond compare.

The greatest wonder, though, was the eve of St. Nicholas Day. Never mind why it was called that. The bishop whose story I later learned was an interloper, good for nothing but to explain why the being we celebrated on that day wore a chain on his wrist. That being was Krampusz, the giver of sweet gifts, half man, half goat, clad in silken garments and carrying a bundle of switches. The color of his feast was a deep, rich red, and all the store windows along our main street were decorated with paper or cloth of that hue. It made the street glow in an otherworldly, all-penetrating, mysterious red sheen. It was not important that Krampusz brought the candy that materialized in our shoes on the window sill the next morning. All I really wanted was to drink in the mood of the redness that oozed from all the cracks of the walls and tinted the snow crunching under foot.

The duality of the pattern was set and the fabric woven by the time we were expelled from Rumania as foreign citizens during the Great Depression that circled the globe early in the thirties. I finished high school in Germany and went on to college, to the Interpreters Institute of the University of Heidelberg. The Nazis were in power, and some of the Christian opposition collected in the Oxford Movement. I joined briefly, but soon drifted away. It was talk and more talk. All the problems of the world would be solved with the proclamation of the Gospel. Their Frank Buchman had been to South

Africa, and immediately, racial tension in that troubled country had melted away. They were lost in a never- never land.

I married an American, had children, suffered through the Second World War, and emigrated to America. For many years, I worked as a translator and language teacher. After sampling the services of the various churches in our neighborhood, I gave up on American organized religion. I had never been fond of social clubs. My children went to Sunday school of the Episcopal church, but after a while refused to continue. "You said they would tell us about God," my oldest, ten at the time, accused me. "But all we get to do is color pictures." The minister came by one day to ask for a financial contribution. As I went for my checkbook, I asked, "Reverend, if I were a heathen—how would you try to convert me?" He looked at me, rather lost, then left politely without waiting for my check. The final blow came when I read a sermon by William Branham, a fundamentalist preacher. "Woman is evil," he thundered. "Woman is lower than an animal. Woman is lower even than a pig. Through woman, sin came into the world. Woman is the vessel of sin."

Yet the fascination with religion remained. I read some ethnographic material, Malinowski among others, and Robert Graves' *White Goddess*, and began putting some ideas on paper. In a fragment from the fifties, entitled "World Without Adoration," I agonized over the question where joy could come from in a world emptied of the divine. In another manuscript from the same period, called simply "Notebook on Religion," I tried to imagine what would happen if scientists would produce proof positive, proof admissible in our century, that the human soul existed and continued after death. It could change our entire culture, provided they would be able to determine what conditions needed to be met in order for that survival to become actual. A veritable utopia blossomed under my pen for, of course, I was the one who set up the conditions: no more killing, kindness to all humans, brotherhood between us and the animals, plants, rivers, and oceans. Some of these ideas I saw emerging later in the counterculture and the environmental movement.

In the meantime, the children grew and began separating from their home as ripe fruit falls from the tree. They left scars behind that continued to ache. With marriage a disappointment and work increasingly boring and burdensome, I decided to go back to school.

This was in 1965, and I was fifty-one years old. "Mature scholars" had not been invented yet, and I felt self-conscious about presenting my yellowed high school and university diplomas to the admissions officers at Ohio State University. But they did accept me as a special student in the Department of Linguistics. A quarter later, I became a regular one. Linguistics had seemed a natural choice, for I had worked with languages all my life. It was the dutiful thing to do. That other needs might also be worth considering did not at first occur to me, although something in me cried out, for what, I did not know. Then one day in the second quarter I was leafing through the university bulletin and that "something" suddenly took shape. It was a course offered by Erika Bourguignon of the Anthropology Department, entitled "Religion in Native Societies." With some trepidation I asked for permission to participate. It turned out not to be just an ordinary course on non-Western religions. Step by systematic step, she led us toward that very heart piece of religious behavior, the phenomenon of the trance. Before long, I became a research assistant on her staff, translating material that she needed for her survey project on the occurrence of his phenomenon cross-culturally. After receiving my master's degree in linguistics in 1968, I was admitted to the doctoral program in anthropology.

As to external circumstances, going to graduate school was not easy. I was divorced by then and had to work full-time to support myself. Ageism was rife and funding agencies did not hesitate to reject applications with the argument that they would not invest in anyone over fifty. So I borrowed—I was close to retirement when I paid off the last of the bank loans —and did fieldwork during summer vacations in order not to jeopardize my job. Not until I was established as a full-time faculty member at Denison University did I receive research money from the Faculty Development Fund.

Being master of my own purse strings had its advantages. As happens often when a person is breaking new ground, I had nothing to say that would have looked impressive on a grant application, only hunches. I was on my own, so I was at liberty to pursue them. Bringing together what I had learned in linguistics and new insights gained from anthropological training, I formulated a working hypothesis concerning the phenomenon of speaking in tongues (glossolalia), by no means only a Christian behavior. According to this thesis, the primary factor shaping the peculiar glossolalia speech patterns was the biology of the trance, what the person's nervous system did at that point. Fieldwork confirmed these suppositions. Aglow with the joy of discovery, I presented my first results at the national meeting of the American Anthropological Association in Seattle in 1968. I was sure everyone would be pleased that at long last we had something tangible to examine. Instead, I soon realized that I had unwittingly stumbled into a bitter controversy in cultural anthropology, namely that of "nature vs. nurture." It seemed so glorious to me as a woman to think that religious experience was not something reserved to disembodied spirits floating in abstract ether, but that our bodies had to participate. After all, does it detract from the beauty of a child's face that you have to open your eyes and activate the optic assemblage in order to see it? Certainly that aspect of seeing was also worth knowing. However, as I became more widely known for reifying something religious, I was attacked in print and on occasion quite angrily from the floor with, "You *must* admit that all this is culture, it has *nothing* to do with the body."

Of course, the role of human physiology does not simply go away on the say-so of some behavioral scientist. And its relationship to religious experience has held my interest to this day. Neither am I alone in this search. After all, what happens to us on the physical level does hold the key to what is later formulated as dogma. It seems that I cannot escape the track laid down in my youth: I study and record the belief systems, but yearn forever to learn more of that very central event, the religious trance, the fountainhead of the primal experience.

This is the natural order of things where religion is actually lived. After all, isn't it an extraordinary matter that groups of Maya Indian peasants in the back country of Yucatán, without a trained clergy or prompting from any authority, should after a day's hard labor get together for almost every evening of the week to "praise God"? Their knowledge of Spanish is faulty, their acquaintance with the Bible passing at best. Yet in face of ridicule and even ostracism from their village, they persist. Why? Because of their thirst for the experience of the Holy Spirit, mediated by the trance.

For my doctoral research, I returned to the Yucatecan Apostolic congregation that I had known from fieldwork on glossolalia. I intended to do a traditional community study. Upon arrival, I found the group in the initial throes of a millenarian movement. With their bodies frozen in stupor or at other times writhing, they were seething with trances and demonic attacks and visions about the end of the world. The fever was accompanied by creative culture change and the formulation of new dogma. Instead of a community, this "crisis cult" became the subject of my dissertation.

During my sabbatical leave in 1975-76, I put on paper a cross-cultural overview incorporating the ideas and observations gained over the years. Instead of trying to define what religion was, I ranged the faiths of humanity, including the so-called "world religions" along the lines of societal types. This pointed up impressive agreements within a type in the use of the trance, in ethics, and in belief systems. It has not been published yet, and I mourn over the rejection this child of my spirit is receiving. Some editors disapprove of the inclusion of the ecstatic experience because, allegedly, it "overextends the category of religion." Others find it too "feminine," as though that were a defect.

I did follow up the changing position of women within various religious settings, finding that with the advent of agriculture, we women lost most of our autonomy. We are just now beginning to recover it, as we break the shackles of that cultural form. In applying a linguistic analysis to ritual cross-culturally, I discovered that its basic outline derived from the birth experience. No wonder that one editor sent it back because it "might irritate too many of your colleagues."

In 1979, the Denison University chose to apply its mandatory retirement rule shortly before it became illegal. Six of us had to go. I was very bitter, feeling that they were cutting me off in mid-course. There was no question in my mind that I would continue to work, and several projects I had already been involved in did make the transition to a different "working" style of life possible. One concerned research on a German university student called Anneliese Michel, who experienced demonic possession and later died supposedly as a result of being exorcized. My analysis led me to a different conclusion, as I outlined in the book published in 1981.

More important in the long run, however, was founding a research institute on my land in New Mexico. It provided not only an institutional affiliation, but also an opportunity to teach and to continue research on the religious trance. In the early 1970s, when I started telling my students about the trance experience I had observed in the Yucatecan Apostolic churches, they posed the question whether it might not be possible to experience something like that also outside of a religious setting. From 1972 until 1976 we worked on developing a method with successive groups of student volunteers. But although the experiences that the students reported as a result of concentration and rhythmic stimulation by the sound of a rattle agreed in many ways with what I knew from the field as well as from ethnographic reports on shamans and other religious specialists, they did not seem consistent enough to me. In 1977, however, I began using a different approach, stimulated by an article of the Canadian psychologist Victor F. Emerson: Instead of leaving the body posture assumed during the trance up to individual choice, I selected some ritual postures from the ethnographic record, and everyone used the same one. This procedure produced the consistency of experience I had been looking for, with various postures mediating different experiences, such as spirit journey, calling of the spirits, and others.

Once again, my initial questions were scientific ones. Why would certain postures mediate particular experiences but not others, while physiological parameters such as EEGs, the blood's biochemistry, and pulse remained the same? I did not know. Why would the same door lead to different parts of the alternate reality? It would be flattering to say that I then took the logical next step and started experimenting with trances myself in order to find some of the answers. It did not happen that way. Instead, in what is conventionally called a conversion experience, that other reality reached out and drew me in. What I had described so many times of consultants in the field now happened to me also: I "strayed" into a trance. What had been comfortable, "objective" observation turned into an apprenticeship, sometimes gentle, sometimes harsh and frightening, in the reality of Amerindian spirituality. Somehow, I found, I had come full circle: On another continent, under a bigger sky, on the sacred mountains of New Mexico and in its mysterious caves, the first cousins of the Krampusz of my childhood lived on and had called me to their presence.

What is thrilling and perhaps hides a promise for the future is the fact that others have answered similar calls. The counterculture tried to learn Indian ways, the literature indicates that the interest in Indian spirituality is growing. If the trend continues, perhaps we will live to see a "re-Indianization" of the continent. Out of it may come not necessarily communities on the traditional Indian mold—that would be too much to hope—but perhaps something different yet also good, a way of life grounded in both realities, good for the soul, good for peace, and good for the earth.

CAROL P. CHRIST

Carol P. Christ (Ph.D. Yale Religious Studies, 1974) is author of *Diving Deep and Surfacing: Women Writers on Spiritual Quest* (Beacon, 1979), and coeditor of *Womanspirit Rising: A Feminist Reader on Religion* (Harper & Row, 1979). A leading authority on women and religion, she lectures frequently in the U.S. and Europe. She was the founder and original cochair of the Women's Caucus: Religious Studies, within the American Academy of Religion. She is cochair of the Women and Religion Section of the A.A.R. She has taught at Yale, Wesleyan, Pacific School of Religion, Iliff School of Theology, and Union Theological Seminary. She is Associate Professor of Women's Studies and Religious Studies at San Jose State University. In the summers she teaches in the International Women's Studies Institute in Greece. Currently she is working on a sequel to *Womanspirit Rising* forthcoming in 1986 and on *Symbolism of Goddess and God in Feminist Theology,* projected for 1986.

LENE SJØRUP

Lene Sjørup is author of *Du er gudinden. Religiøsitet og teologi hinsides gud fader* (Copenhagen, Hekla, 1983) (*You Are Goddess: Spirituality and Theology Beyond God the Father*). She has studied at the Theological Faculty of the University of Copenhagen and at the Graduate Theological Union, Berkeley, Cal. A widely recognized expert on feminist theology, she lectures frequently in Denmark. She is a Research Fellow at the University of Copenhagen on women's theology. She and Carol P. Christ cotaught Religion and Nature, a course in Danish and English at the University of Copenhagen in the spring of 1983. This interview is one of a series which will be published in Danish in her next book.

Darkness and Light:
Interview with Carol P. Christ
(March 3, 1982, San Francisco, California)

CAROL: I'm thirty-six. I'm a white woman. I grew up in the post-war tract home suburbs of Los Angeles in the middle or lower end of the middle class. I grew up in a very conventional family. We belonged to the Presbyterian church, but it wasn't the church of either my mother's or my father's family. Going to church was something everyone did in our community.

From a very early age I felt an importance in spirituality that was never fully accepted within my community. Both of my grandmothers were very spiritual. One was an Irish Catholic, and I spent a summer with her when I was quite young. I can remember going to Mass with her and watching her lighting candles for her son who was in the army, pray her rosary beads, dip her fingers in holy water, and kneel, and rise at different times during the services. I felt it was all very mysterious and somehow very important.

My other grandmother was a Christian Scientist. She didn't talk to me much about her spirituality, but when I was at her house she would often listen to radio programs about people who'd been cured through Christian Science—people who had been dying of cancer or other hopeless cases. Every afternoon she read from the Bible. From both of my grandmothers I picked up an unspoken sense of the importance of spirituality in their lives.

When I was six years old I was supposed to go to Sunday school while my parents were at the church. But there was another church service later. Sometimes I would ask if I could stay. I don't know why I thought it was important, but I remember listening to the parables about the lost sheep and singing the hymns, even when I could hardly read myself. I wanted to be part of what the grown-ups were part of, the real church; I felt there was something going on that was important.

LENE: There was something special and mystical and religious, maybe about the whole thing?

CAROL: Yes. At that time I don't think I could have articulated why I was so interested in it. I don't know if I got it from my grandmothers or I always had it, why I had this sense of wanting to belong to some kind of a community and be part of something that was larger, even larger than all the people who were in that community.

LENE: Did you find it there?

CAROL: I don't really know. When I became a little older I became very aware that in my Sunday school classes most of the people were involved in religion on a pretty superficial level. When I was thirteen, everyone was supposed to get confirmed as Presbyterians, and I didn't want to do it. I said to my parents that I thought that the other kids didn't know anything about other religions, that they were just doing it because their parents wanted them to. I felt that I should know more about other religions before I made such an important decision. I think to me "other religions" meant other forms of Protestantism, probably. Maybe Catholicism. It didn't really mean world religions, which I didn't have much consciousness of—though they might have been in the back of my mind. Joining a church was serious: A person should know what she or he was doing.

LENE: How early did you start having religious experiences —or would you call them that?

CAROL: My memory of my childhood is very vague, and I certainly didn't have a lot of language for articulating what was really going on with me. But I think that my earliest religious experiences were probably in the singing of songs like "Tell Me Why the Ivy Twines,"—"because God made the ivy twine . . . because God loves you—that's why God made you." Something about that always affected me when I was six-seven-eight years old. I don't know if somehow deep down I didn't really feel I was loved enough and this was a larger source of love, or what it was. It did affect me, though.

When I was about twelve or thirteen, and fourteen and fifteen I experienced a lot of death: Not my parents or my brothers, but many of the other closest members of my family died. My grandfather died after having been ill and at home for a very long time. My grandmother died very suddenly, but very painfully, of cancer. About a year later my mother had a baby that I was really looking forward to as almost being my own baby, because I'd already taken care of a slightly younger brother. And it lived for only five days. And then my other grandfather died in a fire. My aunt who was only about forty died about a year after that. This was all within a several-year period. These were my closest relatives, other than my parents and my younger brothers. I think that that gave me a real sense of spiritual depth, also, at that young an age.

LENE: Which kind of depth?

CAROL: I don't think I ever had a "light" attitude toward life after that. A lot of friends I've talked to since say that even in their thirties they haven't experienced the death of someone who was really close to them. And they haven't seen a dead body or been to a funeral. Or only recently. I saw several dead bodies in funerals; death was very real to me.

LENE: But how was it spiritual?

CAROL: I think that it gave me a real sense that whatever the meaning of life is, it is not what people think. It's something much deeper than that. It's not like being invited to a party or even getting married, because your husband might die, or your wife might die. It gave me the sense that there had to be a deeper meaning than the kind of superficial things I saw a lot of people involved in.

I remember being very touched at one of the Catholic funerals when the priest said, "Let us not mourn as those who have no faith." I was really touched; there was a mystery. If you're in touch with that, you won't mourn in the same way. It didn't mean you shouldn't mourn; it didn't say, "Don't mourn, period." It said, "Not as those who have no faith," for whom this is the ultimate devastation; but mourn knowing that there is some perspective in which this all makes sense.

LENE: Were these experiences the reasons why you went into theology?

CAROL: It's hard to say. I certainly never consciously planned to go into theology. In my middle-middle-class, or lower end of the middle-class background, the kids in the family were expected to go to college. As a girl I was groomed to become a high school teacher or grade school teacher, so that I could have something to fall back on until I got married or in case my husband died. My parents were pretty shocked when I started getting more interested in religion than they thought was normal. They never denied religion, but they don't feel it should be a consuming passion, which it was for me for a while.

I had some really profound experiences when I was in college. In my sophomore year I went to Europe. Just before that, I took a class in philosophy from a teacher who was a Catholic philosopher. He told us that St. Thomas Aquinas said that the study of philosophy "is not the study of what man [*sic*] thinks, but the study of where the *truth* of things stands." And that really impressed me. At the tender age of eighteen that seemed so right to me; that was what I wanted to do: to find out the truth of things.

Right after that, I was in Italy for six months. I spent a lot of time in the museums and churches. Looking at frescoes like Masaccio's "Expulsion from the Garden of Eden" or looking at the anguish on Rembrandt's faces really touched me. I felt that artists had understood some real depth in life—like what I had experienced in the deaths. I was also very impressed with the Madonnas of Fra Angelico. That real sweetness always has attracted me religiously, also.

I had deep experiences in Notre Dame in Paris and in some of the cathedrals in Florence, sitting in the darkness and looking up at the stained-glass windows or the frescoes. I had very spiritual experiences that I felt were mediated through both the physical setting of the church and through the people who had been there before.

LENE: How would you describe that experience?

CAROL: I would be alone in a big, dark church. I would walk around immersing myself in the way the light and shadow played on each other. It really fascinated me. And I felt drawn into that darkness, and into the beauty of that setting. Somehow to me, God, which was how I thought then, was part of that darkness, and part of that mystery, and part of that beauty. I would get into a very prayerful attitude. I would go into an aisle with a small altar or just stare at a rose window and meditate. I don't know how verbal it was, but I think I was reflecting on the mystery, the depth, the light, the darkness; and somehow in that light shining into the darkness there was a mystery that went beyond words and touched me very deeply.

LENE: Did you recognize that feeling from other places or other incidents?

CAROL: From the time I was very young I had experiences in nature that I felt were spiritual.

Swimming in the ocean, I would sometimes feel as though I were suspended in a timeless stage, completely at one with the universe. I felt I could die there. If I pictured dying in that moment, it was a feeling of ecstasy and peace, and fullness, and oneness with the universe. I wasn't *seeking* to die, and I was not afraid of the waves.

LENE: Was the experience in the church about death also? Was it the darkness that fascinated you in the churches, the mysterious?

CAROL: It wasn't just the darkness; it was also the light. I was very much in love with the stained-glass windows and the way they let the light into the darkness. I think to me it's always been that relationship between the light and the darkness, between beauty and what you can't see at all. I think that what always fascinated me was the two together. One time in college we were given a sheet of paper and crayons and asked to express whatever was inside us. One part of my drawing was very dark, with deep blues and purples, and one part was light, yellow and pink. When I described it, I said it was not just the darkness or the light that interested me, it was the two being part of the same whole.

The churches were incredibly beautiful. It wasn't just the dark, the tomb, the tunnel. They were also amazingly beautiful and sensual—the paintings, the stained glass windows, the curved arches. The next year in college I tried to write a paper about these experiences. I talked to several professors about them, but they all said, "You're talking about the aesthetic. That's art. I don't know what that has to do with religion." I felt very strongly that the aesthetic was part of the religious. Art had been the mediation, the way through which I had experienced, and the experience was much deeper through beauty and through the sensual.

LENE: You mentioned nature and churches. Were there other circumstances where you felt the same way?

CAROL: When I was in high school I was interested in conservative, Republican politics. I was very concerned about the idea of freedom. From my point of view now, I reject the Republican right-wing view of individual freedom I had then. But I did find a dynamism in that quest for freedom and justice. Later I became more radical in my politics and became part of the antiwar movement and was involved in rallies where we were also concerned about black people, poor people.

I felt a spiritual connection through that, which at that time I interpreted through the Bible: God is on the side of the just. How can God want anyone to suffer? I felt that being part of a group that was working for what I understood to be justice and freedom, righteousness, was spiritual.

LENE: How was it spiritual to you?

CAROL: Well, one way of understanding spirituality is as the connection to something that's larger than yourself. And you can view that "something" as God, or the ground of being, or the Goddess, or the life force, or something else. I think being connected to history and to large social movements can also be spiritual. People also felt spiritual in the Nazi movement. There is a spiritual dimension to being part of something larger. Christians express this as the "community of saints." I hope we can distinguish between destructive and life-enhancing ways of feeling that connection. But I think a sense of connection to history and to community can be spiritual.

LENE: How do you experience the feeling?

CAROL: I can remember being in Washington with 500,000 or a million people at the antiwar demonstrations and feeling that I was with this massive group of people who were all individuals, but who all shared something of the feeling I came with, which was a deep feeling for the people of Vietnam and for their suffering: a desperate longing for them not to be bombed, a not wanting babies to be napalmed. I felt that we were all united in something that was very heartfelt, very deep.

I can also remember wearing a button with a drawing of a baby who was starving in Biafra. I would never do that now, it seems ineffective. But I really felt that by wearing that button, I caused people to think about children starving in Africa, and that some of them would really be moved to compassion and action.

I guess the feeling of compassion, the feeling of being one with someone else's suffering, is part, for me, of what the spiritual experience means.

LENE: Is it fundamentally to you a happy experience, or it it a feeling that you fear?

CAROL: I don't think I really fear it. I think sadness has always been part of it *and* happiness, *both*. They're both together. And I don't think I really fear it. I don't choose to be unhappy in my life. I'm sure there are times in my life when I really resist facing things. I don't say I'm a totally sane, healthy person. But I don't think I really fear being in touch with death or being in touch with sadness. It seems to me that when I do confront pain or death, I have connected to important parts of life, to a part of what life is about. It is important to me to be in touch with things that are real, things that are true. To be moved and touched and to want some kind of justice or compassion to come out of that experience—that to me is an important dimension of spirituality.

LENE: So some kind of ethics come out of it.

CAROL: Yes. I'm not at all comfortable with the term love, but some kind of feeling for other people, some kind of desire to make things better for them. Perhaps empathy is the word.

LENE: How do you feel about organized religion? You said that church meant a lot to you at a certain time.

CAROL: It doesn't anymore. I sometimes get very angry about organized religion—like when I think that the Catholic Church may keep me or other women from being able to have an abortion. Or that it's the right-wing religion, the Protestants and the Mormons, who've stopped the Equal Rights Amendment. It makes me very angry to think that organized religion still has so much power over my individual life and over the lives of other women who have less power than I do. If there is not an Equal Rights Amendment, I will probably still be OK, I will certainly suffer in some ways, but other women have even less power vis-à-vis the system than I do; I probably could find some way to get an abortion if I had to, but other women couldn't. The church is doing this: I could *never* be part of a church that's doing this. I have friends who can; they expect sin to be within the church. But the church has so much power—in Latin American they're preventing women from having access to any kind of birth control; I just could *not* be part of such a system. I can't distinguish, for example, the Presbyterian Church (which I know doesn't hold those stands) from the Christian church at large. The antiabortion and anti-ERA stands of the churches are very consistent with the misogyny that is deeply rooted in Christianity. There are other reasons, too, why I am not a Christian. The Holocaust made me doubt the power of God to act in history and also made me aware that anti-Judaism is deeply rooted in the Bible and Christian theology. From there I went on to question the combination of monotheism, revelation, and chosenness that has made the biblically-based religions so intolerant. Also the core symbolism of Christianity, the worship of Father and Son and the focus on sin and salvation, no longer moves me, no longer seems healthy to me personally or politically. There are many reasons; I could talk about them for hours.

LENE: You mostly spoke of your spiritual experiences as something in the past. Do you still have them? If you do, what do you do about them in terms of religion and religious organization?

CAROL: For a long time my spiritual community was a group of women who like myself were doing scholarship in the field of religious studies. We would all write papers and share them with each other, and that really was my spiritual connection for some time: sharing ideas and stories and experiences, having drinks together, having coffee together, sitting in groups together at night, talking on the phone about how we felt about our lives and the ultimate questions. We met as the Women and Religion Section of the American Academy of Religion, and as the New York Feminist Scholars in Religion, both of which I helped to organize.

Recently I haven't been in as close contact with that group of people, partly because I moved to California, and partly because, as we developed, people in that group became more and more diverse. There was a lot of controversy between socialists and nonsocialists, Christians and non-Christians, etc.

More recently I've been involved in a spirituality group that has developed in the community where I live now. We're a group of women who celebrate the full moons and the solstices and equinoxes, following the pagan year, very much inspired by women's spirituality and Z. Budapest and Starhawk, and also drawing on, from my point of view, people like Eliade and American Indian religion, and all kinds of things that I learned through studying the history of religion, the history of ritual. One of the other women in the group has been in theater, and she brings a sense of ritual as it arises out of drama, playacting. We've a lot of fun in our group, too. Someone is an official Nymph, and she is always making us laugh and joke.

LENE: How does that tie in with your "old" religious experiences?

CAROL: When I was still on the boundary of Christianity and searching for something else but didn't have any way to articulate it, I took a class from Starhawk. Much of what she said named my own experiences. The idea that the Goddess is the life *and* death force tied in with my experiences of the connection between the light and the darkness, color and depths, life and death. And the Goddess as incarnate in nature tied in with my experiences in the ocean. Death as a part of life seemed to be what I had intuitively experienced when I went through all those death experiences. The focus on nature as part of the religious was especially important. I have always known we are one with nature, that nature is a source of our spirituality. Appreciation for ritual, for color, and for playfulness—affirmation that fun was part of it—all seemed right to me. In her classes I kept feeling: This is what I've always believed. And the female divinity was very prominent. I'd been feeling really uncomfortable with God as masculine, with any kind of "generic" masculine pronouns.

So the Goddess was really very familiar to me, but I hadn't heard her named quite that way before.

LENE: It naturally tied in with the things you already knew?

CAROL: Right. And I didn't feel like "I have to think about that, or I'm not sure if I can remember that." It wasn't that way at all. She said what I already knew, what I already thought. But it was being woven together.

Another thing that was important in my quest was the gestalt therapy I did with a woman named Lenore Hecht. She used some bioenergetic techniques, too. Through that I began to understand energy, how we communicate energy by the way we sit, stand, and take our breaths. I became very sensitive to seeing how people who were in a depressed state had very low energy, whereas people who had just expressed their anger or other feelings for someone radiated energy. People are attracted to that energy, whether it is anger, sadness, love—whatever the deep-felt emotion is. The person who expresses it just radiates energy. I learned that you did not have to be afraid of feelings, because there was this energy in feelings.

LENE: What does that energy mean?

CAROL: For me it was important because I'd been—and of course, I'm sure I still am—a very repressed person in a lot of ways. I learned that I didn't have to be afraid just to tell someone I liked them. Even if they didn't like me back, they probably liked to hear that someone liked them. I didn't have to be afraid to tell someone I was mad at them, because through expressing what I really felt I was communicating something deep within me. And most people were attracted to energy, depth of energy. Even if they didn't like what I said, they were still attracted to the idea that I was able to say it. I was attracted to people who were able to do that, too. I didn't have to be afraid to cry or shout.

LENE: So that tied in with your religious experiences?

CAROL: Well, yes. That especially tied in with what Starhawk was saying about raising a cone of energy and about how there is a basic energy in the universe. Through gestalt I had become much more conscious of something I'd already known before in a very inchoate or sporadic way. In gestalt I became very conscious of the presence of that energy and I learned that to some extent you can control it. You can put out more energy and get more energy back. That seemed to relate directly to Starhawk's idea of magic: You can control the energy around you, the kind of energy you put out will affect what kind you get back.

Gestalt and magic didn't seem to be entirely different to me.

LENE: How do you think men's religious experiences compare to the things you experienced?

CAROL: I don't think that there is anything in the world that any human being isn't capable of experiencing. Except, I suppose, very special things: I can't experience having black skin, or a man can't experience having a child coming out of his very body. But I think that the nature of human experience is that it is incredibly plastic. We have incredible capacities for empathy and sympathy for other people's experience. And we have enough in common to understand each other. I wrote my dissertation about Elie Wiesel, the Nazi Holocaust, the concentration camps. I felt that I could really understand his experience from my heart because I did have capacities, no greater than anyone else's, for empathy. Someone can tell their story, and someone else can feel that they're living through it, too.

I also think there are aspects of my own experience that were similar to Elie Wiesel's. He felt betrayed by God as a Jew, I felt betrayed by God as a woman. How could God have let the world be so unjust to women? How could God have let the Nazis be so unjust to the Jews? We came out of a similar background: We believed God was just, that God had some power to act. So, I think that in human experience—I'm using this as an analogy of all human experience—there is enough in common. And there's enough capacity for empathy with what isn't in common. We *can* understand each other's experience, and there's nothing in human experience that anyone of us can't have a great deal of empathy for.

LENE: So you think that men have the same kind of religious experiences that women do?

CAROL: I think some do. I think that in our culture many men's experiences are different from many women's. I don't think it's that way by nature. There might be a certain biological propensity in men to be more aggressive, women to be more passive or more nurturing or something like that. But I don't think these have to define how men and women are. I think that if we look cross-culturally, we see many cultures where men are much less aggressive and much less rational and uptight than they are in our culture.

I think that in general women who have been raised in America, and probably in most of industrialized Western culture, are more open to experiences of mysticism and oneness with the universe than men are. For a lot of reasons. One is that we've been socialized to care about other people. And that opens us to putting ourselves in the place of *the other* whether that other be a child in Vietnam, or a child of our own, or the ocean. As women we're socialized to think from the other side, to draw boundaries: I stop here, and this other thing starts there. I don't think men are incapable of empathetic or mystical experience. Some men had the same kind of mystical experiences that women have had. But I think it's much more frequent with women.

Another way of putting it is that women are open to mysticism and empathy because we don't have very strong ego boundaries. This can be bad: I would like to see women have stronger egos. Not having strong ego boundaries has encouraged that kind of flowing over from the self into the other. Sometimes that can have very negative consequences. Some women don't have any sense of self at all. Their husband leaves them or a child leaves, and they're devastated.

And I definitely think that the things that women have been socialized to be attuned to are the things we all need to be attuned to. And I would have no hope at all if I thought that men are not capable of mysticism and empathy. Because if they aren't, they're going to blow us all up.

SHEILA GREEVE DAVANEY

Sheila Greeve Davaney is Associate Professor of Theology at the Iliff School of Theology. The master's and doctoral degrees are from Harvard where she was also a Research/Resource Associate in Women's Studies. She is editor of *Feminism and Process Thought* and has published in the areas of feminist theology and social theories of knowledge. Her current research concerns the relation of power and knowledge.

Journey from the Heartland

A feminist theologian sounds to many women, including quite often myself, like a contradiction in terms. It is a personal and professional identity that is filled with tension and ambivalence. In this autobiographical statement, I would like to trace how this identity came to be and why, despite its ambivalent character, I believe it is not only an appropriate but also an essential one for myself as a woman committed to the transformation of the social order.

There are many factors that go into the creation of a self: family, economic circumstance, education, political realities, the sheer chance character of experience. One such element that has had tremendous impact, both negative and positive, upon the shaping of the female identity has been religion. In my own life religion, in the form of Christianity, has played a prevalent and omnipresent role. My birth into a Catholic family and education from preschool through college at private Catholic institutions combined to create a religious backdrop against which the development of my self-identity, convictions about reality, and attitudes towards others all took place. In essence, for many years of my life, issues of self-identity were really religious issues for me.

This background of religion functioned on many levels. In the formative years of high school it provided an obvious and irresistible target for rebellion. Being at Catholic boarding school in the sixties, when the church struggled for a new, post-Vatican II identity while still retaining so many outmoded forms of beliefs, meant constantly rebelling against, if not really rejecting, the religious heritage of our childhoods. From skipping mass to ridiculing the church and its views on birth control and sexuality, protest was a form of growing up Catholic.

But if religion was a target for adolescent rebellion, it also came eventually to be for me the context for great personal and intellectual searching and growth. Through a slow and often painful process of transformation, labeled by my rebellious cohorts as "selling out," I came to interpret my Catholic faith as an arena where my questions about the nature of reality and the possibility of meaning might be addressed. I ceased viewing religion as an enemy and began to appropriate it consciously as a ground for my identity. If I had once rejected my religious heritage with a fervor, now I embraced it with an equally zealous wholeheartedness. Where tradition and ritual had appalled me, they now held both fascination and delight. Yet despite this positive assessment of religion, my relation to it was never one of unquestioning acquiescence. Due to an atmosphere of progressive Catholicism (the nuns were far more liberal and full of doubts than their students) and an inherent tendency toward reflection, theological issues were already by the time I was sixteen a source of continual uncertainty and discomfort for me. Questions of meaning in the face of evil and suffering, along with the issues of power and freedom, became a continual refrain in my thinking. And although I viewed the Christian tradition positively, at the same time its response to these issues already seemed totally inadequate.

This combination of a positive assessment of my Catholic faith and a continual questioning of its religious and theological formulations did not seem incongruous to me as I moved into college in the late sixties. My faith, rather than denying the validity of uncertainty, instead seemed to grant me permission to question and eventually to protest. I came to see rebellion as an imperative of faith, not a rejection of it.

In the context of the still lingering civil-rights movement, the war in Vietnam, and the exploding youth movement, this new sense of my faith was radically to change my perception of myself and how I viewed the social order. My opposition to the Vietnam War came slowly and was the result less of joining the "crowd" than of recognizing that the faith I affirmed was irreconcilable with the injustice of that war. Resistance to the war, to racism, and to economic oppression was for many Christians, including myself, the public expression of a revitalized faith. Tutoring in Harlem, working on political campaigns, and marching in Washington all took on the aura of a new form of religious ritual.

If public political protest was regarded as not only acceptable to but demanded by the Catholic left, so too was intellectual protest. As a religion major at Manhattanville College, I, along with many others, considered myself in the vanguard of a radicalized and fully modern Catholicism. We delighted in our heresy and in those heady days sometimes even were convinced that we would be the church's future. Yet perhaps lurking even then was the suspicion that the critical thinking and action that had issued forth from a deeply held faith would one day lead to the abandonment of that faith. Even then, there was the sense that my days of feeling comfortable in and energized by the church were soon to end. The demise of that sense of belonging was to come about in a primary way because of my encounter with feminism.

Already in the sixties and early seventies the present-day women's movement was on the rise, and feminist theory was already taking a radical shape. However, for the most part I was oblivious to the growing movement. This was not only because on certain levels the women's college I attended reinforced traditional expectations but perhaps more because women's colleges in general masked the more blatant forms of sexism that characterized the wider social arena. In an all-female context we were encouraged to excel academically and to set high professional goals for ourselves after graduation. For most of us, the thought that we would be denied access to higher degrees, or to jobs, or to whole professional fields simply did not occur to us. Nor did most of us recognize that the political movements of the left that we so eagerly joined and the sexual revolution that we enthusiastically applauded did not include full and liberating participation by women. The recognition that the New Left was, in sexual terms, a parody of the Old Right, was to be a bitter and painful one for many women.

Thus I approached the end of my college career radicalized politically on a number of issues related to peace and racial and economic justice. But the oppression of women was not on the list of those ills whose alleviation I saw as an important part of my life. Further, while my theological stance had been greatly liberalized, I had yet to examine Christianity's relation to women and had little sense of the profound negative influence theological and religious visions can have upon the lives of those who are shaped by them. Fully embracing the Christian dictum of self-sacrificial love, I was prepared to do battle on behalf of everyone but myself and my sisters.

My first fully explicit encounter with feminism in the context of theological studies came at a weekend for college women in religion sponsored by Union Theological Seminary in New York. Since that time, I have met numerous women who also participated in one of Union's yearly seminars for women and who, like myself, were profoundly changed by it. I began the weekend surprised by and suspicious of the feminist statements I was hearing. I was convinced that these were the carpings of women who simply had not made it. But as I listened to the stories of woman after woman, to the tales of pain and humiliation and of courage and determination, a new awareness began for me. I was deeply troubled by my own ignorance and what had been my facile dismissal of the pain of others. And I felt as well the beginnings of that anger that invades every woman when she recognizes her own oppression. It would take years for this awareness and anger to be given full expression; but though I did not recognize it then, my weekend in New York was a turning point for my consciousness of myself as a woman.

What I did realize after that seminar was that I wanted to go to graduate school. This decision was certainly not clear-cut or without tremendous conflict. On the one hand were my interest in further study and the urgings of college professors. On the other hand, I felt, as did almost everyone I knew, the commitment to political and social action. I eventually opted for a master's program in theological studies at Harvard.

While this decision would set the direction for my later professional choices, I have often wondered if it in fact signaled my retreat from the arena of real social and political protest.

As I began seminary, the question of sexism was an alive issue but one still relegated to the more remote areas of my thought and life. That was all soon to change. The women's community at Harvard Divinity School in the early seventies was well organized, public, and very vocal. Through the disruption of classes, public meetings, and private caucuses, the women continually pointed out the pervasiveness of sexist language, thought forms, and behavior. The fact that there was not one woman teaching full-time on the faculty—and only an occasional visiting professor—served as only one public expression of an attitude of sexism that, if changing, still permeated the entire institution. Slowly, with the help of the continual prompting of other women, I began to understand more fully the dynamics of sexism. Such understanding felt almost like a physical assault. So many things that had once appeared trivial now took on ominous proportions. Sexist language that had seemed unimportant became first irritating and then intolerable. The absence of women faculty and administrators and the presence of a curriculum that was oblivious to issues of importance to women all contributed to a growing personal frustration, disillusionment, and indeed rage.

But Harvard's institutional sexism was not the only source of my disillusionment. Out of a growing woman's consciousness, I came to scrutinize critically both the church that had been my home and the theological tradition that I had inherited from Christianity. With particular sadness and pain I came to recognize fully the role the Catholic Church played in the oppression of women. For it had been my religious self-identity that had originally prompted me to examine issues of justice in relation to others; it had been the church that had first awakened my social conscience and demanded accountability. Now I was to discover that while the church might speak out for justice for others, it was not merely silent in relation to women but an active contributor through church practice and policy to the oppression of women. The post-

Vatican II hope that had infused Mary Daly's *The Church and the Second Sex* was by the mid-seventies turning for many Catholic women into the conviction that if we were to find liberation, it would not be in the Catholic Church. Many feminists have remained within the church and have with integrity sought transforming visions within that religious context. But many others of us have left, some with sadness, others with relief, but all with the sense that never again could we call that church our home.

If my feminism made me something of a spiritual orphan, its impact upon my intellectual development was equally dramatic. When I first began my master's program, I was uncertain in what field of religious studies I wanted to concentrate. My first theology course settled that; I fell in love with theological reflection, with the subtlety of argumentation and the sensitivity to complexity that theology demands. In many ways theology became for me a substitute for the church, an arena where I could once more explore the issues of meaning and value that had shadowed me for years. But my feminist consciousness provided a built-in critical mechanism that raised profound questions about the theological enterprise and prevented any simple or naive identification with this still essentially male context. Through my own reflection and the influence of such women as Mary Daly, the male character of most theological positions became increasingly clear to me. A year spent in a women's theology group coordinated by Judith Plaskow only solidified my conviction that the theological discipline, no less than the church, was sexist through and through. Still, and perhaps oddly to my feminist friends, I did not conclude that theology, too, must be left behind. Instead, by the end of my master's program, I was convinced that feminism needed a theological or philosophical vision and that without such an overarching vision we would fail to recognize and carry out the truly radical nature of our feminist program. I knew even then that, in how I viewed theology, I differed significantly from most male theologians and not a few women theologians. However, it would take several more years before I could with any clarity articulate my conception of this enterprise.

Thus, committed to the doing of theology but frustrated with Harvard, I left the East for a doctoral program at Claremont in California. I was to stay in Claremont for only a year before returning to Harvard, but that year was to have a significant influence on my theological development. At Claremont I first encountered in depth the school of theology and philosophy known as process thought. And while I have been a vocal critic of certain aspects of process thought, I became convinced and remain persuaded that feminism and process thought share a number of concerns and commitments. Each is a critic of traditional Western conceptions of self, God, and world. Both suggest alternative visions of an interdependent, dynamic universe in which brute power is rejected in the name of cooperative interaction. In my thought these two approaches have maintained an alliance of sorts, though here, as always, I remain wary of being co-opted into male thought structures.

That year in California freed me intellectually and emotionally, and I returned to Harvard with a more positive assessment of the possibility of doing feminist theology. I was to remain in Cambridge for five more years completing my doctoral program. Those years both affirmed my vision of theology and disclosed, on a day-to-day basis, the difficulty of being a feminist and a theologian. On the negative side, while much was changing in that environment, much of the underlying sexism remained. Harvard hired a few women, but it would take until 1979 for the institution to hire a woman in the theology department; no role models were to be found here! Courses and doctoral examinations followed the long established pattern of emphasizing white, male, European and North American thinkers. And sexism, though it had shed its more blatant and crude forms, nonetheless still found continual, if more subtle, expression. The women in the department were "encouraged" in our feminist endeavors, while at the same time we were told that feminists would be listened to when they produced work worthy of theological, i.e., male, attention. There were other refrains that we would hear continually in those years: Our feminism was to be applauded but the anger that came with it was "so distasteful and unfeminine"; and in later years as we gained job interviews, our male counterparts continually suggested that we received the invitations because we were women. Underlying all of this was a prevalent attitude, quite unconscious, I think, yet ever present, that the women should be grateful that we had been permitted into a male domain.

The frustration induced by that environment was often overwhelming, and much of the time I was very angry. But if the years between 1975 and 1980 were marred by frustration and occasional fury, they were also years of growth and of celebration and even sometimes of peace. Harvard was changing, too. It had developed one of the most creative programs in women's studies in the country, and the women who came to Cambridge for that program were a continual source of encouragement and tremendous role models of determination and courage. Women faculty and administrators also provided a point of connection; even if they were hired as "safe" women, a few months in that environment usually transformed them into ardent feminists. Over and over again, women faculty, students, staff, and administrators crossed traditional boundaries to work on issues of common concern. But perhaps in those years my greatest sources of both support and challenge were the other women closest to me in the theology doctoral program. For years Linell Cady and Paula Cooley and I were each other's champions, reality checks, and sharers of frustration. We depended upon each other not only in our common struggles but also in our profound differences. To each other we revealed our doubts about being theologians, and through one another's encouragement we gained permission to keep trying to join feminism and theology. And while our extended phone conversations and late night discussions probably prolonged our programs significantly, they helped turn anger into laughter and frustration into stubborn determination. I am quite sure that without the presence of those two women, graduate school would have been, if not an intolerable experience, a far less rich and interesting one than in fact it was.

Nor were women the only ones struggling to understand the implications of feminism and other liberation perspectives for theology. Male faculty and students also participated, though with varying degrees of enthusiasm, in the ongoing effort in light of the reality of oppression to redefine the discipline and their own identities as theologians. Through this continual redefining process, shared by men as well as women, my own vision of theology coalesced. In particular, a ten-year theological conversation with Professor Gordon D. Kaufman has helped clarify my theological vision. As I begin to close this essay, I want to express something of that vision, because it explains why I continue to be a theologian.

For many, theology represents the attempt to translate or redefine historically developed claims into language and concepts appropriate for the present. Hence it is basically a hermeneutical or interpretive process. Underlying this view of theology is the assumption that truth or its approximation has already been disclosed in the past, whether in revelation or tradition or philosophical argumentation. Theology's task, then, is to appropriate, albeit in a creative and critical manner, that supposed truth. When theology is viewed in this way, radical feminists have tended to be wary of participating in the enterprise. Our feminist analysis has uncovered the male character of much of the theological and philosophical traditions. Various ideas of God, self, and world, while often conflicting with one another, nonetheless all bear the mark of their origins in male thought and power. To understand theology's task as either the translation of these ideas into a more acceptable contemporary idiom or the search for a supposedly pristine, and hence liberating, expression of such ideas seems to many feminists a failure to recognize the thoroughly male character of our history and the radical challenge with which feminism confronts the *entire* philosophical and theological tradition that we have inherited. For many women, the past provides a profound lesson in the dynamics of oppression; it does not provide adequate resources for a liberated future. Hence, when theology is viewed as critical appropriation of

tradition, many feminists have, and rightly I think, questioned whether this is a task upon which we should expend our
energies.

There is emerging, however, another view of theology
which is far more compatible with feminist goals.[1] This view,
which I espouse, is grounded in the recognition that human
beings are in the most fundamental way symbol-creating
creatures who live and act within the networks of meaning
that they themselves have created. Embedded in this claim
are two further assumptions. First, it assumes that such a
symbolic framework is imperative for all human thought and
action. Indeed, without some at least implicit vision of reality, of the overall context within which life takes place and of
the human place within that cosmic schema, human beings
would not be able to function at all. Second, this view
assumes that such networks of meaning, such world views, are
cultural and social creations. That is, we do not "read" the
nature of reality directly from reality, but instead, through
human history and culture, we build up, develop, and reinter-
pret conceptions of what we believe existence is really about
and what our human nature, purpose, and meaning consist of
in that cosmic context. Thus, all our world views, secular and
religious alike, are thoroughly human constructions and rep-
resent human attempts to express fundamental convictions
about the nature and meaning of reality. Further, these
visions grow out of, reflect, and most often undergird their
societal contexts and the values and power arrangements of
those contexts. Hence, humans' visions of the nature and
meaning of reality and of human life are not disinterested
accounts of "objective" reality, but value-and interest-laden

1. The understanding of theology as construction that follows has been
   influenced from a number of directions. It certainly reflects the impact
   of feminist theological thought as well as feminist sociological and
   anthropological analysis. However, in detail, it has been influenced the
   most by the theories of Gordon D. Kaufman. Kaufman's interpretation
   of theology as construction has long appeared to me as a compatible, if
   not totally adequate, view for women to consider. For a more developed
   expression of this theory, see Kaufman's *The Theological Imagination*
   (Philadelphia: Westminster Press, 1981).

interpretations of life and its purpose. In this view, truth and meaning are less discovered by humans than created by them.

Beginning with these convictions, I would suggest that the theological enterprise must be reconsidered. This enterprise entails the critical task of examining the historical traditions to which we are heirs in order to determine the forms of human life that they make possible or which they inhibit. In this critical task, knowledge of our history is indeed imperative; failing to understand our heritage condemns us to being forever its victims. However, in contrast to the view of theology as hermeneutics, this approach suggests that no historical form or vision or figure be given an elevated status; theology is not the reexpression of historical truth claims whose validity and appropriateness are assured. Instead, it is in its critical mode the examination of history so that we might gain insight from its failures and draw hope from its relatively few successes.

If the critical assessment of history is an important part of the theological task, its central concern is, I think, constructive. That is, recognizing that we exist in webs of meaning we ourselves have produced, the theologian undertakes the task of self-consciously constructing such symbolic frameworks. Our role as theologians is to contribute to the development of views of self and world that are more adequate to our time and place and enable and nourish more humane forms of existence for today and the future. These visions, like those we have inherited, will be thoroughly human constructions and, as such, relative, conditioned, and value-laden. And while we may appeal to history as a teacher, we will not find there the answers to our present dilemmas. Our inescapable responsibility is to be creators of that which we will call truth in our own age, and such responsibility may very well entail leaving behind our ancient visions of the world.

This interpretation of theology as construction is, I believe, compatible with my feminist self-understanding. But more than being simply compatible, it expresses my deepest conviction that women must self-consciously participate in the creation of our symbolic universes. We have been for too long the victims of male visions of reality, constructed for the purposes of male power and elevated by males to the status of ultimate Truth. Now we must unmask those male visions for the idols that they are, but we must not be content with such critical work. We must also seek the creative vision by which we might live freely, liberating ourselves and our world. Moreover, I am convinced that this work of constructive theology is neither esoteric nor irrelevant to the feminist quest for liberation and wholeness. Instead, it recognizes fully that our visions of reality, self, and world profoundly influence the kind of lives we live. Thus this form of theology can be carried out in the service of concrete social and political transformation.

I began this essay by speaking of the tension that accompanies being a feminist theologian. That tension is real and ever present. It flows from the fact that the discipline of theology most often interprets itself in the hermeneutical mode discussed above; its eyes are still most often fixed on that male-controlled past, even when it claims, as much contemporary theology does, that the idea of the future is central. Further, theology is a discipline still almost completely dominated by men; the number of women is increasing, but for the most part we still work in physical isolation from one another. But perhaps most important, that tension exists because of my sense of inadequacy in the face of the tremendous task that confronts us. For most of my life I "searched for the truth," convinced that if I thought hard enough or prayed with intensity or listened to history, the truth would be disclosed. My experience as a feminist and theologian has called this quest into question. I still listen to my past and to history, and I continue to watch my world to see what I might learn. But instead of waiting for life to give me meaning, I now see my role as endowing the world in which I live with value and significance. I believe we are the creators of the visions of reality that permit or deny us humane existence; each one of us confronts a responsibility whose abdication the world can no longer afford. I have, at least for the present, chosen to embrace that responsibility, if uneasily and with feelings of inadequacy, as a theologian.

For the past three years I have carried out this work at the Iliff School of Theology, a United Methodist Seminary in Denver. The irony that a feminist of my background and commitments should end up teaching in a Methodist seminary has not been lost on friends, colleagues, or myself. Nor is there any doubt in my mind that my loyalties are wider than even this very liberal institution's. But if I worry about the integrity of teaching in a context whose commitments do not always coincide with my own, the honesty that such recognition has produced on all sides has been a source of growth and of creativity. I have further been fortunate to be in an environment where colleagues have encouraged my work and have urged me on in my attempt to redefine the theological enterprise—wherever that might lead. My women colleagues have been especially helpful, providing support as well as being honest in their criticism. They, as did my Cambridge friends, have provided that much needed environment where laughter and anger, hope and despair all can find free expression.

My journey to this place has been a convoluted one. It has entailed the loss of the religious community that shaped me and a movement away from most of the expectations of my past. But it has also been a movement into a self-consciously chosen identity as a woman committed to the transformation of our world into a more human and liberating one. For now, I am living out that commitment as a theologian. There are tensions and even contradictions in this choice. But for the moment, it provides the best place for me to live out my hopes for a nonoppressive future.

MARY ANNE SIDERITS

After earning a doctorate at the University of Michigan, Mary Anne Siderits joined the faculty on the campus where she had been an undergraduate (Marquette University). She lectures on clinical psychology and gender role issues and serves as Director of the Center for Psychological Services. She has been an officer of county and state psychological associations and is currently serving as Secretary-Treasurer of Division 36 of the American Psychological Association (Psychologists Interested in Religious Issues). She is engaged in interview research on gender role issues both in the United States and in Germany. For diversion she grapples with the Renaissance lute and with a contemporary novel.

Of Lost Chords and Morning Faces:
Fragments of a Catholic Studenthood

The mind keeps its own accounts, and there is no anticipating what it will log indelibly and what erase, no telling what will be its final sum. We visit a foreign city, and what is left to memory is not necessarily what the guide books hoard. In the mind's roster of things remembered, the scrap of a face in a brightly bordered window at some forgotten turn may out-rank a sublime cathedral. So with any revisiting of our earlier years: The pattern of remembering is as individual as our handwriting, and it has the quality not of deliberate script but of a document produced at some level beyond the will. All that we keep of the past may, thus, be an unintended brother of the caricature: an isolation of the features that most impressed us.

When I try to assemble the pieces of my religious history, I am confronted by a strange pastiche. The question of whether it is a fair and complete picture of events and persons is in some sense irrelevant. It is *my* picture, the composite that has influenced *me*.

*   *   *

There is a point in childhood, perhaps a point just beyond night-lights and teddy bears, when the child holds on to the waking world by listening, as long as her drowsy head will let her, to what is occurring on the other side of the bedroom wall.

NOTE: All names except mine are fictitious.

This need not be matter for the Freudian romance. There is something special about almost *any* exchange in that other world where one can hear the steps of people and the rattle and click of familiar objects. Even the homeliest of conversations may have some appeal for ears that are trying to decipher them through doors and shadows, but when what is discussed is not everyday conversational baggage, the juvenile eavesdropper is even more intrigued. The voices I remember in this respect were those of my mother and father, and they were talking not about light bulbs and lilac bushes but about words and ideas I was only beginning to understand. Concepts like that of resurrection. What were they saying? I can't recall exactly, but I know they were confronting what was remarkable in their beliefs and weighing the alternatives, and doing so in voices that were calm and unafraid. I did not understand all of their considerations at that time, but I took something away from my nocturnal audience, and it became a permanent possession: the notion that, even among people of faith, nothing is beyond question. And that included the question that fires creativity in science and the arts, "Could it be otherwise?"

*   *   *

Of course, I was to find that the examination of religious belief was not uniformly welcome among my cobelievers. The phrase "presumptuous pride of intellect" has a certain cadence, particularly when delivered by someone who is inclined glibly and smugly to dismiss those who differ (and also those who are different, but that's another issue). Perhaps I did not hear this phrase first from an aunt of mine, but it was on her tightly smiling lips that it acquired a salience for me. It was her regular riposte for any attempt to explore a religious assertion intellectually—and as I moved into adolescence I was inclined to just such attempts. My aunt was to become for me the prototype of those persons who condemn any one who explores positions they consider beyond doubt—

persons whom I would come to call militant fideists, but for whom I then had no ready epithet.

What I was aware of at that time—although I didn't discern it until later—was that these individuals shared a distinctive set. It was not that they were all blatantly negative. Some, to be sure, swelled the ranks of curmudgeons and termagants, but some, like my aunt, were basically pleasant and even determinedly cheerful. What was missing, despite the congeniality and cheer, was a real sense of humor. With humor there is some perception of oneself from a double perspective and a consequent departure from a perpetual earnestness; there is some notion that in any maze worth running what looks like a point of access may indeed be a cul-de-sac. For the militant fideist there is no double perspective, so there can be neither humor nor forgiveness of dissent.

*　　*　　*

On that aunt's account my parents and I set out one fine fall Saturday for the farmlands to the west that had allegedly yielded an outcropping of miracles. The central figure in these events was a middle-aged farm woman whose rural simplicity matched her votaries' images of the young woman of Lourdes. My aunt had entered the circle of this supposed recipient of "apparitions" of the Virgin Mary and persuaded my parents to look into the phenomenon. For my parents anything bore examination, and, besides, the highways lined with autumn foliage were most inviting. For me, half-child, half-adolescent, anything was possible. The child, after all, grows up in a world where each new learning is a kind of revelation of the wonderful, and the world is always assuming new guises of which she had never dreamed. No wonder, then, that there might still be readiness to suspend disbelief, especially since a scientific understanding of the world had not yet prescribed the limits of such a suspension. I say all this simply to make it clear that I would have been ready to accept whatever happened, no matter how strange or how much a departure from the humdrum. And, indeed, I was jolted by what I saw on that visit, but in a direction quite different from any I had imagined.

I perceived not a miracle but a disturbing aspect of human personality new to me. Some in the crowd (and they were not an inconsiderable number) had come expecting certain specific "signs," and they saw what they expected to see. The spontaneous gilding of rosaries seemed a favorite minor expectation, but chief among the anticipated wonders was some sort of solar aberration commonly described as the sun dancing across the sky. (That had happened once before in the annals of the miracle-finders, and the eager souls were awaiting a cosmic rerun.) No thought, of course, of what havoc such a solar dance might wreak in the celestial scheme of things. Astronomical relationships were not of interest to these earthlings with their unflinching hopes for the October sky. (It struck me much later that the phenomenon they looked for was a curious inversion of the Eucharist. Here the substance remained, and its properties were transmuted— surely more of an incompatibility with scientific observation. But there were not many scientists in that crowd.)

Around me (although not from anyone I knew) came the reports of the expected miracle. I saw nothing out of the ordinary. That was a disappointment, of course, but an even greater disenchantment was ahead of me. I had known that I might not be blessed with any special visions. However, if I could not expect to be blessed, I did not expect to be damned either. And yet a remarkable thing occurred among those people who claimed to have been visually favored. There wasn't the joy, the exhilaration I would have expected— nothing even mildly reminiscent of the excitement with which I met the secret workings of a leaf in my biology class. Where was the sense of the wonder of things, and of the God who was supposedly behind this show? What I heard instead was a bitterness toward those whose eyes could not provide the added confirmation. The miracle-watchers looked not for wonder but for certainty—the certainty of being in the divine elite. This was new to me: that the religious attitude might become infected by an animus toward those of a different persuasion. This sobering thought produced a permanent wariness toward any religious response that depended heavily on certainty and very little on wonder.

*   *   *

Trailing an apparition was an exotic activity for which we were not explicitly prepared in the parochial school I attended. What little was said about private revelations clearly indicated that they fell outside that basic receptacle called the "deposit of faith," and we were, therefore, free initially to evaluate them on our own. Quite different were those matters related to ecclesiastical doctrine, where less was left to chance or individual evaluation.

"Grounding in the faith" occupied a regular portion of our parochial school lives and assumed two forms. One was the sort of religion class we had whenever Father came, and the other was the catechism in which we were drilled by the classroom nun. "Father" was actually any one of a series of brown-robed, sandaled priests who came from the friary on the same campus where our school stood. (It was an order noted also for its work with the ghetto poor in our community, and their opposition to social prejudice was happily absorbed with the religious instruction.) They were all gentle and likable men. However, one of them, whom I'll call Father Aquin, is most vivid, probably because (a) to the eyes of the seven-year-olds who first encountered him he was the white-bearded double of the image of God the Father that floated benignly over the altar of our church, and (b) some five or six years later he had the ineffable decency to reassure at least one worried adolescent that the storm of thoughts and feelings with which she was preoccupied were not "evil" but simply the harbinger of her womanhood.

Father Aquin's time with us was spent not just on our routine religious diet but also on the more succulent "mysteries" and other doctrinal intricacies. Many of the children found the latter morsels too difficult to digest, but I remember gulping them. The significance of the "persons" in the sacred triad—now there was something on which to cut one's theological teeth. And of equal interest were the images of people out there somewhere ("scholars") discussing, examining, and arguing about these very ideas. There was, at least, the sense that not everything was finished . . . .

Sister Lumen Dei's catechism lineup could not hope to compete for my attention. There we moved in a slow shuffle to the point where Sister stood—the point at which the ill-prepared, or simply frightened, catechumen underwent her or his individual ordeal by fire. Sister would question, and the pupil was to "recite." The line moved with a speed inversely proportionate to the number of heresies reaching Sister's tired ears. There were a few moments of belated rehearsal for each doctrinal stumbler. A "quick study," I soon discovered that if I positioned myself toward the middle of the recital line, I could master the lesson without sweating over the blue "Baltimore" the night before. Aside from the excitement of performing this maneuver, there wasn't much in that procession to pique my interest. (A few of the standard answers, perhaps, but I'll talk about that later.)

*   *   *

The discrepancy that I see now between Father's and Sister's roles might have made for an unfortunate discrimination between the genders. Was it not Father who soared among the mysteries and Sister who presided over the pedestrian acquisiton of the necessary "answers"? What saved us from making that invidious distinction was the fact that Sister Lumen Dei, swathed in her surplus serge, didn't really seem like a woman to us—rather a representative of a sacred, but certainly third, gender. Oh, we never said that, of course. But I remember how astounded we were when protestant chum of mine described his meeting with one of our nuns. He said that she was a "nice woman," and the phrase stopped us in our tracks. Could one properly call a nun a woman?

Certainly, the generous cut of the religious habit left little room for the revelation of the human body, or even of the all-too-human signs of aging. The well-scrubbed face of Sister Innocence, peering from the starched window of her wimple, appeared detached from what, for all we knew, could have been a graceful neck and shoulders; but that small section also would exclude the neck circle, sagging chin, and wrinkling forehead that would let us know that Sister was growing older. Could that somewhat disembodied face, protected from the earliest signs of aging, have much in common with our future adult selves—supposing, of course, that we did not ourselves move down the impeccable corridors of the nunnery?

*　　*　　*

While in those days the female charges of those same sisters wore nothing like a habit, or even a uniform, there was an unwritten dress code that seemed designed, like the nuns' habits, to minimize signs of corporeal substance that might lead males "into temptation." Strangely enough, this involved stretches of flesh not ordinarily thought to be among the most provocative: the shoulder ball and the area between knee and ankle, for example. Thus, sleeveless tops were frowned upon, knee socks were preferable to anklets, and hems always ran below the fashion. This might have been the occasion for no more than amusing maternal compromises, had it not been for the tacit message about sex roles that these restrictions conveyed: In the realm of sexual activity, there were those who needed moral protection and those responsible for providing it. And, in some contrast to other realms, here the man was seen as vulnerable, while the female of the species had to be the limit-setter. As I look at it now, there was almost a partitioning of personality, with the male conceived as the representative of drive in the relationship and the female as the agent of moral values. *She* was to play superego to *his* id. This role construction—foreshadowed in our grade school dress code—was elaborated in our adolescent years. Fresh from their copies of *Modern Youth and Chastity,* teenage girls were implicitly counseled that a cool head was to be the most important part of their anatomy in the sexual relationship—at least before marriage. (With marriage the girl was to change her role from that of nay-sayer to obliging partner, again because the male lacked genital fortitude. In either case, his sin would be upon her soul, and she must learn to make the role adjustment.) Could this role asymmetry be compatible with real communication in a relationship or with the balance of emotional release and responsibility that should be the lot of both male and female?

*   *   *

As I hinted earlier, among the material we memorized for Sister Lumen Dei and her successors were some ideas that grabbed me and didn't let go. Now I recognize that all of these more compelling ideas had to do with individual latitude. There was the matter of mortal sin, for example. Objectively, there were certain sins so grave that they were said to warrant eternal damnation, certainly a fearsome thought. But there was an interesting proviso. From the standpoint of the subject, no offense was mortal unless (s)he perceived its gravity. And there was the possibility of perfect contrition. If the penitent could truly muster love (rather than fear) of God as the basis of reform, even the most serious sin could be absolved aside from the confessional. The bypassing of the confessional was not the most important issue. Indeed, I found that the ministration of that sacrament could often be downright comforting; witness my reference to Father Aquin's solace at the burgeoning of my sexuality. What was important, it seems to me, was the emphasis on what occurred within the individual (as distinguished from what was done outside).

The third piece of doctrine that I particularly fancied had to do with the fate of those who were not Catholic. Early in my formal schooling I had been taught that I belonged to the "one true church." Since this was by dint of circumstances that had preceded me (I was what has rather inaccurately been called a "born Catholic"), I considered myself just plain lucky. However, I felt uneasy about those who didn't enjoy the same good fortune. "Outside the church there is no salvation" sounded rather grim until one learned that the "church" could be defined liberally enough to include persons of good conscience, regardless of affiliation. Again, it seemed that individual motivation was more important than any of its props.

*   *   *

Motivation was an important precursor of one of the privileges I later learned was accorded to scholars: the privilege of taking an intellectual risk. During my formal education "the Index" was still a force in Catholic intellectual life. (The *Index Librorum Prohibitorum,* I was to discover, was actually a rather small book, its size not at all commensurate with its formidability.) Those works it explicitly listed and the others that were proscribed in principle were supposedly dangerous to faith. That made especially heady the experience of having blanket permission in certain courses at my Jesuit university to sample those forbidden books when the reasons for doing so were serious, i.e., for scholarly purposes. Among those of us who were regarded as serious students, Father Buchmann became a minor campus hero because he managed to get some of these works on the open shelves of the university bookstore.

I remember Father Buchmann in another setting, remonstrating with an official of one of the leading fellowship foundations: "What do you mean, women aren't candidates for this fellowship?" For Father B. neither books nor women deserved segregation. (The situation wasn't quite that way in every corner of the university. One of my philosophy professors was reputed to have a bias against women students. After performing well on several of his exams, I found that Dr. Strand's bias was at least partly penetrable. He developed an invariable roll call in his solicitation of discussion: "Mr. Stover, Mr. Boscobel [and so on, through a number of the prominent males] . . . , Miss Siderits, and ladies . . ." Perhaps for him intellectual women, like the nuns of yore, were a third gender. However, even that was preferable to the situation in another classroom, where I, fortunately, never had to sit. Indeed, how the females sat was reportedly one of the major concerns of Father Toohey, who continually admonished them to "keep closed the gates of hell," a not-too-subtle injunction to cross their legs. It is easy enough to say that Father T.'s behavior was both atypical and pathological. What is significant is that no one did anything about it. We were inured to the image of woman as sexual culprit.)

*   *   *

A peculiar mosaic of recollections, as I remarked earlier. Is there any pattern in it? What I find is a recurring tension between inducements to protection and the encouragement of openness. In some quarters there was a fear of intellectuals or a concern about preserving a unanimity of religious views. Yet from the very early stages of my religious instruction there was time for the intellectual components of faith. Those who stumped for protection against undue intellectual experience also were vigilant for what they considered the undue experience of feeling, especially sexual feeling. Yet there were others, like my white-bearded confessor, who were able to accept the naturalness of such feeling. Mystical experience could lose its freshness and become vicarious and peremptory, as it did with the sun-watchers. Yet some religious life flourished in the province of the individual.

Such tensions can, at worst, produce what psychologists call a double bind, the impetus to act in apparently contradictory directions. However, at best, they promote a sense of dramatically different options in religious pursuits and of the necessity of choosing between them. My own reaction seems to have been of the latter stripe. I opted for individualism and openness, quite possibly because of the attitudes I sensed in those who represented, if only unconsciously, those options. Humor, compassion, enthusiasm, a sense of discovery—this is what I perceived in those who were not fixated on protection and authority. Perhaps I simply found that constellation of attributes attractive, or perhaps they resonated profoundly with what was earliest in me by virtue of temperament or domestic experience.

The voices of my parents are stilled, but I have retained the attitude that nothing is beyond question. Professionally, this has led me to examine societal assumptions that, while not specifically religious, have implications for persons in the religious community. I have focused my inquiries particularly on the artificial human limitations imposed by gender stereotypes and on the consequent need for role liberation. Among the students most interested in these questions are a number of contemporary sisters. No longer enveloped in the serge of Sisters Innocence and Lumen Dei, they are sometimes painfully aware of their femininity and its implications. Not so well disposed to the examination of gender roles are persons like Dr. Strand, who inveighs against liberation, currently revealing his biases without the peculiar roll call of my college days.

In my personal life, the openness to questioning has led to an interest in a variety of religious perspectives and a view of religion less burdened by prefabricated doctrinal formulations. I have never returned to those farmlands where, as a young teenager, I watched the sun-watchers. However, I now recognize that my experence there spurred a continuing concern with the psychology of religious belief. The past summer this concern has taken me from ceremonies at Lourdes to the cave paintings at Lascaux. At the former shrine I stood on different ground from the blue buggies of the afflicted, as we dealt in various ways with our various hopes. My companion, an anthropologist with no religious training but with a tentative belief in God and an abiding belief in elderly aunts, carefully secured a bottle of Lourdes water for the now aged aunt who has remained so wary of intellectuals. (Her opposition to differences of religious opinion has intensified, and she now assigns diabolical origin to all opinions that differ from her own.)

Father Aquin, who stimulated a seven-year-old's appetite for the intellectual evaluations so foreign to her aunt, celebrated his sixtieth anniversary in the priesthood a decade ago. At that time he seemed both touched and surprised by the postscript to the erstwhile seven-year-old's card of congratulations, in which she expressed her appreciation for his sensitive treatment of the uncertainties associated with her sexual discovery as an adolescent. That kind of sensitivity is sometimes wanting at my university, where the majority of students are involved in premarital sexuality but that fact of campus life is too often ignored, save for denunciations of sinfulness in certain quarters.

Father Buchmann, who represented intellectual openness in my later education, is still teaching on the campus where I encountered him. He need no longer monitor the campus bookstore; "the Index" is among ecclesiastical antiquities. Young women of promise are now fully accepted as candidates by the fellowship foundation that once disappointed him, but I have thought warmly of his efforts when I have sat on the campus board for the selection of local nominees.

In all of this the evaluation of religious experience may seem undesirably contaminated by the psychological attributes of those who embody it. I think not; but, then, I am a psychologist and inclined to emphasize the personal. By their works you shall know them—and that seems to include what one works in oneself and in others.

L. REBECCA PROPST

L. Rebecca Propst received her Ph.D. in Clinical and Social Psychology from Vanderbilt University in 1975. She spent five years at the Psychology Department at Ohio University, and is currently Associate Professor of Counseling Psychology at Lewis and Clark College, Portland, Oregon.

Her current research interests include an examination of the role of the patient's religious values in the psychotherapy treatment of depression. This has been pursued through psychotherapy outcome research.

She has published numerous articles examining religious beliefs within a cognitive-behavioral therapy context and is currently at work on a book examining the role of spirituality in cognitive-behavioral therapy.

Personal Empiricism

I currently hold a position in a graduate program in counseling psychology in which I teach a variety of counseling courses and thus am involved in training future psychologists. I also have a small private practice doing primarily psychotherapy of depression and marital counseling. The majority of my clients come from a Christian religious perspective.

The major focus of my interest at this time, however, is exploring the nature of the psychotherapy process and the role the individual's Christian spirituality may play in that process. This has been the focus of my research and writing for the past several years. I prefer to approach the question of the role of spirituality in the psychotherapy process from an empirical standpoint. "Empirical" in this context means that I use psychotherapy research methodology, complete with statistics and control groups. Rather than discussing the pros and cons of the value of the spiritual in the psychotherapy process, I prefer to set up procedures whereby I can actually observe what happens to various individuals when different emphases are present in the psychotherapy. I have defined spirituality in my psychotherapy research as the process of giving allegiance to a transcendent other outside of oneself (i.e., God).

The question of the therapeutic value of reliance on "another" is an important question in mental health. Most psychotherapy researchers and theorists regard the healthy individual as one who is autonomous. This healthy individual has a greater sense of self-efficacy or self-control and thus does not need to rely on another. A major question for me is "In what sense does spirituality subtract from or add to this sense of self-efficacy?"

I am most interested in observing how various kinds of spirituality affect what actually happens to individuals. I am less interested in some of the current philosophical discussions of the relationship between mental health and spirituality. I do enjoy, however, finding parallels between some of the contemporary psychotherapy procedures in the research literature and some of the earlier literature in the tradition of Christian mysticism, such as St. John of the Cross.

In both my religious experience and my academic pursuits, I often find myself sharing the perspectives of the apostle Thomas, and define myself as an empiricist. By empiricism, I mean the belief that the major source of knowledge is experience. I must experience it to believe. Generally, data I use as a basis for knowledge has to come from either my senses or from other people's senses. Someone has to have seen it, even if I have not. I am less trustful of rational and philosophical argument. Usually such an argument, if it is good enough, can prove any point.

As is the case with all people's orientations, I probably picked up this strong "show me" orientation from my parents. My parents are not religious. They are working-class semi-Appalachians. Semi-Appalachian means, in my family's case, two things: We grew up on the fringe of the geographical area of Appalachia, and I was as a child influenced both by mainstream culture and the more rural, simpler Appalachian culture.

My dad, before he retired, was a coal miner. My mother is a housewife. My parents sent my brother and me to church because that seemed to them a way to give us some training in "how to behave." My father especially thought that "it would keep my brother from becoming too rough." It must have succeeded. Both my brother and I have become solidly middle-class.

My mother thought that religion was for the wealthy. "You have to have nice clothes to go to church," she often commented to me when I asked her to attend church with me as a child. She felt the value of the church was social and emphatically denied that there was any life after death. "After all," she said, "when people die, they go to the grave."

She often made fun of a Jehovah's Witness neighbor who asserted that she would never die.

My father was similarly oriented. He felt very uncomfortable in church and usually limited his religion to discussions with the other men in the mines as to whether there was really a soul. He had never seen one, so he was not sure. He did have one strong faith influence in his life, however. That influence was his mother. She had managed to raise nine children in a one-room shack in a mining town in Appalachia, be a Pentecostal minister, and maintain a caring, giving attitude toward the neighbors. At her death he asserted that perhaps her prayers had kept him safe in the mine when he had had some close calls and that he had often wondered about that.

I can divide my early religious experiences into two kinds: those associated with the formal church and my personal experiences.

The church we were sent to as children was a small fundamentalist Baptist church. It was a source of both conflict and self-esteem for me. The church was a source of self-esteem for me, because I could usually excel in the Bible contests. I was also successful at the Bible memory work. When I was a child, my identity as someone who was smart, at least originally, came from the church.

The church was also a source of conflict, however. Because my parents did not attend church, my brother and I often felt left out. As children we did not belong to any nuclear family or small group in the church. Everyone else "got" to be in families. We had no family pew to sit in on Sunday morning. Additionally, I was often embarrassed about where we lived compared with the houses in which the other kids lived. The church in the United States is middle-class. Even those churches that seem to be working-class are aspiring to middle-class values. This idea probably continues to goad me. Christianity must show up as a force for political and social good in a society. It must make a difference. It must not be aligned with the comfortable status quo.

In addition to the institutional side of religion, however, there began to develop inside me a personal approach to Christianity. At age eleven I received a Bible as a prize for perfect attendance at summer church school. I then proceeded to read it every evening on my own and keep a diary about what I read and my feelings about God. God at some point became a real experience in my life. God was someone whom I conversed with, argued with, and cried to. In many ways, Christ (God to me) seemed much more accepting than my parents. Those early devotional periods were not exercises that I did because I *should* do them to be a good Christian (thank goodness), but something I looked forward to.

I can still remember one of the doors in my bedroom that opened to the outside and was left open in the summers with only a screen. I would sit on the floor in front of the screen for hours and look at the stars at night and "have discussions with God." I was careful not to let my parents know about my "private devotions," since they would think I was "odd" or a religious fanatic. This personal quiet "experience of God's presence," especially in the outdoors, continues to be an important part of my spiritual life.

As a high-school student, I had decided that I wanted to be a missionary or Christian education director (acceptable roles for women). I was especially interested in becoming a missionary doctor because that would combine my growing interest in science with my interest in God. After all, I had read some exciting biographies of Protestant saints (the missionaries) and was quite impressed by them. When I approached my parents with the idea of attending a Christian college, they reacted very negatively. After much conflict with my parents, especially my mother, I decided to attend the hometown State University. It seemed affordable and I could live at home. I was also able to get a small scholarship that covered most of the minimal tuition. It had never occurred to me, coming from a working class background, to seek out a more prestigious university, except for a Christian college. Colleges were colleges. As I was one of the first among all my numerous cousins to attend college, any college seemed a big deal.

As I reflect back upon it, in many ways I was in an advantageous position to develop my own religious perspective. I was not forced to imitate the religion of my parents. For me, being religious was not simply living up to others' expectations. It was, instead, being able to listen to my internal core. At the university I became very much involved with a Christian student group. I decided that perhaps, instead of being a medical missionary, I would be a missionary of sorts in the secular world of the university campus. I decided I was interested in college teaching. My choice of the discipline of psychology came about by accident. I could just as easily have chosen biology.

In the early seventies it seemed that American society and I went in opposite directions. When I graduated from college in 1970, many of my classmates wore black armbands in support of the Kent State rebellion. I did not. I was not interested in politics, but rather in my own activities and graduate school. My attention was very internally focused on my experience of God and my vocational direction. By 1975 society was becoming decidedly less political and more interested in middle-class values. I, however, was beginning to experience a transformation. My old empiricism was beginning to come back to haunt me. If Christianity does not make any difference in the political and social sphere of the society, then it does not make any difference. I was becoming more radical politically and began to be interested in issues of social change.

In graduate school I began to experience conflict between my role in the church and my role as a graduate student. In the church I was expected to be a passive, nonintellectual listener. The church found it difficult to accept me as anything but a pew woman. I was certainly not seen as a leader; women did not do such things. As a graduate student, on the other hand, I was expected to be an active leader. The conflict and the anger between these two roles (and cultures) began to intensify. Not until I actually began my professional career with a faculty position at a university four years later, however, was I able to put my finger on the exact causes of the conflicts that occurred during graduate school.

During my graduate school days, because I did not have a full consciousness of the difficult position I was in, my anger exploded into a rejection of both the church and God. It was not that I no longer believed in God. It was just that God was not someone to be trusted. After a while, however, the anger ripened into unbelief. At the same time, my peers and colleagues in the graduate program in psychology weren't exactly thrilled to have a "religious person" in their midst. I obliged them by trying not to show that part of me too much.

At this difficult time in my life I began to be aware of the sexism that existed in my graduate department. (Other female graduate students commented later that they had been surprised I had been so naive regarding the sexism in the department.) At this southern university in the early seventies, most professors gave conflicting messages to female graduate students. These professors saw themselves as training academic leaders, but they weren't so sure about their female students.

At this point of my unbelief, I felt acceptance in neither the church nor the graduate department. In many ways the lack of acceptance in the church was more difficult to deal with.

Thomas Merton, a Trappist monk, writes that there are three stages in Christian conversion: intellectual conversion, moral conversion, and, finally, falling in love. With Christ I had a relationship of intimacy and love. Yet, when one becomes angry in a relationship, a certain distance evolves. After a period of emotional distance in any relationship, the relationship dissolves. I began to feel very much alone. I recall during this period looking up at the stars one night and shuddering. Life seemed so empty. I felt alone in the universe. My entire reason for existence seemed shattered. I suppose I was being haunted by my empiricism. I was expecting some difference between the church and the society. I did not experience any.

During the next year, I did come in contact with individuals who were quite caring, especially when I was having some financial difficulties. One summer in graduate school, I had no place to live and no money for apartment rent. I vividly recall attending a prayer meeting of one group. Not only were they giving of their materials, but they were very expressive of their emotions. I noted in my diary that I felt so far away from these people and so different from them. On the other hand, it was obvious from their behaviors that spirituality meant something to them.

Their kindness led me to cry out again to God. God answered. I do not know that I could say how. But if experience is a source of knowledge, then God was there. God and I continued our arguments throughout graduate school. In fact we had quite a stormy relationship. But, the relationship *was* re-established. Adrian Van Kaam, professor of formative spirituality at Duquesne University, speaks of discerning the spiritual in everyday life. God as a force behind the experience of everyday reality again became a reality to me.

As I moved into my professional career as a university professor, the sexism I experienced again became an issue for me. I discovered much to my discomfort that sexism existed not only in conservative religious institutions; it existed also in mainstream Protestant churches and—horror of horrors—in that most holy of institutions, the university.

In the past seven to eight years, I have been involved in many denominations, both Protestant and Roman Catholic. Unfortunately, the common thread I find running through them—more subtle in some groups than in others, but always there—is sexism. There is sexism in the sense that I know that any claim I have to a certain religious vocation is never taken quite as seriously as if a male has made the same claim.

Because of this sexism, I tend to stay on the fringes of any denomination. I never feel quite able to accept any as my own. Perhaps again it is the old conflict I felt as a child. I am just not part of the family of any particular religious group. This state of affairs results in a certain alienation. It also means, however, that I have been able to see beyond the institutional church and touch a personal God. I have found God in the Episcopal service, the Roman Catholic mass, and the simple worship of a Mennonite congregation. God is there, but paradoxically God is also absent. Worship services are often devoid of God.

When writing an autobiography of this sort, I must report if I have actually ever seen God. I would say I have. It happened while I was on my clinical internship. I was working with a young adolescent patient who was accidentally tranferred to a back ward of regressed schizophrenics. One day as I went to visit her, I saw a very small nun attending to the patients who were there. She very lovingly picked them up, fed them, and changed their diapers. The patients were in advanced catatonic states and not capable of responding in any way to acknowledge her care. She continued the care, however, as if each patient were Jesus himself. I left the unit quite stunned. Any doubt in my mind before going into the unit that there was a holy presence in the universe was no longer there when I left the unit.

I suppose I continue to be a paradox, however. Even as my faith grows, my relationship with the institutional church gets weaker. I don't really want it to be that way. It just is. Sometimes I look at the church and really wonder about the spiritual reality behind it. At the same time, abbeys—part of the institution—have become a very important place for me to go to cultivate my relationship with God. They offer a quiet place.

At present there are for me three sources of my religious belief and experience. The first source of my belief, and perhaps the most important, is my observations of the behavior of others. If Christianity is valid, it must make a difference in the behavior of others. I did my Ph.D. dissertation in the area of social psychology of attitude change. One maxim in the literature of this area of psychology is the importance of behavior for determining beliefs. I do not look at what people say they believe; I look at what they do. I have found some evidence in people's behavior for a spiritual reality. There was the nun. There was also the faculty couple in college who invested a lot of time with the students. There was that group in graduate school, and there is my husband. There are Mother Theresa and the Catholic Worker Movement. Beyond those, I can think of people who have chosen to live lives more simply and have not got caught up in the materialism of our culture. They have done this with a religious motivation. I will continue to look at these people to strengthen my own belief.

A second source of my religious commitment is my own experience of the presence of Christ. Christ has usually been a loving presence in my life. Christ brings a very gentle, delicate feeling that cannot be contained. I sometimes want to leap with excitement. On the other hand, often the presence of Christ is also a quiet feeling, and exuberance seems inappropriate.

Often, I yearn for more closeness with Christ and can certainly identify with St. John of the Cross in *Dark Night of the Soul.* The soul rushes out to meet Christ with all the anticipation of meeting a lover and then is lost in the love of that relationship.

Despite the importance of both people and experiences for me, sometimes they fail, however. At times, I meet individuals who sadden me with their "religious" approach to life. I become hurt and confused about the reality of Christ.

At times, also, it is hard to feel much emotion. It is hard to feel that anticipation of the presence of Christ, especially when I am caught up in a busy schedule, with the demands of students or writing and research projects. There does not seem to be anything left to invest in my relationship with God. Confusion, darkness, and unsureness result. I can often see such brief dark nights of the soul as indeed a lovely gesture on God's part to increase my yearning for God. At that point I must wait. The scriptural writer put it well—"Be still, and know that I am God. . . ."

At times I give in to the darkness. I may feel desolate. That is when I realize that there is a third reason for my Christian faith. When I encounter Christians whose behavior seems inconsistent, when my experience and feelings seem numb, I am still left with the resurrection of Jesus. The essence of my Christian faith has to be the visitation of God to earth in the form of Christ. The evidence of that visit for me is the resurrection.

This might seem like a very orthodox belief for someone who has a tangential and troubled relationship with the institutional church. However, experience, not philosophical speculation, has to be a basis of knowledge for me, and I suppose I count the experiences of the primitive church as valid.

Wolfhart Pannenberg, a contemporary German theologian and certainly no fundamentalist, asserts that the resurrection of Christ seems the most probable explanation for the events in primitive Christianity. He cites the reports and the *experiences* by many early Christians of the appearance of Christ to them and the bold faith of those who had been so timid. (*Jesus, God and Man*, Lewis T. Wilkens and Duane A. Priebe, translators, Philadelphia: Westminister, 1978) Perhaps I have been attracted to Pannenberg's writings because he is like me. He is almost alone among well-known contemporary theologians in his assertion that religious history must be open to the same empirical scrutiny and standards of truth as secular history. Without the resurrection, Christology would be an uncertain discipline. Philosophical speculations do not have the impact of an event that has been experienced with the senses. I must agree with the apostle Paul and assert that "if Christ be not risen from the dead, then my faith is in vain" (1 Corinthians 15:14).

The stories of other gods rising from the dead have never been a problem for me. Pannenberg asserts that the evidence for the resurrection of Jesus is the type of evidence that historians usually deal with, whereas the old mythologies make no claim to the same sort of historical framework. Additionally, however, perhaps these older myths also contain truth. J. R. R. Tolkien commented to C. S. Lewis that in some way these older myths were also true. "Just as speech is an invention about objects, so myth is an invention about the truth" (*Tolkien, The Authorized Biography*, H. Carpenter, Boston: Houghton Mifflin, 1977, p. 147). The truth was the resurrection of Jesus.

My present religious experience contains both hope and struggle. I am still struggling with my own spiritual direction in God's kingdom. There is the struggle between the life of the academic who seemingly just "thinks about things" and the world of "doing good works and deeds." I am usually most impressed with the physical sacrifices and behavior of others rather than their ideas, so I need to examine my own life and vocational direction. Perhaps I should exchange academia for a life of "working with the poor or dispossessed." Academia seems a most unlikely place for me to live out the model of the Christ-figure. I guess I cannot get away from my empiricism. Is my everyday behavior any different? Though the church often seems more interested in its own welfare than the welfare of those it touches, I nevertheless see signs of life. These signs challenge me and give me hope. "The created world awaits with eager expectation the day when those who are the (daughters and) sons of God will be displayed in all their glory . . . , the hope that the created world will be liberated from this slavery to decay (and oppression) . . ." (Romans 8:19,21).

KATHRYN ALLEN RABUZZI

Kathryn Allen Rabuzzi has taught English at Syracuse University for five years. She is currently working on several articles for the Macmillan *Encyclopedia of Religion,* edited by Mircea Eliade et al, and her second book, *Mothers and Heroes,* in which she constructs a gynocentric framework for examining the lives of women without contaminating biases of masculine standards. Her first book, *The Sacred and the Feminine: Toward a Theology of Housework,* was published by The Seabury Press in 1982.

Glass Flowers

I first met Sherry Goldman when we were both nineteen and newly married, she already visibly pregnant. I was still unaware that I was, too. I haven't seen her now for over fifteen years, except for one brief, disastrous encounter in the late '60s. I wonder what she will be like this time.

My husband hesitates briefly before he lifts their brass knocker. From within a dog barks; otherwise, it is still. Will they have furniture this time?

The door opens. It can't be Lenny. . . . No, it is a stranger, dark and deferential. As he ushers us up the stairs, it occurs to me that he is their "man." At the top, Lenny, looking as I remember him from postcollege days, greets us warmly. And Sherry—she's gorgeous, her hair shiny black, her body slim in a black jumpsuit, her neck sporting a red satin ribbon.

We introduce our respective children, who know each other only from photo albums. Uneasily—or am I imagining it?— we group ourselves, suburban style, by age and sex, Sherry and I attempting to catch up as their maid passes Brie and French double cream in the wake of the man's passing Pouilly Fuissé.

Long after we have returned home and stopped talking about our brief reunion, I find myself drawn back to it, to Sherry in particular. Not needing to perform household chores now that her husband is a millionaire several times over, and unable from chronic migraines and dizziness to work at a career, she now apparently does nothing, not even grocery shopping or shampooing her own hair. I shake my head in disbelief: She was the one who was a feminist long before the word was fashionable; she was the one who became hippy, along with her entire family, in the '60s; how could this remarkable transformation have taken place? My only clue lies in the few words she said just before we left. "I have no belief. Like so many Jews I know, I have nothing. And after the Holocaust. . . . How can there be a God who let such a thing happen?"

What can I say in response? I don't "believe" either, but I do have faith. It seems to me that Sherry not only lacks belief, but faith as well. What haunts me, as I search out the milestones of my own faith, is the age-old question: How can this—whatever the "this" of my own or anybody else's faith —hold up in the face of an event as monstrous as the Holocaust? Indeed, what *is* my post-Holocaust, decidedly secular faith?

*   *   *

In Pär Lagerkvist's telling, Barabbas misses the exact moment of Jesus' resurrection:

> Now it was getting light, and soon the first rays of the sun were thrown on to the rock out of which the sepulchre was carved. It all happened so quickly that he couldn't quite follow it—now of all times when he really should have had his wits about him! The sepulchre was empty! The stone was rolled away on the ground below and the carved-out space in the rock empty!'

For me, such an essential "missing" occurred in the opposite phase of the faith cycle, the time in which faith dies rather than kindles. For me, a setting, not a rising, sun transfigured "reality." How it happened I can only piece together partially in retrospect.

One day, sometime in my early or mid-twenties, I took out from the public library Jung's *Modern Man in Search of a Soul*. As I began reading it, I experienced an uneasy feeling of déjà vu. Could I possibly have read this book already? I couldn't remember ever having seen it before. Yet as I continued to read, strange bits and pieces of experience jiggled loose in my mind. I felt myself carred back in time to a point when

God lived for me in the sky and his only begotten Son miraculously came to earth, born of a virgin mother, to live in a strange, faraway land whose people were qualitatively different from anyone I knew. These were people who seemed to disappear just as most of the strange sounding lands they lived in did when "history" started. These were people I learned about only in Sunday school, never in school. There I learned about seasons and dinosaurs, cavemen and Mesopotamia. But all these things I believed in equally because various teachers told me they were so.

Alongside these believed-in things were others, *not* believed in for just the opposite reason. Somebody—teacher or playmates or Mommy—had told me they weren't real: Santa Claus and the Easter Bunny and fairies. Deep down underneath all these believed-in and not-believed-in things, however, was another layer entirely. I had never talked about this layer to anyone. This was where I *knew,* without anyone ever having told me, what things were really like, no matter what I gave assent to in school or with my friends. There I knew that fairies actually were real—oh, not that I had ever seen one, but I just knew they were "there" somewhere, just as I knew that there was a "golden" quality to much of existence: to the sugar house, the birches I loved to bend long before I'd ever heard of Robert Frost, the stone wall, frost flowers on the windowpane, the smell of pine needles underfoot, the first hepaticas in spring. And I knew, too, that there were black things: Maggie giving birth to dead kittens on the dining room rug one day at lunch; Jiggs catching a mouse and crunching its bone in his mouth; the hideout under Gordon's back porch; the girls' room in the basement with its evil-sounding, not fully understood graffiti and two stinking toilets; being chased home from school by Arnold's gang; being called "Jap" by Nancy Lambert because my home-knit hat was "funny."

But worse, and more puzzling, was the grayness in which most people seemed to exist all the time. That feeling sometimes came over me in a car on a rainy day when everything seemed to float away for no reason at all, taking with it all the happiness in the world. It also came with certain kids I was supposed to play with because my mother said I must: All they seemed interested in was telling me how much silverware they had gotten last birthday for their hope chests, and when asked by a grown-up what they wanted to do when they grew up, they invariably answered, "I want to be a Mommy and have five children." The grayness also accompanied teachers like Miss Barnstable, who taught me to pronounce "mischievous" as "miss cheeveeus" even though I knew she was wrong. And it came with Great-aunt Florence's gifts every Christmas: nylons when I was seven, *Wee Tales* when I was eleven.

As I read on in *Modern Man in Search of a Soul,* it came to me that this world of grayness was the only one I knew anymore—my world had grown utterly devoid, not just of its former goldenness but, worse, of the very possibility that such color could exist. Blackness was equally impossible. I shook my head in bewilderment. How long had I lived in this miserable world of gray? In it I merely existed; just getting up out of bed every morning was often a major accomplishment.

This was a time of getting up, making breakfast, calling children and spouse, eating breakfast, sending spouse off to work, gathering children for *Captain Kangaroo,* cleaning up the kitchen, showering, dressing, taking children for a walk, running errands, coming home for lunch, putting children down for naps, playing with them, picking up, fixing dinner, cleaning up, and falling asleep over the paper. It was a time when *I* had no future: Never would I go back to school. Never would I get a chance to live something called *my* life. Reading my college alumnae bulletin tormented me: Helen Beadle has just completed her Ph.D. in Asian Studies; Joy Chan is working for ITT in London; Lois Feinberg has just been awarded a Fulbright to work on her second novel; Kathryn Allen Rabuzzi, who dropped out after only two years, is at home with hundreds of toddlers, expecting a dozen more in April, awaiting the day when her husband completes his millionth year of medical training.

Through all these gray years Sherry commiserated with me. It was she, in fact, who loaned me the copy of Tillich's *Dynamics of Faith,* which still sits, unreturned, on one of my bookshelves.

*   *   *

Now, many years later, the earth once again lives for me, and I walk in the presence of spirits. The change began with that terrifying shock of reading Jung, the book that I now know plunged me into my initial prolonged experience of grayness. How and why did that book land me in purgatory? I can't tell you. Of the return I can say a bit more, though it was not by imaged paths. The return was a *via negativa* that plunged me ever deeper into grayness until out of that deepening lack of color, as if it were a kind of counterimage, color miraculously returned.

It was a long journey, over a period of years, composed of many parts. Vastly unlike my gradmother's way, marked by talismans such as Norman Vincent Peale and Peter Marshall, mine is littered with the likes of Gabriel Vahanian and Samuel Beckett. Instead of leaving the gray plain to emerge in a sunny glade, I penetrated more and more deeply into the grayness. Now and then a sparkle of color pricked through the fog. . . .

Religion 102. This must be it. But it's all dark in here, and I can barely see to find a seat. "Is this Religion 102?" Ignorant as I, my seatmate sits in the dark. Suddenly a screen in front bursts into life, covered with dancers. Surely this is not the right class, but I can't see to get out. Fifteen minutes of Jose Limon, and the lights flick on. A professor stands and asks, "What does all this have to do with religion?"

Dance and religion . . . I had never made such a connection. There were many such unexpected connections for me in that course. One day the professor suggested that for some people the *study* of religion might be religion. I could accept that. But something was still missing and took a few more years to appear. That "something," a post-death-of-God and response in the sort of world that Sherry's question emerges from, is the closest I can come to answering her question.

In one of my earliest recollections I am four years old, holding on one side the hand of my mother, on the other, that of my aunt. We are walking up the steps of Harvard's

Peabody Museum to see something very special. All week my aunt, Caroline, has been telling me about the GLASS FLOWERS. Glass flowers: every night after my prayer I see them in the dark. They glow like the special fruits on the trees Aladdin discovers when he descends into the cave: ". . . the trees . . . were loaded with extraordinary fruit of different colors on each tree. Some bore fruit entirely white, and some clear and transparent as crystal; some pale red, and others deeper; some green, blue, and purple, and others yellow. . . ."[2] On the top step, just before Caroline opens the heavy door, I glance at my sapphire ring which I have been allowed to wear for this very special occasion. The flowers will be far bigger and brighter I know.

We arrive. I look around, bewildered. I can see nothing but *real flowers*. "Where are the *glass* flowers, Caroline? I don't want to look at live ones. You promised me *glass* flowers, Caroline; you promised."

No amount of adult explanation assuages my disappointment. I am totally unimpressed by the skill of the artist in making these glass flowers virtually indistinguishable from the flowers in Mama's rock garden at home. If I had wanted to see *real* flowers I would have chosen a real garden, not a dusty old museum. I wanted to see flowers that looked like *glass,* flowers glowing the way my sapphire does in the proper light.

*   *   *

It is years later. I am a freshman in Cambridge. My roommate says, "Let's go to the Peabody and see the glass flowers."

Glass flowers: The name is magic. I don't know why. Of course I will stop studying Plato and go with her. In my mind I envision intricacy and vibrance: glass, still glasslike in its semblance of flowering. I imagine rows and rows of flowers in the style of the Tiffany glass panels I love in the Metropolitan Museum in New York.

Not until Ann and I have plunked our quarters in the turnstile and wandered through two full rows of disappointingly "real" flowers totally unlike my Tiffanyesque expectations do I suddenly recollect my earlier experience. I stand, stupid with disappointment. I fix on a rose so perfect a bee would be fooled by it. "My glass flowers," I think, "I wonder if I will ever find them." For even now, after my second disappointment, I believe they exist somewhere.

"Come on, Ann, let's go. I don't like it in here. These flowers are a real bore."

*   *   *

A few years ago something strange happened. I awoke one morning to discover that an ice storm had pelted our house in the night. From every window ice had transformed trees into glistening baubles. As the sun spread, ice turned to rain, and the trees dripped shards of fine glass. I was entranced. Not until I assumed the day's tasks did it occur to me: These are my glass flowers. Unlike the glass flowers that looked so real that they disappointed me, these real trees looked like glass and delighted me. Aladdin's cave could have been no more enchanting.

What I have just written is a fiction. By that I don't mean a complete invention; everything I mentioned actually happened. But it is a fiction in the sense that it is a creation of my imagination: an imaginative shaping of what most persons rather vaguely speak of as "reality." There are other terms I might have chosen: revelation, symbol, story, and ritual. But revelation and symbol too strongly suggest traditional religion; story and ritual are more generic than I intend.

In my fiction, my active participation in an external event infused meaning into my world. What happened was neither so remote from me that it left me totally untouched, nor so deeply within that it had no reference external to me. Though my fiction never mentions such words as "deity," "belief," or

"salvation," it is for me a faith story, an external manifestation of religious consciousness as such consciousness may be
experienced by someone like me or Sherry for whom traditional (patriarchal) theology no longer works.

But why do I tell you this particular fiction when there are
hundreds of *known* fictions to choose from? My choice is
deliberate. Were I to tell you a story by Flannery O'Connor,
enact a play by Ntozake Shange, or recite a poem by Erica
Jong, I would give you an artistic end product. But to convey
my understanding of the consciousness that grounds my faith
I insist that it is first of all the *process* that matters, only
secondarily the product; sometimes, in fact, there *is* no product for me. Through my fiction-making *process,* whether I
produce a tangible product or not, I engage myself with the
world; it is the process by which I become who I am. When I
gaze up at the sky and see pictures of giants devouring small
children, I am engaging in fiction-making; when I peer at the
arthritic couple in the booth next to mine at McDonald's and
decide from eavesdropping that their oldest daughter is having an affair with her best friend's husband, I am engaging in
fiction-making; when I gaze into the mirror and transform
myself into a future distinguished professor, I am engaging in
fiction-making. But when I participate in this process, aside
from those rare instances that I share, no one except myself
knows that is what I am doing. So it is almost impossible to
capture this process whereby I create the fictions that reveal
me to myself. Perhaps for that reason it is more customary to
look at the products, not the process, to reveal an individual's
faith story.

Some of these products reveal "the word of God"; others
manifest "the sacred"; still others evidence "the demonic."
But I take my cue from aesthetician Benedetto Croce: I feel I
must go a step further and include in my investigations the
process, rather than repeatedly singling out products, most of
which belong to that tiny, mostly male, elect whom Western
culture calls artists.

But my Crocean approach raises two significant problems
for me. First, if I have no product by which to judge my faith,
how can I know the process is actually happening? And

second, if the fiction-making process is a behavioral manifestation of religious consciousness, what distinguishes such consciousness from any *other* kind of human consciousness? These, in my judgment, are the crucial questions for considering the meaning of my religious consciousness, for I am an individual who from a traditional religious perspective would be called a nonbeliever.

I think my fiction itself provides an answer. Certainly that fiction exhibits characteristics traditionally considered secular. As such, it may reflect a purely aesthetic consciousness, having no meaning apart from its capacity to delight my senses. Or it may be a purely psychological fiction in which my childhood fantasy has found external completion and verification in adulthood. Or it may be no more than an inconsequential personal anecdote.

But these responses leave me unsatisfied. Having lived out my fiction, I *know* it is a religious experience. My problem: how do I justify that claim? I can, of course, use terminology such as "revelation" to name the appearance of the ice storm; "transcendence" to describe my ultimate reaction; and "grace" to encompass the fact that I experienced the final episode at all. But I am also somewhat uneasy with this way of looking at it. I keep wondering if using conventional terminology does not violate the integrity of the actual experience. Because this is *not* simply the same old story. And yet it is also not purely secular as we used to use that word when we neatly dichotomized experience into sacred and secular components.

I prefer to move in another direction. If I am bold enough to assert that religious consciousness is not some special kind of human consciousness set apart from other forms, but is human consciousness itself, then my problem disappears. Let me explain: In an older world view, whose traces still haunt me sufficiently to cause these problems under discussion, I could utter such words as "God," "religion," "faith," "grace," "salvation," and know that I would be understood. I could also assume that whatever else religion might be, here in the West most people would accept some definition that referred to a relationship between god and human or, more recently for some feminists, between goddess and human. But once the god/dess term disappears or mutates (as it has for me and some of my contemporaries like Sherry), I am left in an almost impossible predicament. If "god" automatically triggers off responses of wholly other, male, transcendent, omnipotent, and the like, I cannot meaningfully use the name. If I substitute "goddess," I may feel more comfortable intellectually, but emotionally the words remains too self-consciously a word for me, conjuring up images too specifically anthropomorphic for me honestly to give assent to. Only if the "rotted names," to borrow from Wallace Stevens, are reinvigorated with radically different meanings can they relate to what constitutes faith for me. I find myself drawn to a conception of deity expressed by science fiction writer Stanislaw Lem in his brilliant work *Solaris,* where he speaks of "an imperfect god, . . . a god whose passion is not a redemption, who saves nothing, fulfills no purpose—a god who simply is."[3] That image allows me to reimagine and relocate deity, even to see myself incarnating it, as Naomi Goldenberg so persuasively argues in *Changing of the Gods.* This conception of deity is very different from the old image of a radically other, transcendent God located far off in the sky somewhere that I learned very young I must "believe" in. By making this shift to an idea of deity I can and do have faith in, I am not merely quibbling over terminology: I am talking about what constitutes for me an utterly changed reality.

My fiction of the glass flowers has led me into this changed reality at a time and place in history when "faith" as it used to be construed scarcely works any more. The meaning I found in my fiction is the closest I can come to answering Sherry's question. That it does not match the magnitude of her query, hence is no answer at all, is very much to the point.

REFERENCES

1. Pär Lagerkvist, *Barabbas* (New York: Vintage Books, 1951), p. 46.

2. "Aladdin: or, the Wonderful Lamp," in *The Arabian Nights* (no author or editor listed), New York: Grosset & Dunlap, Publishers, 1946, p. 230.
3. Stanislaw Lem, *Solaris* (New York: G.P. Putnam's Sons, 1978), p. 206.

DODY DONNELLY

Dody Donnelly, adjunct faculty member at San Francisco Theological Seminary, holds the Th.D. degree in Historical Theology from the Graduate Theological Union, Berkeley, and the Ph.D. in Latin, Greek, and Ancient History from Catholic University, Washington, D.C. She is presently West Coast Director of Women Today West, an organization helping people help prisoners through education and job training.

Dr. Donnelly also writes, lectures, and offers workshops and retreats for laity and clergy. She is interested in synthesizing psycho-theological-sexual dimensions of personality in a spirituality of sex and spirit. Her *Radical Love* was published by Winston Press in 1984.

Current interests include theological education for all people as continuing education. She is also a consultant to pastoral and education systems in program design and team building in the areas of theology, spiritual direction, and prison reform. Her book *Team* was published by Paulist Press. She has created programs for spiritual renewal, social justice, meditation, prayer retreats, and the theology and spirituality of peacemaking.

Gaily in the Dark

G. K. Chesterton called the great Gaels of Ireland the men that God made mad, "for all their wars are merry, and all their songs are sad." Somehow or other, my Irish song has been merry. As one of my superiors put it: "You, Sister, are choleric, with a deathless dash of sanguine!" And that sanguine has always pushed me back to "merry" when the choleric—and the melancholic—got out of hand. Who knows how long the spiritual glider will sail from cloud to cloud? In any case, I know I am loved.

I was born in San Francisco atop a windy hill under a full moon the North American Indians label "Ripe Berries," with the raspberry my plant-herb and the mighty sturgeon my totem. At six months old, I left for Ireland where I imbibed green, farm sounds and smells and the adoration of my grandfather for about two lovely years. But since the British and my dad didn't see things alike, he sailed us all back to San Francisco.

Dad, a North-of-Ireland Catholic from the Donnellys of Lough Neagh, knew a faith in God that translated into action. I can still hear his tread in the hall, his knock on our bedroom door every First Friday morning: "OK; it's six o'clock!" And off we went to early Mass at Salesian Corpus Christi. We never minded, for he went, too.

Confession each month before First Friday was routine; we all trooped over to chruch with no thought of our "regimentation." We rather enjoyed time out from classes. I loved to chat with my confessor behind his dark curtain. His broken Italian-English and musical background translated my name "Dorothy Donnelly" into "Hello, Dorotee Do-re-mi!" as he slid back the screen and I told him my monthly horrenda.

Catholic school years introduced me to the saints: to St. Joseph (that was my father's name, and my teachers were Sisters of St. Joseph of Orange, California); to the Little Flower of Lisieux, a powerful role model for me; and to my lifelong friend, Thomas More of Chelsea. I promptly fell in love with a man who could joke while climbing the Tower Hill scaffold, and devoured biographies of More with a passion that one day resulted in my doctoral thesis in classics, translating his lively Latin answer to Martin Luther.

Though Thérèse de Lisieux controlled my early teens, she had to give way to basketball, study, social life, dating . . . the world! But to my real surprise I did enter the convent in Orange after telling myself I would try it out for a few weeks. Little "Tess" and Tom More had taught me that Christian life was heroic, exciting, and hard, too. More said, "A man can lose his head—and still come to no harm!" So, even sweating out meditation, hands deep in big, black sleeves in the blazing Southern California afternoons, I somehow enjoyed it all; it was all for getting to God by thinking straight ahead.

Fortunately my emotional side emerged and I felt God's love, the early "gustos" or sweets Teresa of Avila describes. My spiritual life, so-called, was suffused in a warm glow of devotion as a novice who never quite understood why we did what we did, but still managed to enjoy most of it. Though Scripture in those days was not a part of our training, I somehow arrived at final vows deeply in love with the Psalms, those heart-openers that saved me from the "points" of meditation, though the period prior to vows was heavy with questioning about the seeming coldness of our personal relationships. I was accused of having a "particular friendship" for another nun, and suffered deeply from separation from her loved company when I changed houses after final vows. As a maturing human being, I met the real ambiguity of a system that taught us to love. . . . But not necessarily one another? Not our own companions? It was a puzzle.

Once out in the field, I taught and taught and taught: ten years in elementary, ten in high school, five in college, studying all the while through an A.B. in English literature that took me twelve years of summer sessions and Saturday classes. My eager, inquiring mind ate up study but was luckily balanced by daily meditation: a place to stop, to breathe, sometimes to sleep, but at least to center and to be with God. Spiritual reading each day pushed me mightily, feeding both heart and mind.

Three academic degrees later, I went through reentry pangs after finishing a Ph.D. in Classics at Catholic University in Washington, D.C. Residence there was pure joy—a chance to devote myself fully to my intellectual goals, to broaden my horizons, to meet new friends whom I still cherish, and to change my view of myself and my environment. After some trouble in gaining permission to accept it, I went to Rome on a Fulbright for postdoctoral study. There an explosion of consciousness pushed me into deeper reflection about the meaning of the church, religious life, and my role in it. So my teaching at my college reflected this new openness —and so, threatened some people, to my surprise! Result: A year later, while I was away teaching summer school for Catholic University, I received a call from a friend shocked that I had been removed from the college! She knew it before I did. I was now reassigned to the high school I had left for studies, but the male principal, a priest who resented my closeness to the students, told me that he had no job for me— except typing class four times a day.

In numbness and shock I packed myself out of the college. But then out popped the pot of gold. Sorting my notes and materials, I found I had another book in all that stuff. My first had been the manual for Young Christian Students, *How*, a guide for workers training youth. Now teaching typing four times a day gave me leisure to write my second little book, *Sister Apostle*, published by my social action mentor and saint, Father Louis Putz, CSC, of Notre Dame, editor of the then Fides Press. I'll never forget the night he called and told me that my manuscript contained two books, *Sister Apostle* and a revision of *How*. I was just leaving my family home in San Francisco for my father's wake in a sad, gray January day. The book appeared on the campus where I was teaching summer session the following July. Then the ceiling collapsed.

Though I had been exiled to high school teaching for only one year, my return to college teaching involved painful conflicts concerning teaching theory about the formation of young religious and my role on the formation team. In *Sister Apostle* (1964) I had pushed especially for training through group discussion. That then fearsome idea aroused opposition and threatened the team. One superior, questioning my suggestion in the book that the nuns' personal mail no longer be opened and read and that stamps be readily available, asked in shocked tones: "Do you realize, Sister, how much postage we'll have to pay for?" It seemed useless to note that my idea was not about postage, but about *trust* as a shaper of the nuns' self-concept. The book caused a storm. Some responded to me with a boycott and silence; others accused me of disloyalty to the community. My support came from outside.

My pain was deep, because I had expected understanding and found so little. But as always, God could use that book as She alone knew how. Cardinal Suenens of Belgium read it, had it translated into French, and met me in Berkeley. Through his personal delegate sent to the motherhouse, he invited me to be on an advisory committee in Rome for the next session of Vatican II (1965). His answer from my superiors was a flat no, to the amazement of his delegate. But even as I reassured her and took her to vespers in our chapel, I felt sure God had a good reason for that refusal, painful though it was. I soon discovered why. My dear friend and younger sister wrote to tell me she had cancer. That was October 24, 1956; she died in my arms on Christmas Eve. She was more important than any Vatican Council.

However, that book caused wider ripples yet. Another dear friend, a newspaper editor, after reading it, suggested that I needed a sabbatical year studying theology—the secret dream of my life! Since my sister had died only a year after my father, death was doubly near and incomprehensible. I did need to reflect. What theory did we Christians hold about death? What help could theology and Scripture give me? In trepidation, but trusting in Her, I applied for a sabbatical year at the Graduate Theological Union in Berkeley. Just as I had been the first Ph.D. in our community, I now asked for the first sabbatical. Wondrously and kindly my request was granted, just at the moment all religious communities turned to self-study, at the order of Pope Paul VI. So all during my Berkeley studies, I also as chapter delegate helped prepare the renewal and rule changes for our order. This was a draining and fear-filled project for many, but my enthusiasm for change carried me though exhausting chapter sessions. In one week's time we went from habit-garb to self-selected contemporary clothing, to the shocked disapproval of the Los Angeles chancery officials.

Doubting our seriousness, they asked us all to fly back to Orange and go through the decision on the habit *again*—just to see if we all still meant it! We all *did,* and I felt a thrill of hope that we nuns could take charge of our own space. Much improvement was still made in living conditions, freedom of choice, growth opportunities, and structures. But my hope dimmed somewhat the next few years as people reacted to the reforms and settled into the status quo.

Meanwhile, the department of classics closed at our college, and I was asked to stay on in Berkeley and complete another doctorate, this time in theology! I felt one was enough, but remaining in Berkeley was worth the trouble of getting a second; the environment was vital, a cultural smorgasbord loaded with chances to grow. And not least among these was the blossoming Charismatic Movement moving strongly in the Protestant groups at our Union. So I began to study my spirituality in the light of what it would mean to really surrender one's life to the Spirit. In despair of ever passing theology comprehensives, huddled in a big chair in my tiny apartment, I told God that She *had* to take care of this. I could not! Out of that dark, winter day came a faint beginning of letting God run my life, deepening when I went through the Life in the Spirit seminar with my friends and experienced persons praying over me. Tears of joy signaled the melting of fear of the future and the inflooding of God's empowering love. I was learning to trust again.

And suddenly, too, I learned what theology was all about as I met and taught with my colleague, Father Don Gelpi. The Jesuits in Berkeley had asked me to teach for them. Don's own deep faith and his courses soon sparked my writing of *Team,* later published by Paulist Press in 1977, a book of theology and practice about how laity and clergy together might renew the church.

Yet again, my newfound theology and my trust in the Spirit led me to pull no punches in *Team.* I named the church, priesthood, and religious life as structures that needed healing. I pleaded for equal, intensive training of the laity as the church of the future. As the reverberations began, I moved to have my tenure decided a year ahead of time. This entailed creating a tenure committee, since I was not only the sole woman full-time on the theology faculty, but also the only non-Jesuit. My theological understanding was ever deepening, my teaching was Spirit-filled, my publications were multiplying—but the answer from the tenure committee was no!

I was in tears over what I felt was an unjust rejection. Urged on by friends, I reapplied the following year under a new president; but again the answer was no. I had threatened the system, yes, but I was also personally unacceptable—much too open, too free, too critical. The written report of the committee made fascinating reading—and does even today—but how grateful I am now for that loud no from God! That no thrust me into the ecumenical world and forced my further growth in trust, in prayer, and in theological understanding.

That denial of tenure allowed me a year for discerning what was next. Pacific School of Religion, my Protestant alma mater, asked me to head a task force for a "religious-formation program" in their seminary, a sight unseen among Protestant schools in 1976. Lack of understanding what "spirituality" meant led to strong faculty opposition there, but we made a good beginning of a program, introducing yoga, marriage counseling, and meditation groups and underscoring the vital connection between personal spiritual formation and ministry. Paradoxically the formation of Protestant seminary students had been relegated to chapel services or counseling, so our beginnings found little understanding. But the seeds were planted and are flowering today, thank God!

When an offer of further consultation there came in September of 1977, my eleventh year in Berkeley, it was not for me. I felt that I was being called to blend findings from psychology and theology in the study of human spiritual development. I began studying my lifelong friend, Thomas More of Chelsea, at a request from his 500th Birthday Committee, and finally delivered a paper on "The Size of More" in the St. Thomas More College quincentennial conference, a debt of love paid to my role model and inspiration. Though I had done my classics doctoral thesis on More's response to Martin Luther in 1962, this later chapter, subsequently published in a collection, supplied the theological understanding I had lacked in dealing with his thought and spirituality as a classicist. His awesome conscience loomed ever larger in my consciousness.

My global consciousness grew with my trip to the Soviet Union with Sister Ann Gillen for the National Task Force on Soviet Jews. There I felt the pain and terror of my Jewish brothers and sisters longing for transport to Israel but barred exit. Thence I found myself back in Geneva and was invited to Accra, Ghana, so that more *women* theologians would be involved in our planning of the Plenary Session on *women* at the Nairobi World Council Assembly. There I had a profound experience of a more pervasive male blindness to the need of women for equality and representation in the church. Now, ten years later, that Ghana World Council conference is just beginning to bear fruit for women's spirituality and presence in the People of God.

Denial of tenure had meant I would never have the leisure of paid sabbatical leave for further research. But that same denial actually gave me time to write many articles, begin another book, accept lecture offers in many places including Canada, Europe, and Central America, and travel extensively in the Middle East. For me, 1978 proved an *annus mirabilis.* God had given me a richer sabbatical than any academic could have envisioned. My prayer grew in gratitude and joy, and I learned to trust even more!

During this period I had the advantage of excellent guided retreats, inspiring liturgies, and theological deepening; but once I left Berkeley, ministry became the central focus of my religious growth, as I moved closer to my mother. As our relationship deepened, God taught me more and more about aging, fear, the strength of faith, the armour of hope. When my marvelous mother died in December 1981, we had traveled a long, hard road together. But we are closer now than we ever were before her death, as she prays for me and I consult with her—a powerful lady!

But being with my mother during those three years also brought home to me my limitations, my naiveté, my inexperience with the realities of life. Those realities had begun to appear during the years from 1967 on when I lived alone and had to learn how to relate to that unknown species, the male. I had to live an adolescence I had literally skipped, and I fell in love now and then with plenty of learning, pain, joy, surprise, and understanding with each relationship. All along went the deepening of my self-image: I was God's beloved woman and God was busy about my total education. I knew God was loving me in each person who loved me, and She was loving them, too.

Another school at the Graduate Theological Union asked me to begin teaching a class in psyche and spirit each winter; so for ten weeks each year I was immersed again in spiritual formation, this time with thirty people, ages twenty-two to seventy-two. I plunged into the Western mystics, discovered something of what Teresa of Avila was really up to, went after the Protestant mystics as well, and applied this to my doctoral thesis in theology on St. Augustine of Hippo, my psychologist-saint, whom I had met first while studying his Latin *Confessions.* Now he was master guide in the spiritual life.

My training in theology, now done by *life* and seldom by professor, continued. With Father Don Gelpi I taught the history of the priesthood; it only deepened my lifelong desire for the theological training of the laity, the deprived masses of the church. We tried to put that course into a manuscript; though it was never published, it had done its work in my education. My book *Team* showed that effect in my pastoral theology, a Spirit-based approach to ministry for all—with *everyone* using the gifts of God and having access to *training* whether or not preparing for ordination.

Along with that lay emphasis came a dawning realization of the plight of the most neglected layperson: woman. I began to teach a course "Masculine/Feminine Spirituality: Myth or Reality?" and on we went for some six years, the content always evolving as the number of men gradually equaled the number of women in class. We worked out what we had experienced about gender difference and how it might apply to how we loved and envisioned God and one another. Ever deeper grew our realization that self-image profoundly controlled how we acted as men and women.

We finally got in touch with the incredible amounts of conditioning we had imbibed from North American culture, our churches, our families, our own false self-images of what it meant for us to be men and women. And yet how different our personal experience of that phenomenon really was for each of us! That experience started more wheels turning. How could we heal our images of self and our images of God, who seemed to come off in all this as anti-sexual . . . the very God who invented sex . . . and us embodied humans! How could healing come? What needed to change? What did I need to research? How could I pray my way with God to some questions that would produce new attitudes, new ways to accept our embodied humanity as God's precious idea? Another book was being born.

In 1974 a study of masculine/feminine spirituality seemed a strange bird in the course offerings at the Graduate Theological Union, so few were the female students—and even rarer the female faculty. But out of that work, especially the historical research on women's history and conditioning, came deeper realization of how I myself had been so socialized. My research into the history of priesthood and lay ministry suddenly merged with feminist studies, and the picture of women's subordination over centuries became part of my daily consciousness. So part of my course involved helping women get in touch with the tyranny of thought and custom that had conditioned them to compete with each other from the subconscious. This behavior appeared to me so destructive, because no conscious guilt seemed attached to obstructing the path of another woman—only a confusing, feverish, competitive anger that seemed almost without a cause.

When I discovered this disease in myself and observed its virulence in other women, I resolved so far as God would help me, that I would never put down another woman. My spirituality quietly blossomed to embrace in their total humanity my sisters, the women of the world, not as competitors, even if unconscious ones, but as allies, as coconspirators fighting for the saving of the planet.

Only in 1980 did I complete the first draft of a manuscript I then called *Sexual Spirituality,* later published by Winston Press in 1984 as *Radical Love.* Like most sturgeons (the Native American would say) I took a long time to mature, and especially to integrate sexuality and spirituality. What an enlightening, painful-joyful experience that long trip has been, thanks to the ever-guiding, patient Teacher Herself!

Yet, on the other hand, how much pain, misunderstanding, and plain unreality have woven their way through those years of mine! Slowly I learned not to lay unreal expectations on others to fulfill my needs or desires. Cherishing the differences in others became a major theme of my spirituality. Each person was a gift of unique value sent into my life; my Teacher invited me to accept them and not demand they measure up to my image and likeness.

Early in my stay in Berkeley I met two fine men, exresidents of San Quentin Prison. Working with their chaplain, we set out on a new path with the course, "Ministry to Captive Structures," training graduate students preparing for ministry to understand and minister to prison residents. The program included visits to three infamous dens: Folsom, San Quentin, and Vacaville prisons, including the then unused gas chamber soon to be reactivated. Gradually we brought together a theology of the U.S. prison system that challenged it to total reform—not too popular a move, but since that time to some of those students, an important one. In my own prayer, I saw the prisoner as the poorest of the poor the gospel calls us to help, for they cannot even ask us for the cup of cold water. Soon my work with women merged with the prison concern and centered into forming a group, Women Today

West, a branch of Sister Margaret Traxler's Institute of Women Today, to raise public consciousness about women in prison.

Meeting the prison system head-on—its autonomy, its unaccountability, its arbitrariness—burnt my soul and has kept me to the challenge ever since. Women in prison remain a deep concern in my spiritual journey, and I mourn the little capacity I seem to have to help them; but prayer remains a vital way, as do the classes in meditation I've been happy to give within prison walls. Lectures, lobbying, and involving other women in training prisoners prerelease are very important to me, and I feel compelled to give them more time.

In my book *Team* I had suggested that people could work part-time so that we'd have time to grow our gifts, learn an instrument, minister, just pick the daisies, and, especially, pray and contemplate the glory of the universe. Loss of tenure signaled that I should put my life where my theory was, so I now live by the phone and the mailbox, trying to listen to whither the Spirit blows. So off I go to anywhere, so long as She can use me. The world conference on team ministry chose to fly me to Brussels as a result of *Team*. Doing consulting with groups trying to be ministry teams has been very rewarding.

More and more, the lectures, workshops, and retreats seem to be about meditation, prayer, and mystic experience as rallying points. This pushes me to stay close to God, asking Her before each engagement to open the hearts of my hearers, to give me the words She wants for them, and to leave the results to Her. This makes possible the many such works I do now respond to, but always my extroverted self must fight to make time to be quiet with God, to rest in that center of light, and to listen carefully to Her leading.

In New York, for one such lecture, I met Morton Kelsey, who invited me to work with him in our current "Companions on the Inner Way" conferences at San Francisco Theological Seminary. For the first time, this winter ('85) in Berkeley I'll teach "Spiritual Friendship," to me a strange development, since I've felt that both the retreats I am called to give and

the personal spiritual guidance I now do are somewhat unbelievable. When I was first asked to give a retreat, it seemed
just right and all wrong. My background of thirty years of
making retreats (under priests always) left me a bit non-
plussed by the idea. How would I do that? What would I do?
But when I learned to give to God the people I'd meet, and
looked back over what had seemed to help me, it worked itself
out. I was an interested, absorbed spectator, clapping for God
about Her fancy footwork with the retreatants.

In the praise of God I enjoy in prayer, I find it especially
satisfying to include bodily prayer, meditation techniques
that involve entering the soma as sacred space, fasting, yoga,
and nature walks. Most of all, I love to use music, that
powerful touch on the unconscious, to relax us, to open up our
blocked places, to let God in. I am the retreatant most
blessed.

Spiritual guidance is a chance one by one to meet God in
Her world. Trying to listen to the living Spirit in the other
person is my challenge in walking with another as spiritual
companion, especially when I know so well my own inadequacy. Fortunately, we don't walk along because we're superior, but probably because God wants us to do the learning
that meeting another yearning, striving, loving heart can
demand.

Out of all this living has come a demand deep within to
follow more closely, to simplify, to let pretensions go, to be
what I appear to be or to drop such appearances. Now,
through consultation, discernment, prayer, I feel that the
many courses I've taught are finally being assimilated by this
sturgeon, whose bony plates of armor seem to take an axe to
sever. Yet they also serve as protection for the sensitive child
within me. I now feel that God is calling me again to put my
life where my mouth is. After twenty years of calling for the
empowerment of the laity, of women, of the prisoner, now God
says, Why not be one? Tossed out into the deep water in 1967,
this sturgeon, in typical retarded sturgeon fashion, took a long
time to absorb the lessons of the ocean; but I praise God for
the discovery through some long discerning and much help
that my seventeen years of living alone have been graduate

work. I have been mercifully taught to share and am now hoping to share all I earn and have with those who need it, especially women and prisoners. And what I know must be shared. Who I have become may be shared—and all this as She reels in or releases the long, long lines attached to my heart.

My book *Radical Love* calls me to Canada this year and all over the U.S.—and somehow to London, where I visited the women entrenched in the rain and mud around the U.S. missile site. Somehow the theology of peacemaking seems the fruit of so many of my studies and experiences. Radical love is Christ's forgiving love in the gospel; I must try to live it, share it, receive it, and, most of all, allow myself to be, with Dante, "glad in the glad sunshine" because I'm alive. I am incredibly loved by such a One, and I want now only to answer that love by loving God's beloved ones, my brothers and sisters everywhere. I am afraid, alone, poor, but rich in Her love. I know She wants my trust, the gift that thrills Her heart, because trusting Her means I believe that this Lover is faithful—and that is Her name.

APHRODITE CLAMAR

Aphrodite Clamar, a clinical psychologist, received her Ph.D. from New York University and is currently engaged in the practice of psychotherapy in New York City. She has done research and published widely on families constituted in unusual fashion (adoptive and stepfamilies, for example) and in areas of concern to women. A special interest has been the impact of religious socialization on women's lives.

American Athena:
A Modern Woman
and the Traditional
Greek Orthodox Church

Greek Orthodoxy is my religion. I was born to Greek Orthodox parents; adopted by Greek Orthodox parents; baptized
Greek Orthodox and reminded regularly, by my parents, that
though they sent me to a Methodist elementary school and an
Episcopal Sunday school—all for expediency's sake—I was,
first and foremost, Greek Orthodox. My parents were proud
of their heritage and hoped that their only child would share
this pride.

My parents backed their pride with something more sub-
stantial than hope. My father and maternal grandfather
were among the founders of the Holy Cross Greek Orthodox
Theological School in Connecticut (later moved to Massachusetts). When I was quite young, before we moved to Florida—
where I became part of the Southern Protestant religious
community—my father had been president of the Greek
Orthodox Church in Worcester, Massachusetts. Even in Florida, away from their roots, my parents continued their contact with the church by entertaining and lodging visiting
church hierarchs. I remember as a little girl staring at these
black-clad men with long beards and dark eyes—overpower-
ing figures who frightened me no matter how warmly they
spoke or how much they tried to encourage me to talk to them
in Greek.

While I lived in Florida, these contacts with the church
grew more and more irregular. There was no Greek Orthodox
church in Lakeland (where we lived), and Greek Orthodoxy

began to take on the flavor of a fairy tale—a colorful story that was interesting but hardly real. I was exposed to it just enough to be convinced that it existed, but little enough to be ignorant of its beliefs and history. I did learn to speak Greek at home, but I could neither read nor write in Greek; similarly, I identified with a religion about which I knew little of substance.

The years passed. My father died when I was eleven, and shortly thereafter my mother and I moved to New York City. I now lived near a Greek Orthodox church and could attend whenever I wanted to. Feeling like a stranger in the midst of a crowd, all of whom knew one another, I began to attend holiday services. Stranger or not, I found myself immediately attracted to the ritual with its backdrop of colorful vestments, incense, flickering candles, somber icons, and chanting. While my Greek might not be good enough for me to understand completely the priest's sermon or the psalter's intoning, I was definitely "hooked" on the pageantry, mysticism, and tradition.

Enchanted, I watched the men of God—wearing the embroidered, gold-and jewel-encrusted robes of God's authority, ornate skirts swishing about their black shoes—perform their holy offices in the sanctuary. Flanked by their serious-faced assistants, the altar boys, secure in their service to our mother-church, the priests moved easily in and out of the holy altar—an area that was forbidden to me as a menstruating female. In fact, I learned soon enough from my mother that no women at all were permitted into the sanctuary. Post-menopausal women (preferably sexually inactive widows) might be allowed the privilege of cleaning the altar and its artifacts. But then cleaning is a woman's job, even behind the altar. The responsibility to intercede in my behalf with the Almighty was reserved for men assisted by boys. Mystery and drama predominated. I watched from the audience, much like a spectator at the opera.

Recently my friend and contemporary, Constance Callinicos, in an unpublished reminiscence, described the effect of this ritual on impressionable girls:

The division of male and female, begun in childhood with the knowledge of every little girl that her brother, younger or older, is special as is every male in her life, comes during puberty when pubescent boys are recruited into the all-male service of the church, into the hallowed ground of the Holy Altar, which is forbidden to females. At the same time the pubescent girl is learning of her unclean femaleness, and the restrictions imposed upon her. Brother is dressed in fine brocade and given a censer to hold, a candle in a gold candelabra, Holy Words to read from the Bible during services; she is cautioned not to defile Holy Icons and Holy Bread while she bleeds, nor is she to kiss the hand of any priest or other Holy Man during this dangerous time.

I understand this now, but I gave little conscious thought to these subliminal impressions at the time. They were to lie dormant until twelve years ago when I was preparing to marry. My husband-to-be was both Jewish and prominent in the professional Jewish world. While deciding on a wedding ceremony and ferreting out the religious traditions we would maintain in our home, he invited me to convert to Judaism.

The decision about whether or not to convert—and if so, when—would be truly mine to make, he assured me. By this time my mother had also died; I had no siblings or close relatives to put pressure on me one way or the other, nor ties to a priest who could advise me or influence my decision. I was on my own.

Forced to come to a decision—to leave or remain in my church—I entered a period of reading, questioning, seeking. Immersed in a mass of books and periodicals, I studied both religions but made no decision to convert.

In the meantime, I got married. I now began to visit Israel regularly with my husband. I would now see the places where the events in the New and Old Testament took place. History stared me in the face at every turn. Sunday school stories, vacation Bible school studies, and classroom ditties about Jesus suddenly came alive. Jerusalem, the Via Dolorosa, Gethsemane, Bethlehem, the Burning Bush at the monastery of Santa Caterina—they all existed. Even biblical characters took on a personality of their own, as I walked the roads they trod, sat beneath trees like those where they rested, rubbed my hands on stones they knew, gazed at the same rivers and deserts they saw. No longer the fairy tales of my childhood, the Bible and its stories became "real" to me.

As a result of my readings and travels, I developed an increasing understanding of and respect for Judaism. Along the way I wrote a paper on psychotherapeutic concerns of Orthodox Jewish women, which I presented at an annual meeting of the American Psychological Association. This paper was to become my entrée to the Jewish feminist world. This, in turn, led to friendships with Jewish feminists and leaders and gave me the opportunity to observe the movement toward equality for women within Reform and Conservative Judaism.

At the same time, it seemed to me, Greek Orthodoxy was continuing on the course it had set generations ago. Greek Orthodoxy still shuns the social, sexual, and feminist revolutions that are apparent not only in the United States but also in western Europe and Israel. There does not appear to be a discernible feminist movement within my church—none of the organized pressure I have come to expect from Jewish women. As far as I can determine, if I wanted a role within my church, I could be a Sunday school teacher, choir member, or volunteer in the philanthropic Philoptchos Society, whose stated aim is "to preserve the sacredness of the Orthodox family, perpetuate the Christian concept of marriage and upbringing of children and through it perpetuate and propagate the Greek Orthodox faith and traditions in conformity with its doctrines, canons, discipline, divine worship, usages, and customs." In my life, my role as a Greek-American woman is to raise the children; in the church, to raise money, educate children, or sing. And since I'm tone deaf, singing is definitely out.

Greek Orthodoxy, it seems, clings proudly to its traditions —many of which, I learned, stem from the earliest, most primitive form of Christianity. Viewed historically, this tenacious adherence to tradition makes sense. Persecuted by non-Christians and rival denominations of Christianity, the Orthodox church defended itself by revering tradition.

Today, however, these threats to the church's existence can hardly be said to exist. Must the church continue to act with such rigidity? One of the church's cherished traditions, I read, sanctifies and perpetuates women's second-class position within both church and society. Eve's disobedience is still blamed for the expulsion from Paradise. The church fathers still believe in a special "female nature," a divinely ordained inferiority that makes women physically, morally, and intellectually less than men. Thus St. Cyril of Alexandria could write: "The male must always rule, the female must everywhere stay in second class." Carried to its ultimate, this saint's dictum empowers a male priesthood with the weight of authority and tradition, while admonishing the female congregant to bow her head to laws written and enforced by men in an androcentric culture.

This brief, superficial description of the tenets of Greek Orthodoxy can only hint at the complex history of this church. Nevertheless, it does touch on some of my concerns. Not only is there no feminist movement within my church; it will be extremely difficult for such a development to take place. The Greek-American women I meet are intelligent, well-educated, articulate participants in the world around them. They have choices. Among their choices: to accept things as they are; to marry out or assimilate with the greater American society, ultimately drifting away from their historical past; or to learn from their non-Greek Orthodox sisters how to organize and push for change. It is too early to predict which way we will go.

Why Greek Orthodoxy does not reach out to us, its women, is a question the patriarchs of the church will perhaps one day be required to answer. Why we are not making the demands our Jewish, Catholic, and Protestant sisters are making is yet another and perhaps more poignant question that I ask myself. From my own experience, from the interviews I conducted, and from the conversations I held, one conclusion emerges: For the modern Greek-American woman who has received a university education and entered business or a profession—whether or not she combines it with marriage or family—the church has lost much of its relevance and no longer has the primacy it held for her mother and grandmother.

In the course of determining my religious future, I reflected on my religious past. How deeply, I wondered, had Greek Orthodoxy helped to form my personality? How insidiously had it influenced the choices I made? How did it circumscribe my sexuality? How had it defined my role within my family and group—as daughter, wife, hostess, woman professional, and friend? How much of the influence was cultural and how much religious? In this last question, perhaps, lies the core of my dilemma—Greek Orthodoxy is an integral part of being a Greek-American. More than a religion, it represents my cultural heritage. A potent ingredient in my identity, it assures my membership in a universal family whose behavior and attitudes I understand—even if I don't always agree with them or like them.

In short, my religion is both an emotional and cultural connection. While I may recognize its limitations, I must still bow to my own deeper spiritual needs. The ancient ritual and mysticism of Greek Orthodoxy add significantly to the meaning of my life. They underscore my connection to an ancient people, to an ancient culture and civilization. I cannot easily dismiss—not by marriage, nor by dint of intellect, nor by a conscious effort to take a giant eraser and rub out my past. Without the religion of my ancestors I would be bereft of my history—feeling, perhaps, as an orphan loose in the world.

My personal decision has been to remain in the Greek Orthodox church and to participate as well in my husband's religion with him (as he does with me)—in essence, to maintain a dual-religion household, where each of us is free to partake of our religion and culture as we wish or need.

I have made one more decision: to encourage other Greek Orthodox women to articulate our dissatisfaction with our church and to let the hierarchs know we seek changes.

Scripture (Galatians 3:28) makes it quite clear that "there is neither Jew nor Greek, there is neither slave nor free, there is neither male nor female; for you are all one in Christ Jesus." It is my hope that Greek Orthodoxy will one day act in accordance with this truth.

MARY LOU RANDOUR

Mary Lou Randour, Ph.D., is a psychologist with a long-term personal and professional interest in women's development and role in society, and in existential psychology. This year she is a Clinical Fellow with the Clinical Program in Psychology and Religion (Erikson Center), offered by the Harvard Medical School, Department of Psychiatry, at the Cambridge Hospital. In addition to her clinical work at Cambridge Hospital, she is a Postdoctoral Fellow at the Center for Research on Women, Wellesley College, where she is assisting with a research study on women and stress. While at the Center, she also is developing a clinical research project on agoraphobia. *Women's Psyche, Women's Spirit* is the title of a manuscript she is finishing. Based on original research she conducted over the last two years, she hopes it will be a published book in the near future.

An Exploration of Faith

The question of faith is the most personal of all possible questions. So I trust you will understand, dear reader, that I must explore this question of my faith assuming no audience, no reader over my shoulder. My reply to the question of my faith is for me and for no one else. However, as I pause from this exploration of my faith, I can share with you all that I have discovered thus far, for whatever use you can find. In the hope that we can sometimes learn from others, I offer you the fruits of my search as of now, in the form of a letter to myself.

Dear Mary Lou,

I'm struggling with the most basic question of my existence: What is my faith? As I began to earnestly search for what this means to me, I kept stumbling over the whole concept of faith. What is faith? I wondered. I didn't feel I had any. I turned to the dictionary for guidance. Here I could at least find some starting point. This is what I found:

> Faith: A confident belief in the truth, value, or trustworthiness of a person, idea, or thing; any set of principles or beliefs.

I read this definition with relief; here was a definition of faith that was at least familiar to me. This seemed like a possibility. Until then I feared the worst—that I was devoid of faith. Even though I consider myself a modern feminist thinker (a post-Christian feminist, in my more daring moments), I realized that my relief over finding the dictionary definition of faith was a sign of my unwitting equating of faith with a belief in the scriptures of an organized (read: patriarchal) religion. My intellect had long ago rejected the idea that faith was defined exclusively by an attitude of reverence and devotion toward the God of the scriptures. But other parts of me, less accessible to my own reason, still clung to a traditional view of faith (such is the perdurability of our childhood teachings).

I have to give up my childish interpretation of faith because I can't love both myself and the scriptures (where virgin daughters are offered to the men of Sodom by their father so he could protect the male travelers in his house [Gen. 19]; where a Levite's concubine is given by her master to a group of men who rape her throughout the night until she dies [Judges 19]; and where a woman who, in order to protect her spouse, grabs the testicles of the man he is fighting with is punished by having her hand cut off, "without pity" [Deut. 25]), and I can't accept the God of whom they speak. Yahweh is too fierce, too homicidal, too harsh. I don't know Mohammed, but his devotees in Pakistan today are trying to convert their version of Moslem law into state law that specifies that in a court of law the testimony of two women is equal to that of one man, and in all of Islam menstruating women are still forbidden to enter a mosque. Even the gentle Buddha referred to women as the source of all sin and temptation. The Hindu texts do the same. And while Christ was kinder to women, given his culture and his times—some even call him a feminist—he is still a symbol of the patriarch.

I need a doctrine and a practice that include and honor the female and femaleness. No religion that I know does that. If I am to think of my godliness, my holiness, which I believe we all reach out to do, then I need a concept of God that, if not female, at least manifests aspects of femaleness. Of course, I don't have to anthropomorphize the deity; I have alternatives —to see the divine as "currents of energy," as a verb, as the ground of being, or as the great powers of the universe. But that's difficult and I'm still working on that one.

As I said, I was becoming disheartened when I first started pondering the dimensions of my faith, until I turned to the dictionary. Of course, I thought, I do have belief in the truth, value, or trustworthiness of some person, idea, or thing. And I do have a set of principles or beliefs.

My anxiety about having no faith stemmed from my loss of any hope that I will ever have a mature faith, as traditionally defined, in the God or creed of any religion that I know. And I don't know yet what, if anything, replaces this loss. Somehow, without wanting to, and although sometimes trying not to, I have turned away from the Christian faith I was raised in. I have experimented with other traditions, but none have satisfied. My feminist consciousness—a consciousness that has made me aware of the power and the glory of my self and introduced me to my right to integrity and authenticity—has led me to this explicit rejection of all major religions. My dissatisfaction with Christianity occurred before I had any formal or conscious knowledge of feminism, but both, I think, grew out of a sense of alienation. As an adolescent I struggled with my Christianity. I fervently prayed and, in vain, awaited feelings of devotion, awe, and trust in God. Instead I felt fear, guilt, and a general sense of shame and worthlessness.

I accepted the responsibility for my inability to accept and to live unquestioningly with a Christian faith. I understood that it was only human to doubt; but my doubts were always stronger than my faith. And underlying the doubt was a vague, inchoate sense of alienation from Christian doctrine and ritual. Now I understand that this sense of alienation was simply a healthy and valid distrust of an exclusive male theology that could not, and did not, touch my heart or hear my inner voices.

I did not feel comfortable with my growing sense of estrangement from the faith of my fathers and tried a variety of strategies to still my persistent doubts. One strategy was my conversion to Roman Catholicism at the age of 21. I took instruction, received my first communion, ritualistically participated in a number of confessions, and then retired from the faith six months later. My inability to keep up what was for me a charade was greater than my need to find comfort in some Christian convention.

After this futile attempt to stay within Christianity, my next confrontation with faith was resolved by joining the ranks of those in the most modern of religions—therapy. My faith in therapy at least allowed me to chip away at my feelings of worthlessness, shame, guilt, and fear and offered self-acceptance, trust, and understanding of self. As important as therapy was to me, because of its exclusive focus on self, it wasn't enough. I needed to move beyond myself, to transcend myself, to unite with something larger and beyond myself; van Kaam talks about moments of inspiration to go beyond the form of life we are at home with, to a new form that discloses more of the original, or holy, life form. I was and am looking for such a moment.

I turned toward the East and began to read mostly about Buddhism, a little about Hinduism. At first Buddhism seemed safe. There was no god to assign gender to. The path to enlightenment was through meditation. Self-reliance and responsibility were stressed; there was no power outside of self (or rather, no self) to invoke, cajole, or plead with. As I began to meditate, I found this practice beneficial in opening my awareness. I still do. My first problem with Buddhism arose when I was told that it was best to have a meditation teacher who was experienced in the practice. At one level this made sense to me, yet on another level I knew I could never find a teacher from among the male monks I knew who would understand, let alone answer, my spiritual needs as a woman in this world. I also was troubled with the fact that all the Buddhist monks I met or knew about were men; I later learned that there are women who are Buddhist nuns, but they have less authority, autonomy, and prestige than their male counterparts. The final blow to my exploration of Buddhism fell when I read excerpts from some of the Buddhist texts. These texts describe the Buddha as passing a test by thwarting the advances of a group of women on his path to enlightenment and later, after enlightenment, as repeatedly warning his monks to shield themselves from the vices and defects of women. As in other religions, so in Buddhism women are seen as the source and manifestation of all the sin and temptation of the world. Women are maya, the veil of worldly illusion that conceals the ultimate reality from our view. With deep regret I realized that Buddhism, like all other major religions, was indelibly stained with misogynism and gynophobia.

As I read next the teachings of Hinduism, I was still angry, although not surprised, to find women presented as defective and corrupt. I tried to excuse the treatment of women by noting that some of these texts were written thousands of years ago; I also tried to justify the rampant antifeminism found in Hinduism with the fact that there were strong images of the feminine in their mythology. Sometimes Shakti and certainly always the bloodthirsty Kali are powerful symbols of the feminine. There is to me a schizophrenic treatment of women in Indian thinking, where, on the one hand, women are seen as vile and corrupt, but, on the other, the divine has aspects of the feminine. More current examples of this ambivalent view of women can be found in the writing of a modern-day Indian siddha, or holy man. He advocates equality, the interrelatedness of all things, and reverence for women. At the same time, he equates women with eating, sleeping, fearfulness, sensuality (in short, the world) and men with mastery of the senses, courage, dispassionate devotion, love (the spirit). When a woman is detached, a renunciate, solitary, holy, she is described as being like a man. When a man is caught in addiction, sunk in worldly life, full of lust, he is described as a "stupid woman." There may be plentiful and powerful images of the feminine in Indian mythology, but these are images and not real women. Real women are seen as the embodiment of worldly pleasures, of failings, and, again, as the source of sin and temptation. Women are the embodiment of that which must be overcome or transcended.

Ultimately I could find no justification for this attitude toward women. At least my interest in Hinduism was abandoned with less regret than my leave-taking of Buddhism. I was always suspicious of the Hindu practice of separating the sexes during worship, and I was equally suspicious and uncomfortable with the elaborate homage and fervent devotion I saw paid to Indian gurus.

Later, as I refected on my brief experiment with Eastern thought, I realized that the Eastern emphasis on the interaction and interdependence of dualities—a needed counterpoint and corrective to dualistic Western thinking—breaks down with the consideration of sensuality and spirituality. Even in the East sensuality and spirituality are dualistically split. (The one exception is Tantrism; but Tantrism is an esoteric tradition.) For example, celibacy is more highly valued than sexual expression. The holy people (mostly men) of the East are expected, for the most part, to lead a celibate life. It is understood that lay people, or householders, are distracted from the purely spiritual life because of their family responsibilities. But in one's later years an exclusive focus on spirituality is recommended. This exclusive focus means an elimination of the sensual, the sexual, and the physical from one's life. For holy persons and lay people alike, the emphasis in the East is on transcending sexuality.

Another example of the denigration of the physical can be seen in the Eastern scheme of chakras, or body energy centers, in which reproduction and sexual gratification are considered lower forms of energy. The goal is to transcend the lower chakras, or the physical, and to operate out of pure spirit, associated with the "higher" chakras.

The requirement of celibacy and the association of the physical with lower forms of energy are examples to me of nothing more than the worst (or best) of dualistic thinking. And as in all dualistic thinking there is an ordering of values. Physical processes are not only in opposition to spirit but are also inferior to spirit. In feminist theological work spirit and flesh are emphasized as being parts of the same system with neither accorded higher value. In Mother Goddess worship and in the practice of witchcraft, as I understand it, the physical is celebrated and seen as both a path toward the spirit and at one with spirit. (It also is not surprising that the Goddess is the center of worship in Tantric rites.) It follows that it is women who refuse to split flesh from spirit. Women, both in the East and the West, have been associated with the flesh, and because of this association, have been disgraced and held responsible for sin and temptation.

I learned other important lessons from my exposure to Eastern philosophies. I learned to redefine, or at least rethink, what it means to be holy. Eastern religious people, who are sometimes credited with great psychic and physical powers, are also often referred to as holy. But I began to wonder how a person could be holy and at the same time belong to, and not speak out against, a tradition that finds women defective. Would a person be considered holy who belonged to a tradition that referred to Jews or Blacks as defective? I doubt it. I don't think one can be holy and work, without comment, in a tradition that holds a group of people as inferior or evil. These men may have great powers, but I concluded that this does not necessarily mean they are holy. To me holiness requires loving and honoring all life; and it may, and probably would, require transcending or reforming one's tradition.

I also learned about my unconscious acceptance of assumptions. I accepted the stress of Eastern philosophies to eliminate self or ego as an appropriate and desirable goal. Later, as I read various feminist theologies, I had my first encounter with the view that women do not need to give up their sense of self; for them (or rather us) our work is in another direction. Our work is to develop a sense of power and of self. This proposition was a revelation to me. Other implications from this insight unfolded. The whole emphasis on self-negation in the Eastern philosophies is based on an appropriate conclusion, but it is a conclusion derived from male experience. In the male tradition, Valerie Saiving suggests, sin and temptation are defined as the will-to-power, the "imperialistic drive" that is directed at others; men forget that they are not the whole but only part of the whole. Their sin is pride, power, arrogance, hubris. Women have never been put in the position to have enough power to abuse. For women, sin is based on different circumstances, and because of that, sin may be defined in a completely different way. For women, sin may be the denial of self, the abnegation of self, the lack of a will to mastery. Women do not need a practice that encourages the loss of self, for too many have been denied the opportunity to discover a self to lose. All existing major theologies—Buddhism, Christianity, Hinduism, Islam and Judaism—are written by, for, and about men. They are based on male experience, and their doctrine and ritual reflect those origins.

After casting away all major religions of the East and West, what am I left with? I stare into a void. What will happen to me? An experience of nothingness, we are told, typically precedes a spiritual awakening for women. We are also told that impasse and crisis are often turning points in both personal and spiritual development—as though we must be stripped bare before we can perhaps see the world differently, more clearly, and with fewer distortions. So I confront the void, this experience of nothingness, with uncertainty, some anxiety, and some hope that I will pass through suffering to a more complete, pellucid view of the world.

But still, when I allow myself to understand the totality of my rejection and what meaning it has for my ontological and spiritual being, I shudder with my aloneness. At times it is hard to feel correct, or justified, in taking such an extreme stance. But that is where my truth has led me and where I must stand, for now. But am I truly alone? I always have my self, and isn't that all any of us ever has? Is it not an existential fact that we are alone? Sometimes I want my mother, my father, my husband, my friends, to walk with me through whatever "valley of the shadow of death" I may be experiencing. But mostly I understand, and will always have to struggle to accept, the existential fact that I am alone. I may accept my aloneness, but sometimes in the stillness I hear the cynical lament of the Peggy Lee song "Is that all there is?" In answer to this cynicism I cannot give up the hope—or is it faith?—that there has to be more than billions of past, present, and future souls who take form and then perish, with no connectedness to one another or to the world they live in. There must be, I think, some connective tissue, some cosmic web, that unites us all. Could there not be a silken, shiny thread that unites all—woman, man, child, animal, insect, plant, flower, and rock—who live now, have lived, and will live?

Do I have only this vision of a shiny, silken thread to hold onto? What else do I have that offers me support, that helps supply meaning to my experiences, that gives me a frame of reference for looking out into the world? I have what all women have always had: I have other women as my friends, as my community. The patriarch has been unable to quell the strength of women's friendships; in fact, living in and under an alien and unfriendly system has encouraged women's solidarity. Like many women, the process of my self-affirmation began when I found the company and support of other women who had as their conscious goal to examine their lives and to decide for themselves who they were, who they could be. Feminist theologians talk of a "new naming" and that was our task, to name the world anew for ourselves. Without other women and our awareness as women, I would be lost in an alienating patriarchy. The company and support of other women confirmed my unwillingness to accept my self as inferior, or stained, or to be used in relation to the male (as Mrs.), or to be related to as an object (through rape or *Playboy*). With other women I was able to say no to those images of the patriarch that would demean, dismiss, or destroy me. With other women I found the strength and wisdom to begin a new naming. My spiritual searching is guided by my feminism, with my feminist perspective providing the parameters for my spiritual process of becoming. Like Mary Daly I look for the unfolding of God in a new space/time that is found in the center of women's lives. What I have learned from my sorority is to look within myself, and within the lived lives of other women, for that connective energy that unites us all. I no longer look up to the transcendent sky-father for guidance and meaning, but rather within and around the living of expressed life. I look at the elegance and serenity of the here of lived lives in the present of this experience. There is comfort inside this community of women. It is my bulwark against the worst of male culture. It nourishes and soothes my woman's spirit. It clarifies my vision, feeds my courage to be, and wipes away the lies of a male culture that hates and fears the other.

But can I stay here within this protective womb of womanliness? A large part of me wants to; it is my home. It is where I found my self. But now that I have reclaimed my self, it is time to reclaim the world. I walk away from the nurture place of women's friendships with great sadness, for I am only recently healed from the sometimes brutal blows of a world that does not love women. But still I am drawn to the world, away from my first home, because it is in this world that other women live who have not had the hope, time, or place to affirm themselves, as women, with other women. Also, in this world are the men who suffer under the brutal weight of a society that chooses death before some false notion of dishonor, that kills in the name of life, that brutalizes and objectifies in the name of sex and passion. I live, as other women must, in the tension between building and protecting my sense of self and confronting the challenges of the world. My sense of self is built on my identity as a woman. Yet I also search for the universals of human life so that eventually what I learn from my experiences and the meaning that I assign to them may also be appropriated by other woman and by men, and so that I may benefit from the experiences of others, women and men. I want to feel safe in the world with both women and men.

I am living on a spiritual boundary. One side of the boundary I know; it is the land of the patriarch. The other side has no name. I only know what it is not. It is not Buddhism, Christianity, Hinduism, Islam, or Judaism. As I look toward the side of the boundary with no name, I have an ineffable feeling about the possibilities of being. I have the freedom (and the burden) to name the world for myself.

J. BARDARAH McCANDLESS

J. Bardarah McCandless is a Professor of Religion at Westminster College, New Wilmington, Pa., a liberal arts college of the Presbyterian Church U.S.A., with responsibilities in Biblical Studies and Christian Education. Education background includes A.B., Oberlin College (History); M.R.E., New York Theological Seminary (formerly Biblical Seminary in New York); Ph.D., University of Pittsburgh (Religious Education and Educational Psychology). Among her memberships are Phi Beta Kappa, Pi Lambda Theta, Association of Professors and Researchers in Religious Education, and Society for the Scientific Study of Religion. Publications include *An Untainted Saint . . . Ain't—Practical Piety in Timely Rhyme* (Dawn Valley Press) and articles published in the *Journal of Pastoral Counseling, Religious Education,* and *Journal of Religion and Health.* Her current interest is in interrelationships between theology and psychology.

Adventure in Faith

Jesus got into my thinking at an early age. He was a friend to little children. And I felt very little as an only child growing up in a twelve-room house with an overly conscientious mother. My mother and I also felt lonely—she for a husband who was frequently away on business during the week and I for a father.

But Jesus was an ever present, loving companion. According to family lore, one day in my fourth year, as I was stomping up the center hall stairway in a huff, a visitor said that Jesus would not like my behavior. Stopping halfway up the broad steps, I swung around, shook my curly head, and announced, "I'm not skeered of Jesus."

Jesus also cared about little girls' problems. One weekend my doll's eyes fell to the back of its head. I asked my father to fix them. When he gently explained that he couldn't help, I consoled, "Don't worry. Jesus can fix them. Jesus is God's carpenter."

God was a natural part of our home life. My parents were sensitive, loving people who adored each other and adored their child. They wove their Christian ideals so naturally through the fabric of everyday life that I do not remember their verbalizing them with me except in grace before meals, a desire for Sunday church worship, and bedtime prayers or Bible stories.

My parents also respected each other and other people. Although in personality my parents were two evenly matched but loving tigers who could disagree sharply with each other or with others, they did not put others down. With me, they used firm discipline but generously gave me themselves, their time and attention, more than things. My parents' love for each other and for me laid a strong foundation for my life and deepening religious faith.

Yet my father's frequent and unavoidable absences during the week placed on both of my parents a strain that communicated unintended messages to me. Out of those unintended messages were born ghosts that not only shadowed my nursery days but also, without anyone's knowledge, haunted me for almost half a century, eventually raising painful religious questions.

My formal schooling began when my well-intentioned mother turned a guest room into a school room and taught me kindergarten and first grade. She wanted to avoid my "catching germs" from the children who attended the school a half block away.

When I was seven, we moved to western Pennsylvania to be near my father's work. Here second grade in public school opened up a world of new adventures. By high school years, although faith in God still underlay my thinking, the real glamour and fun in life came from the school newspaper, yearbook, numerous committees, and dreams of government foreign service. But none of these filled a loneliness I hardly dared admit.

In the summer before my senior year in high school I attended a church conference in the nearby mountains. Desperately wanting friends, I was startled one evening to hear a speaker read Jesus' words, "Seek first the kingdom of God and all these things shall be added unto you."

"Could God add friends to my life?" I wondered. "Wouldn't serious commitment to God separate me from other people?" Whatever they meant, the words called to something deep within me. I joined other teenagers in a candlelit circle under the evening stars and made an intentional choice to accept Jesus as my savior and to follow where he would lead. In time that commitment would lead me not only into rich friendships but also into many struggles. What did it mean to seek God's kingdom first?

During college years, in a private non-church-related college, some of my acquaintances rejected Christianity, thinking that faith meant committing intellectual suicide, wearing blinders, and refusing to ask questions of life. A few verbally religious friends said they would rather help others than spend their time studying. My hunger for new intellectual experiences could accept neither view. God had given us minds. Therefore, as Christians we had the right, even the responsibility, to think, to explore.

Exploration led me into a history major, investigating medieval Europe and the development of British constitutional government, with side trips into French literature, the art of Giotto and Ghirlandajo, the music of Bach's "B Minor Mass" or Beethoven's "Appassionata Sonata," and voice lessons that struggled with "Caro Mio Bene" and other beginning Italian art songs. Although motives can be easily confused, I believed that God called us to develop our abilities to the highest point possible, not to inflate our pride but to prepare those abilities for God's use in the world.

My religious journey in college years was in many ways a rebellion into deeper faith. My parents' nonverbalization of faith led me to want reasons for faith. Why did Christians believe as they did? What was the basis for their faith? A freshman college religion course added further questions. Was the Bible just the record of human beings' search for God, as we were now being taught, or was it God's message to human beings as I had heard in Sunday school? Was the Pentateuch a mere patchwork of human inventions labeled J, E, D, and P? And were the Gospels only haphazard, cut-and-paste productions? Was Jesus only a great human being and not God in human flesh? Questions with which the church had long wrestled now became mine and demanded resolution.

But questions from upperclass psychology majors challenged my faith even more. Several majors lived or ate in our small dorm, with its round dining room tables, and peppered meal-time conversations with terms like "repression," "regression," "defense mechanisms"—uttered in such tones of condemnation and condescension to underclassmen as to denote the emotional equivalent of theology's "unforgivable sin." Heaven forbid that anyone develop a defense mechanism—whatever that was.

The impression was also given that religion was a crutch, God nothing but a projection of wishful thinking, and religious commitment a sign of neurosis. Of course no one bothered to define the term "neurotic"—but the tone of voice said that whatever it was, it wasn't good. Being religious, I didn't appreciate the condemnation but was curious to learn what the students meant.

After a time, doubt wrestled with faith and asked if God really did exist. Could a transcendent being exist beyond the reach of our intellectual proofs or test-tube measurements?

A few religious groups on campus steadied me, but by my junior year a deeper question gnawed within me. One day, after an hour of frustrating work on a Mozart aria in a conservatory practice room, I sat down at the piano, stared blankly at the music and asked, "What is worth living for? What is worth giving my life to?" Nothing could give an answer—not my current history major; nor the fun of bikeriding with friends; nor the usefulness of working on charitable fundraising drives and helping at a local orphanage.

So I finally answered, "Nothing," then in a few minutes added, "except Jesus Christ." But that idea didn't make me very happy. It seemed to demand giving up too much, though I couldn't say "too much of what" would be given up. At this point, contrary to the words of the psychology majors, the call of Christ felt more like a painful cross than a supportive crutch.

But theology often comes alive in midnight hours. A few months later a neck injury put me in the hospital for a month to spend many hours lying flat in bed with my neck in traction. I felt irritated and useless as hours crawled by. The doctor even forbade writing a sympathy card to a friend because writing would strain neck muscles.

In the silence of one night I asked, "Does God love a person who can't *do* things for others?" In answer I remembered words heard at a recent conference, " . . . by grace you have been saved through faith; and this is not your own doing, it is the gift of God—not because of works, lest any man should boast. For we are his workmanship, created in Christ

Jesus for good works, which God prepared beforehand, that we should walk in them." (Eph. 2:8-10 RSV)

That was it. Our salvation was *given* to us through Christ, not earned through our works. Our works were our grateful response to God's salvation, not our payment for it. With this thought I could relax—until the next theological questions boiled to the surface. And boil they did.

For weeks after the hospitalization the doctor forbade reading and writing to prevent strain on my collar-bound neck. So to pass the time I stirred puddings for my mother, explored our suburban neighborhood on foot, listened to the liquid silver rustling of wind through the willow tree behind the house, and kept on asking questions. Could one safely believe in something for which one could not give complete intellectual reasons? The classic arguments, cosmological, teleological, etc., could point to but not prove the existence of God. Could God be trusted to exist as a reality?

One spring morning I wakened unusually early, feeling especially discouraged by the tedium of recovery and impatient to get on with living. But something about this day was different. I felt in imagination as if I were standing on the edge of a cliff and a voice were asking me to step off the cliff, holding only to God's hand. After long hesitant moments, in prayerful imagination, I reached out for God's hand and stepped off the cliff. In the following days God's hand held. God was real. A new step of trust had been taken, a "leap of faith" some would call it. My intellectual questions were neither squelched nor answered but for the moment transcended by God's love.

A year after these religious experiences, I attended a summer conference for college students that pulled together all my previous religious experiences and proved to be the turning point of my life. For a month, on a wooded island in a northern lake, students clambered over rocks, canoed on the lake, attended Bible studies, argued about the world situation, and prayed.

Through these days two ideas flooded my thinking—one was the love of God and the other was a call to accept the lordship of Christ over my whole life, to seek his direction for all my plans and ambitions. In one way the idea was frightening, but in another it made sense. It meant surrendering the direction of life not to another human being or to an institution but to Christ himself, as that direction could be found through active seeking of God's will through prayer, study of the Bible, conversations with others, and hard study of relevant issues.

The struggle with God ended early one morning as I sat quietly on the lakeshore. God won. For the first time ever I felt the inner "peace that passes understanding." In the coming weeks all parts of my life—academic, musical, social —drew together into joyful new purpose. Intellectual questions, though not all resolved, were viewed through the prism of a new perspective.

The following year, after graduating from college, I was vocationally sure of only two things—I did not want to be a suburban housewife, (though sharing a profession with a husband would be all right), and I did not want to be a public school teacher. Although "religious" work had no appeal, an inner nudge into some sort of vocational Christian work was growing so strong that to draw back seemed like running away from a challenge. When my pastor learned of this feeling, he said, "It sounds to me like God's call." I agreed and made plans to enter seminary.

Years later I would wonder whether the "pull" into religious work was really from God's call or from psychological needs. Still later I would realize that God can work both by means of and in spite of our psychological needs. How else could God work through people?

With no desire to be a minister but possibly a desire to work with college students, I entered seminary to study the Bible and theology in order to share with others the adventure of new life in Christ. Our seminary had other women students and several women professors. Students were preparing for work in this country or in missions overseas—the women in educational work, the men in both education and ordained ministry. Conversations among the women dealt mainly with questions of marriage, effectiveness in vocational work, and balancing marriage and a vocation. Ordination of women was not yet a burning issue in the early fifties.

The field of Christian education offered contact with people but it also called for skills in teaching and group leadership, skills that, for one more drawn to historical research, did not come "naturally" to me. But I figured that if God gives one a job to do, God will supply the means with which to do it.

After seminary I served as Director of Christian Education in two suburban churches in Pennsylvania before entering the field of college teaching. Possibly because I was in a typically female field, I was not sensitive to sexist discrimination, aside from the salary scale, a problem everywhere. I felt far more discriminated against for being single than for being a woman. But in spite of all, I enjoyed the constant challenge of working with children, youth, and adults.

In the early sixties I moved into college teaching in biblical studies and Christian education in a then (but not historically) all-male religion department. I felt accepted as a person and not as a token woman. The presence or absence of a woman was not an issue—though I was warmly welcomed by the dozen other women on the faculty of this church-related college, a college which had admitted women students since its founding in the 1850s. Thus, up to this point, study and work in the field of religion posed little difficluty to me as a woman.

My real struggle with religion arose from inner experiences. For since Christ had become a deeper reality to me at the summer conference before my senior year in college, life had continued to bring deep joy and purpose. As I worked on conquering shyness with people my own age (older people had never been a problem), new friendships had been formed that brought the sharing of fun as well as serious thought and attempted service for others. Christ had changed my life in many ways.

But I made one mistake. I thought that since Christ had renewed my life so profoundly, he had automatically healed all inner hurts of the past, or so I understood the verse, "If anyone is in Christ, he is a new creation. The old has passed away, . . . the new has come" (2 Cor. 5:17). After a decade of college teaching, I learned that such healing was not necessarily so. With a doctorate completed in religious education and educational psychology, one semester I finally had a sufficiently light teaching, speaking, and singing schedule and the emotional security to investigate a question that had "bugged" me for fifteen years.

Fifteen years before, while working as a director of Christian education, I had had a medical problem for which doctors had made a wrong diagnosis that frightened me. A case of chicken pox had sapped my energy and left my throat burning for months after. Rest gave no relief. After many unsuccessful attempts to get relief, I made one more effort. The diagnosis was, "You're in excellent health. The problem is tension from going too hard. You'd better slow down." After all the extra rest, the diagnosis made no sense but did trigger big trouble.

For no known reason, the word "tension" set off near panic inside me that plagued me day and night for the next five months. While still working at the church, I carried on a running argument with doctors. Finally, one doctor discovered a toxic condition from deeply imbedded, pus-filled tonsils. He removed the tonsils. I got well. The panic ended immediately. Physical strength returned gradually and steadily. But the memory of the near panic lingered on and triggered questions that later doctoral study and reading books on pastoral counseling failed to answer. Why did the word "tension" frighten me? What caused the terror inside me? Through the next happy, busy years of working in a church and then teaching in college I had tried to forget the whole thing. The memory had left a painful voice crying inside me that after a time I had squelched by labeling it "self-pity."

But now, after fifteen years, I felt safe enough to ask what had happened. A friend who was also a pastoral counselor helped me search for an answer, an answer that in time would both challenge and deepen my theological understanding. Gradually the answer looked like this. Fear of the word "tension" was fear of the truth: That enormous tension did exist, not from going too hard but from trying to hide unknown rage over unknown childhood hurts. The rage had been kindled by unintentional teaching in childhood that emotional pain must not show or be felt, which also meant that emotional pain must not be healed.

The phrase "tension from going too hard," when applied to what I thought was physical illness, sounded as if the doctors were saying, "The problem is emotional." If that were true, then it would mean that I had let emotional pain show and, even worse, had asked for its healing. Thus I would have broken two of the most basic rules accidentally ingrained in childhood and would thereby have almost unleashed both a child's fear of parental judgment and a child's forbidden rage over the parental rules. My unexplainable five months of terror thus arose from the fear that a child's forbidden rage might explode into consciousness.

Surprisingly, the disturbing mealtime psychology discussions during college years alerted me now to possible clues to underlying hurt. But the first discoveries challenged my theology. Hadn't Christ changed my life bringing new joy and purpose in living? Didn't the crucifixion release us from bondage to the past? How could unknown rage from unknown hurts still lurk in hidden depths?

Gradually, the answer came clear to me. A very young child may gain mistaken, distorted, or frightening ideas— such as fearing abandonment when its mother tarries too long in the next room or, although physically present, is emotionally absent. An under-two-year-old may learn from inappropriately timed punishment from either parent that it is wrong to miss an absent parent and wrong to want a parent's love. If too frightening, these ideas and their accompanying feelings of fear or rage may be buried and find only indirect expression in an adult's life. Before these distorted ideas and buried feelings can receive the message of Christ's love, they must generally first be brought to consciousness. In the light of Christ's love and adult understanding and expression, the forbidden feelings can lose their threatening power.

Sometimes one's theology can form a barrier to that healing. Biblical ideas may be drawn like a magnet to strengthen unconscious efforts to hide unknown pain. Verses like "The joy of the Lord is your strength" and "Rejoice in the Lord always" and warnings against anger or dishonoring parents—all elements in constructive religious experience—can be used destructively to hide pain.

Looking backward to childhood need not be dishonoring to parents, as some people fear, if its purpose is not to blame others or to shift responsibility from oneself but is rather to trace a problem to its source with the intent of understanding and correcting it. A person is responsible to use information from the past to overcome, not to excuse, present difficulties. One can still honor parents by recognizing that they did their best in the midst of difficult circumstances.

I learned that while some theological ideas raised barriers to healing, others can shape tools to demolish barriers. The promise of God's forgiveness and acceptance of us—not because of our goodness but because of Christ's love and death for us—can give the courage to cut through fearful clouds of guilt rising from unknown childhood "crime"; and the idea of original sin—that all our goodness is tainted, imperfect—can ease the pain of discovering that hurt could occur in the midst of our parents' best-intentioned goodness.

Furthermore, the presence of Christ can give strength to withstand the onslaughts of pain wakened from long buried hurt. Christ has been called "God's empathy for us." As Christians interpret Isaiah 53, Jesus was "a man of sorrows and acquainted with grief." In Christ God suffers with the sufferer. Thus the sufferer is not alone. Christ's love also can help to draw the venom from old wounds and then to blunt the daggers of memory. And through the resurrection Christ offers hope for new life.

Thus theology was a constant guide on my journey to and from the past. I found the power of Jesus Christ to be valid in the depths of personality as well as on the level of everyday experience.

The goal of my self-exploration was not to "find myself" but to "free myself" for more effective living for God and others. Exploring the past has made me more sensitive to others' tears cried in laughter or loss buried in depression. The exploration has also helped me at last to confront the old psychological idea that "being religious is a sign of neurosis" and realize instead that the problem lies not in *being* religious but in how one *uses* one's religion. One may use religion in either healthy or unhealthy ways. These ideas have contributed to my teaching in both biblical studies and Christian education.

My overall plans for future teaching, study, and writing have also grown from this adventure of discovery and liberation. One area of study is adult Christian education. I am concerned about the adults in our churches who may be emotionally imprisoned through their distorted views of some New Testament teachings and thus squelch all anger; deny a legitimate self-esteem even though Jesus said, "Love your neighbor as *yourself*"; or assume that Christ has so changed their lives that they no longer have or should have unpleasant feelings.

Some adults may also have concepts of God and themselves that are haunted by what can be called "unholy ghosts of childhood." Such persons may say, "I know God is a loving God and I want to love him, but I can't." Or they feel that God can't really love them.

At a time of increasing awareness of child abuse and the strains of single parenting and other forms of lonely parenting, a further concern of mine is for the church to provide emotional support for parents of preschool children. Church-sponsored day-care centers can make excellent contributions to young children. But more efforts are needed to help the parents of these—and other—preschool children to develop parenting skills and to understand parental contributions to the child's interrelated emotional and spiritual development. We in the church should assist parents in laying foundations for their children's lives so that from childhood roots persons may draw more strength than pain for later living.

Gradually I am also giving attention to another area of liberation—the women's movement. For a long time I was puzzled by some of women's complaints—other than differential pay and limited vocational avenues. I was puzzled when some feminists said, "Learn to think of yourself as a human being first instead of woman." Since I had been raised to think of myself first as a human being, and second as a woman, I could not understand that other women did not feel the same way.

I had been offered role models of women who "did" things, served important causes in the world. Perhaps I heard the voice of my mother's own unfulfilled adventurous spirit. My mother greatly admired her older sister who, although a wife and the mother of four children, used her Phi Beta Kappa education to serve her local and state communities and was a member of the national board of the YWCA. And in her hometown she was publicly protesting the mistreatment of black- and brown-skinned people long before the civil rights movement of the sixties.

Further messages I had heard were: don't get tied down too early to a husband and children; take secretarial and book-keeping courses to be able to handle financial matters and support yourself (lest a college education be unmarketable); drive a car to be independent. Since my childhood was sup-posed to have been over-protected, I assumed that other girls received these messages plus many more that pushed them toward independence. Furthermore, both my parents warned me against autocratic, dominating men. Fortunately I have not felt put down by male friends or men with whom I have worked. However, brusque encounters with some other men I may have written off as arising from the men's rudeness, rather than from my being a woman. Thus, the early protests of feminists were a mystery.

I was also mystified at first by feminist theologians' pro-tests against the maleness of God. However, my sympathies were jolted awake in reading German feminist theologian Dorothee Sölle's objections to concepts of male power and especially to the concept of God as divine superpower. She wrote, "My objections . . . began to make themselves felt *when I was in Auschwitz* (italics mine)."* At the word "Auschwitz" I suddenly heard what many women had been saying. If the male behavior at Auschwitz was only an

---

* "Paternalistic Religion as Experienced by Women," *Concilium*; Theme— God as Father, March 1981, Seabury Press, New York, p. 72.

extreme form of common male behavior known to many women, and if that behavior had colored their concept of God as male, then the protest of many women—theologians or not —made sense.

Further excursions into feminist theology have helped me recognize the need to:

- observe how the equality of men and women described in Genesis 1:27 contrasts with the lowered status of women in Genesis 3 after the Fall;
- note the maternal characteristics attributed to God, as for example Isaiah 66:13, "As one whom his mother comforts, so I will comfort you. . . ;"
- ask why society emphasizes Eph. 5:24, ". . . let wives be subject to their husbands," but neglects Eph. 5:25, "Husbands, love your wives, as Christ loved the church and gave himself up for her";
- wonder about the difference between Jesus' respectful treatment of women and women's lowly status in the later church;
- look at problems raised if God is equated with such power that persons are forced into infantile, helpless dependency.

I also struggle with language about God. The use of familial (father-mother) language for God makes problems for some people, especially if the word "father" conjures up the image of the dictatorial, patriarchal father. For me, however, the situation was different. When I first heard God being referred to in a worship service as "she" or "mother," I left the church remembering my delightful but overcontrolling mother and thinking, "If God were female, I would have had no hope." As a child, I had wished my absent father were there to defend me from my mother's unintentionally excessive control and had apparently seen God as the present defending father, the protector from, not the perpetrator of, tyranny.

The problem of God-language is not easily solved. Replacing the family or personal images of God with terms like "light" and "wind" in one sense stretches one's concept of God; but it runs the risk, I fear, of reducing the personal God of the Bible to an impersonal cosmic "it." Surely this is not the

God whom Jesus addressed as "Abba." I yearn for an all-purpose pronoun to incorporate he/she. Nevertheless, although we can never capture the Creator of the Universe in the created work, our struggle with words may lead us to deeper understanding of the nature of God and the nature of human relationships with that God and with one another.

In summary, from childhood, God has been a part of my daily experience through hours of joy and also through those hours when despair and hope dance on a knife-edge. Questions, doubts, and answers have resulted in new questions. Following what I perceived to be God's direction, I have been led to outward study and teaching and to inward exploration. More work lies ahead for me. I cannot predict the future form of such work in a world crying for the assurance of God's care. But I believe we are most empowered to meet the needs of a crying world as we confront and cooperate with the loving, forgiving, healing, and challenging God as seen in the face of Jesus Christ. Herein is my hope and prayer.

RITA BRESNAHAN

A counselor and an educator, Rita Bresnahan has been involved in feminist spirituality for a number of years, creating and celebrating women's rituals in conferences and retreats across the country. Rita brings fresh perspectives from her synthesis of psychology, spirituality, and feminism into her teaching, her therapy and consultation sessions, her groups for women in transition, and her many workshops and seminars. Particularly does she utilize imagery and ritual to prime natural sources that speak to us at/from our depths, connecting us to ourselves and to one another, effecting transformation.

In 1982 Rita moved to the Seattle area, where the misty mystic nature-spirit of the great Northwest continues to be her most constant teacher and companion.

Spirit Journey: Ebb and Flow

At the age of thirty-six, I walked unnoticed out the front door of the Franciscan mother house I had known intimately for eighteen years. Just as resolutely as I had signed a few minutes before the document granting me a dispensation from my religious vows, I crossed out with an angry definitive slash the life I'd lived there, as if it belonged to somebody else. I crossed out, too, the nuns who remained, together with all the ideals and associations connected with that eternity of dissonance and self-desertion. Closing that door marked the official start of my second life, and all the fear and panic of beginning a new life flooded over me. I'd like to remember my step as light and airy when I headed to the waiting car. But I felt no sense of joy or of freedom. Only a heaviness. A terrible heaviness.

I'd turned eighteen in that place. From a strong Irish Catholic family, shy, naive, and untried, I had dutifully "followed my vocation"—the call from God, eagerly exchanging my "Rita" for the romanticized, detached "Sister Mary Sharon." When I left the order, I'd known sister Mary Sharon longer than I had known Rita. In fact, Rita was nowhere to be found that leaving day. My adult identity fell away when I stripped myself of that familiar habit. No one was inside. "Who can I be," I'd ask myself, "if I'm not a nun—not a teacher?" Neuter: certainly not a woman. Having revoked my vows, no longer a good person. Who then?

For many long months I was unable to answer that haunting question, struggling as I was to survive in an alien world. My growth had been stunted in many ways during those years; the day I left the order I was instantaneously whisked back in time—a thirty-six-year-old woman just turned seven-teen. Never had I felt so painfully self-conscious, never so ugly, so scared, confused, and dependent—so totally inade-quate to meet the world.

Straddling two worlds, I didn't know who I was, what I could do, what any options were. After an eternity of acting and thinking like someone I was not (even believing at most levels that I *was* that shadowy someone), I knew no way of unearthing the real essence within. That new Rita was a mysterious, elusive creature, one I had never met before.

How could that nun-shadow—a shadow that for eighteen years had clung closely to the walls, moving only when directed by the authorities in her order, changing shape, alter-nately magnified or diminished, as the light allowed—be transformed into person-substance?

What compounded the tortuous struggle to infuse sub-stance into shadow was that now "Rita" refused to allow any part of "Sister Mary Sharon" to re-enter her new life. "Rita" was embarrassed about that convent life, that "spiritual life" —angry with it. With its guilt and self-betrayal and free-floating fears, it was excess baggage. So I buried it.

Over the following years a recurrent dream plagued me. Still in the order, fully habited and veiled, blindfolded, I would be lying in a narrow white metal dormitory bed with huge concrete blocks placed all over the top of my body, my arms and legs strapped to the metal slats below. Nobody remembered I was in that dark, closed room. Time and again I'd awaken with a jolt, sweating and shivering, relieved to discover that I was only dreaming, was no longer a nun. Yet I was somehow still bound; for the immobilized, helpless, alien-ated mood stretched into my days. What still had a hold on me? How could I loose myself from that?

I moved from Illinois to Colorado, hoping that a change of locale and the mountain air would grant me a freedom I had not known. In Colorado I avoided anything smacking of reli-gion. I forgot about the order, convincing myself I was no longer affected by that unlived life there. One piece of con-vent identity I retained was my need to be perfect in what-ever I did. Driven to achieve, I became successful—

professionally, socially, economically—in every way possible. At least that's what it looked like from the outside. But inside, in spite of "having it made," in spite of traveling extensively and long vacations, I grew increasingly restless, dissatisfied during those six years. Something was missing.

At the age of forty-three, the possibility of lung cancer reawakened my habit of soul-searching. In the weeks of testing and overwhelming anxiety before the operation, something inside me changed. After the benign tumor reprieve, I turned my life around, not knowing *toward* what destination. I knew only that it was *from* the parameters I'd allowed to define and confine me: role, status, money, having to have the answers, having to be perfect. I resigned from my position with the mental health center with no clear notion of what I was going to do, or why I had made that choice. I knew only that it *was* important and that the time was right. In my journal at that time I quoted Goethe: "Whatever you can do or dream you can, begin it." I did not know what I could do, nor even what my dream was. Nevertheless, I did begin it.

That departure from old patterns, from established expectations, from having to have everything in place, became a quest to discover what was truly important to me. Once that was in clear focus, I trusted myself to have the integrity to live accordingly.

I set off vagabonding, leaving my home in Boulder, Colorado, and heading to the West Coast, with visions of catching a freighter to the Orient. My first stop was Salt Lake City. I had anticipated that my stay there would be brief and insignificant, but it became a time of tremendous meaning. I reclaimed an integral part of myself there—the religious, mystic, spiritual self that had in some way reigned supreme for eighteen years but that I had carefully and deliberately abandoned and denied upon leaving the convent.

It happened in the Mormon Tabernacle, where two friends had taken me to hear the *Messiah*. I cannot describe the process that began inside me, nor how long it lasted. I only know I crossed some unnamed line, felt myself suddenly open once again to spiritual levels of experiencing and knowing. Such a relief to be free again . . . tears streaming down

. . . allowing the spirit to encompass me, without all the resistance and negative overlays. Just reclaim, embrace, the spirit within. It had been there as a constant, of course, perhaps even growing more insistent as its years of denial continued.

I was deeply touched by each section of that oratorio: the voice crying in the wilderness . . . people walking in darkness seeing a great light . . . eyes of the blind opened, ears of the deaf unstopped, lame persons leaping . . . the tongue of the dumb singing. And each of these spoke of me—now opened, unstopped, leaping, singing. . . . "Behold, I tell you a mystery. . . . We shall be changed in a moment." I was changed. In that moment I understood that what I had actually meant to renounce years before was the *religiosity* of those years: the hypocritical, authoritarian, guilt-inducing, sanctimonious manipulation that bears no relationship to the spiritual. A realm of phoniness where so much was mouthed mechanically, preached and practiced and imposed under the guise of good—yet whose end result in so many cases is a devastating one: That is what I had rejected.

But much of what had been called evil and traitorous—the questioning, the renouncing of my vows—on that day became not only acceptable but holy. What had earlier looked like betrayal was, ultimately, only truth. I was following my own truth. And whatever God is—truth, wisdom, oneness, healing, trust, congruence, life, meaning, love—that is the faith I profess, the religious life I now choose to lead. It was, and is, impossible—indeed, immoral—to deny that.

Buoyed up by this new discovery, I headed on to the West Coast, where I gardened for my rent in Berkeley, struggled with a deep love, worked on the bottling crew in a winery, decided against hopping a freighter to the Far East in search of lost treasures. Periodically, during some twenty months of vagabonding, I crisscrossed the country, finding myself back in Illinois—a surprise even to myself. Roots country, yes, where I had grown up and where my mother and brothers still lived. Ten miles away loomed another magnet for me, the pull and push of which I did not fully acknowledge: the mother house. I carefully avoided that area of the city as if it were condemned; the times I did approach within even blocks of those areas, there welled up in me a feeling of nausea, a sense of my own powerlessness and absorbing fear. Tenaciously, something in that place held me in its grasp.

Gradually, near the end of my vagabonding, tiny flickers of light began to illuminate the darkness of those eighteen years. The first was provided by a workshop in which we participants were encouraged to look with new eyes at the background learning and context of significant people in our lives. Flash: the nuns from my order are mere human beings. And women—I couldn't believe they were women too. Even those who had been in positions of authority and with whom I had known such conflict? They, too, could be scared and confused, and very uncertain? Lonely at times, longing for the comfort of a human touch? Suddenly the bete noire was tamed, lost its hold over me. The order was no longer an all-powerful judge disposing of me at will. It could not swallow me, suck me in, consume or punish me. "It" was powerless. I held my power in my own hands.

I was reading Ursula LeGuin's *Earthsea* at the time, and she, too, spoke to me deeply in her compelling trilogy: As long as one flees the shadow, she is powerless against it. In the turning about and confronting it, calling it by name, embracing it, one finds one's own strength and becomes whole. It was not the Reverend Mother I'd been afraid of but, rather, something unnamed inside myself.

Shortly after that workshop came an invitation from a friend still in the order to visit at the mother house. It was not the first such invitation, but it was the first carrying the welcome of a new administration, and the first I'd felt inclined to accept. I toured the mother house with her, awkwardly meeting the nuns again, revisiting sites of my immense joys and deep hurts, remembering what I had tried to forget. It felt reminiscent of going through a loved one's personal effects after a death. But here I was—both the deceased and the survivor. At the time of that visit I was in no condition to decide what to keep and what to dispose of.

That same weekend, we went to see the movie *Julia*. The opening scene struck me forcefully, particularly in the context of the convent weekend: the solitary figure in the rowboat out on the lake, and Hellman's words, taken from the frontispiece of *Pentimento*: "The old conception, replaced by a later choice, is a way of seeing and then seeing again. . . . The pain has aged now and I want to see what was there for me once, what is there for me now." Ah yes, what was there for that painfully shy, confused, but intense and sensitive young nun—and what is there for her NOW! At that moment I determined to open myself to that gift.

I was at the time a doctoral candidate in psychology and was studying how the process of change comes about, especially for women in their mid-life years. One focus for the study was women who had left the religious orders. My doctoral advisor and colleagues challenged me: "What about interviewing those who *stayed*? Haven't there been great changes *inside* the religious orders as well?" "Yes, but. . ."

No excuses were sufficient, particularly to quiet my inner divining rod that discerns what is right for me at any given time. It hovered and trembled and finally dipped down: BACK TO CONVENT. "All right, all right!" I hollered. And gave in.

Yet how could I, still harboring much of the old anger and bitterness, return, if even for the three to four weeks that would be needed? In such a charged situation, how could I be objective, as befits a psychologist? In examining my own changes, I drew a blank when it came to the convent years. Getting in touch with that past was much of my reason for returning. But how would I know when I was ready?

And then came the dream! I was fully habited and veiled. Smiling broadly, laughing. And DANCING! My body was moving freely! Through psychedelic swirls. No longer strapped down. No longer in the closed darkness.

I wrote the president of the order asking to spend a few weeks back at the mother house. By return mail, without requesting an explanation, her unequivocal response was "Come!" That note of welcome brought with it relief, but unbearable anxiety as well. Relief, because the connection had been made and I was following my own sense of what I needed to do. But also anxiety: Could I survive the ghosts of my past? Would reviving them jeopardize the security of the now? With this ambivalence I crossed the threshold of the mother house once again, nearly ten years after I had angrily left it all behind.

I was totally unprepared for the enlightenment that came during those four weeks.

What struck me repeatedly was how the nuns who stayed and I were really on the same journey. Quotes from letters sent to members of the community by Sister Joan, president, revealed how many metaphors we held in common: ". . . the quest for understanding requires that we give up the search for certainty and go on a voyage of discovery . . . letting go of what we have for what we do not have . . . deeper solidarity . . . ministers of healing . . . moving toward new visions, open to where they may take us provided we are willing to move in darkness and uncertainty . . . hoping to see many hidden barriers released and lifted, wounds healed, harsh judgments let go of . . . growing awareness of what it means to be a woman . . . and freedom to be oneself." So, they, too, had leapt over many walls. How dramatically my perspective changed, from seeing them as so different from me, to seeing that we are all sisters, pilgrims traveling together. "Sister" now is much more than a title, a form of address, but speaks tenderly of the bond between us. For we are all sisters, we who were "Sisters" for eighteen years without touching upon so much of what sisterhood could really mean: the kind of love and support and trust and sharing at the core that began to manifest itself those weeks, reconnecting us gently but irrevocably to one another.

Gradually, following those weeks at the mother house, I could begin letting discounted parts of myself return. In the past, certain of my behaviors and attitudes had been referred to as "nunny," and I hated it. Even when a friend had insisted, "But Rita, it's your 'nunny' parts I like best!" I had still cringed. I felt it meant naive and innocent, Pollyannaish. "Nunny" also meant being reflective, often seeking solitude. It meant a heightened sensitivity and response to the needs of others, a way of being of service. For years I had withheld myself, had performed no such action that might give me away, make me feel "nunny" or be perceived as such, thus unknowingly crossing out another important part of myself. A graduate student in one of my classes helped me understand what I was about, without the "nunny" label: "Rita, I have felt more ministered to in your Tuesday night class than I ever have in the Sunday morning pew." At the last class session I received a card quoting Camus—"In the midst of winter I finally learned that there was in me an invincible summer"—with the added note, "Rita, this is what your class has meant to us." The light began to dawn. I welcomed my "nunny" self back: she who is not only quiet and meditative and introspective, but she who responds to what she cares about, offering an ambiance of love and tenderness that nourishes the depths.

The enlightenment embedded in my return to that formidable site also assumed another critical form. By reflecting in silence and through tears I began to understand the movement and the meaning of my own life process: what had brought me to the convent at that tender age, what had kept me there such long years, why I ultimately had had to leave it all behind me, and what forces had drawn me back for the reconciliation. It was a seeing with new eyes and fresh perspectives—a coming into a new kind of ownership of my life.

For me, the core issue in the journey revolves around sorting out beliefs about "the way the world has to be," as I had been taught to view it. Once I had started to question, my whole world began to topple. When that "crack in the cosmic egg" appeared—when I realized the extent to which I had been lying to myself, denying my own authority-—there was the unspoken but haunting and pivotal question: Can I trust myself to know what is real for me, what is true, what is right? Or do I have to continue to rely on someone else to determine that for me?

In my struggle with traditional religion, that was my ultimate dilemma: the discrepancy between the what-should-be of dogma and what I knew in my depths to be true, as my life experience revealed it. The mistake had lain in cutting myself off from my feelings, from my own experience, in attempting to build a spiritual life before I understood or appreciated my humanness. My "spiritual life" cannot exist in a vacuum, split off from the rest of me. The highest goal in the convent had been somehow to "rise above" the humanness, to "conquer" it. However, at the height of my "religious perfection" era, when I *had* risen above, I had felt curiously hollow and shallow; I had felt, ironically, that I had somehow lost my soul. Not in the sense of having committed some act that meant I was irrevocably damned but, rather, that the very depths of my being were closed off to me.

Was I "wrong" all those years? Were they a "waste"? Not at all. The key is not to see my earlier perceptions and choices as "wrong" but to be able to say of them, "It was important that I entered the convent and that I dedicated my life to the church for eighteen years. But it is also important that I left the order. Life changes. So do I. I love myself where I am, at each step of the way, for I understand how I got there. Each was right for its time. I can understand my decision at age seventeen. I understand—and honor what it was that I needed and what I wanted at that time—given my upbringing, my assumptions about the world, my resources." That may be the secret in dealing with past issues or commitments: not denying them their place in time, but transforming them into what makes sense for me now—values emerging from my own experience as opposed to "shoulds" imposed from without. Coming to terms with my past and understanding the assumptions in which I was immersed lay the ground for knowing my present, for understanding myself. Leaving the order did not constitute failure; nor would staying necessarily have meant success. Both were simply life experiences—choices, as are all of the paths along which we travel. The ultimate "failure" is not to allow myself to "know" with a deeper knowing, not to learn from experience, to fight the ebb and flow of my life.

It is this process of ebb and flow that best symbolizes the movement of my spirit-journey. Many months ago a force I called "my water-spirit surfacing" brought me to the Northwest. Now each day deep and mysterious waters graciously present to me the gifts of life itself—ever present though ever changing; gentle, wild, daily reminders, magnificent manifestations of the ebb and flow that makes all things one. I am learning not to separate my world into what is spiritual and what is not, for I perceive and embrace the sacredness in the stuff of even the most ordinary of happenings. I also know myself to be a part of a larger whole, part of a community; and that is much of what my life, my vision, is about: fostering relatedness that emerges from honoring the place where each person stands, from sharing vulnerabilities as well as strengths, from honoring the darkness as well as the light, from being open to lessons from all quarters.

A popular phrase used in the sixties and seventies to describe nuns who left the orders was that they had "lost their vocation." However, the concept of vocation is richer and fuller for me now, more encompassing than ever before. Rather than thinking of vocation as a calling from God, from outside myself, I experience it as a continuous and ever-changing process of moving to the quiver of my own inner divining rod, to the truth of my own inner wisdom. These quivers are marked by an everyday sense of reverence and mystery, of caring and wonder and exploration. They emanate from a life-affirming and joyful sense of my own spirit, or our interconnectedness to one another and to the universe itself.

And so it is.

MARY JO MEADOW

Mary Jo Meadow (Ph.D. in Clinical and Personality Psychology, University of Minnesota, 1976) is Professor of Psychology and Director of Religious Studies at Mankato State University (Minnesota), where she has taught for ten years.

She is first author of a textbook, *Psychology of Religion: Religion in Individual Lives,* and is author of *Other People,* a self-help book for women on dealing with problem relationships in the context of religious values. She is currently completing an annotated bibliography of works on women and religion and has several other books in progress.

Mary Jo has served as President of Division 36 (Psychologists Interested in Religious Issues) of the American Psychological Association and has held other offices in the APA. She was president of the Upper Midwest Region of the American Academy of Religion and served for two years as co-chair of the Women's Caucus of the AAR. She established the Women's Caucus in the Society for the Scientific Study of Religion and has served a variety of professional societies in various capacities.

Mary Jo has written many journal articles on spirituality, religion, and women's issues. Her special interests are women and religion, spirituality, and religious development.

Scenes from a God-Search

Nearing fifty years old, I look back on the child and the young woman I once was. For as long as I can remember, God and I have not been able to leave each other alone. And on that bitter cold winter day in St. Louis when my parents baptized me into the Catholic church, an enduring love-hate relationship with institutional religion was born.

I have searched with all my heart for God and have often not liked the God I found. I have bent myself in "sweet surrender" and have angrily challenged. I have felt pursued by the "Hound of Heaven" and have struggled in the grip of a god who "deserves" to be rejected. Through it all, one thing has become clear. I am so constructed—genes? early experiences? temperamental inclination?—that the search will not, cannot, be abandoned. Images of God may be found and rejected, replaced and revamped, sometimes absolutely lacking—but the search goes on.

Three stages seem to predominate. In the beginning, God was like a plume of smoke rising up and disappearing into the heavens. The smoke was sometimes white, sometimes black, sometimes threatening, sometimes comforting—but all I had to do was to turn and look, and it would be there. Then my column of smoke disappeared, and I felt as guilty as if I had killed God.

It took time and suffering for God to reappear—and in a different guise. God became like a protective cloud that was always over my head. I could not always "see" God, but God was always there in a manner both intimate and obscure. God was a felt presence in which I could "wrap up" myself, lose myself. God hovered over me unfailingly.

Then that presence abandoned me—or I it—and when I looked for my cloud, it was gone. I tried filling myself with many other things. None of them worked. Words begin to fail as I get too near the present time. How much easier to look back to the distant past and understand than to explain one's current situation! To the extent that God is present, God is now like a fog—a dense, impenetrable fog in which I cannot see anything clearly, in which I stumble around and stagger blindly, in which I am not even sure that that which is there is God.

Well—enough preamble. On with the play!

Act I:
The Column of Smoke

My childhood religiousness began intensely. My parents were nineteenth-century Catholics in many of their outlooks. Their faith pervaded our entire lives and was strongly dogmatic, legalistic, and miracle-seeking. What potential I had for a "religious temperament" was reinforced strongly in every possible way. I was captivated by an elusive goal of goodness and God-givenness early in life. I delighted in biographies of saints and other Christian writings. In my own small way, I tried to imitate the goodness that thrilled me

I am seven years old. I read a biography of St. Rose of Lima. Her willing endurance of suffering—even her seeking out ways to prefer herself least—greatly impress me. For weeks, I follow her practice of trying to choose the most stale pieces of bread for oneself.

I also became fearful of making a mistake or doing something that would put me beyond God's reach. The sisters at my Catholic school told horrible stories about usually good children who committed a mortal sin and then made a bad confession—only to be hit by a car and go to hell. I made the "Nine First Fridays"—several times, just to be sure—which guaranteed one a priest and a chance to confess before dying.

I am nine years old. I am curious about my body and explore "down there" to see what it is like. I know that I have

done something horribly wrong! But how can I tell the priest,
who was a man, about this? In the confessional, I tell him that
I was "nasty." He asks me what I mean. I can only repeat
that I was just nasty. He asks, "You mean like unkind to your
friends?" Relieved to have some way out of the situation, I
mutter, "Yes"—and live for some time in fear that I have
damned myself to hell, even long after I could rationally
argue against this conclusion.

I was an intellectually bright child whose capacity for logic
and scientific reasoning far outstripped her understanding of
mystery. I had many collisions with my parents over their
literal beliefs. I also challenged them about practices I considered superstitious. My parents discussed such issues as
whether or not you could eat canned beans on Friday if you
removed the pork piece before you heated them. By poring
over the Bible, they drew many conclusions about what must
happen before the end of the world. They invited people into
our home to lecture on miraculous occurrences, bearing with
them relics of saints, various healing oils and waters, roses
that never died from religious shrines, and similar valuables.

I am eleven years old. My parents have a woman lecture
in our home about a statue that sheds tears over human
sinfulness. She even carries a tear from the statue in a small
test tube. We take up a generous collection for her before she
leaves. I am quite upset. "But can't you see? All she has to
do is go to the sink and put in another drop of water whenever
the one in her tube dries up. A tear couldn't last all that time
even if a statue could cry!" My parents are unimpressed and
consider me sacrilegious.

My parents had high apocalyptic interest. They were especially fascinated by appearances of the Virgin Mary. Their
all-consuming interest in these led them to visit many religious shrines around the world. Excitement ran through our
house when a woman as near as Necedah, Wisconsin, reported
visions. Thus began a series of pilgrimages to Necedah. I
went only once.

I am thirteen years old. At Necedah, we must park our car
some distance away. We walk down the dusty farm road. All
around, people are selling cheap plastic rosaries, religious

medals and scapulars, and other goods for exorbitant prices.
I start feeling sick at the stomach. Surely this circus show has
nothing to do with real religion! We crowd around the fenced-
off farmyard and watch the seer come out and stretch up her
arms. Although we see nothing extraordinary, we are told
that a vision took place and that we are to pray the rosary for
sinners. The next time my parents go to Necedah, I stay home
in St. Louis at my grandmother's house to listen to the World
Series. My parents and siblings come back with stories about
how the sun spun around in heaven, came close to the earth,
and then moved back, all the while shooting off purple sparks.

By my mid-teens, I could no longer intellectually support
any of my parents' religiousness, although I kept up outer
practices to maintain peace. We made occasional forays into
arguments when I could not contain my exasperation with
some things, or when they got too fearful that I was damning
myself. A nun who occasionally visited the family warned
them that I was straight on the path to hell. I delighted in
being outrageous in front of this nun. Many of my concerns
were "prophetic" ones, however, in that they referred to
issues with which the Catholic church has since dealt.

I am fifteen years old. My father asks me to read an article
by Father Richard Ginder in Our Sunday Visitor. *Ginder*
says that he is grateful for the Index of Forbidden Books
because he would not want to read anything that might
endanger his faith. I am incensed. "But that is not intellectu-
ally honest," I yell at my father. He is equally incensed. "If
you valued the gift of faith given you as you ought to, you
would feel like Father does."

I became increasingly distraught over religious issues.
Clearly, my parents' faith would not work for me, but I knew
no other. Just as clearly, I yearned for the absolute, for
goodness, for the way. I came close to despairing of ever
finding what I sought. Ambivalently, I sent away for and
read reams of material about cloistered religious orders where
perhaps I might find God. At one point, I told my parents
that I was not interested in God if God is how they saw God, if
God is waiting to pounce on us when we try to be honest with
ourselves, if God wants such silly things from us. They told

me that I cannot decide how God is, but must learn to love God as He [*sic*] is. Yet I *am* interested in God—and am in great pain and confusion.

I am sixteen years old. It is Good Friday afternoon. I go into my bedroom and lock the door. "God, I do want to belong to you, but I am just so confused and I don't know how. I don't mind paying what it costs—I am willing to suffer with God, but things just don't feel right. And I don't know what to do or where to go or who to talk to." I stretch out my arms to the side in the form of a cross. I stand in the cross shape for a long time, until I am in such pain that agony is not too strong a word. I collapse on the bed and cry.

Shortly after I turned seventeen, I fell in love for the first time—with a young man who turned out to be a "professional" seducer. I sensed that "loss of my virginity"—a terrible catastrophe for a young Catholic girl—was creeping up on me and tried to talk to my mother. She could not handle it. The next day Gary "had his way" with me. As the summer crept on, I kept myself frantically busy and became more and more confused and self-hating. My mother grew increasingly fearful as I kept late hours and starting running with a crowd of which she did not approve. She talked me into meeting with a priest known for having a "way" with young people.

I am seventeen years old. I face the young priest with whom I am to talk and give him facts. Yes, I am going with people that the church would not approve of; the group includes gay men and "promiscuous" women. They drink a lot also. Yes, I have accepted a lot of their life-style. Yes, I know the church would consider me in mortal sin. For over two hours, I am stony-faced and matter-of-fact. Finally, I break and start to weep. The priest asks if he can hear my confession. I cry out that there is no way I can go through all of that again. He gently assures that that is not necessary and leads me to the confessional for absolution, asking only that I tell him I am sorry for all that I have already told him.

At the Jesuit college I attended, I found a Catholicism quite different from that of my parents. I entered a world of scholasticism and casuistry that did not offend my intelligence as had my parents' faith. I adopted a very intellectual, emotionally cold, and "respectable" religiousness. I was a top student, had a nearly full-time job, and led an active social life. Finally, I met a very important young man and we loved each other deeply. This was my first experience with a truly emotionally intimate relationship, in which anything and everything was safe to say and think. But one emotion connected with religion had not been stilled—guilt! And Frank and I found it impossible to keep our emotional closeness from wanting physical expression. We went to confession together, prayed together, attended church together—and then again "sinned" together.

I am nineteen years old. In desperation, Frank and I have decided to talk to a Jesuit priest whom we both like and trust. We explain our problem. He advises me to date other young men, and Frank to stay away from female company for a while. I am torn. I love Frank, but cannot tolerate the guilt. I send Frank away.

Two years later, ready to graduate from college, I chose to marry another young man who "respected" me enough not to touch me before marriage. The intensity of a relationship like Frank's had been too painful, and this man was a "good catch" by general standards—what did it matter that we had not established the emotional intimacy Frank and I had had?

I am twenty-one years old. I am married, pregnant, and in danger of miscarrying. My parents' God—the only God I have really known—rises up to threaten me. Perhaps I am being punished for my wickedness. "Oh, God, protect my baby. Don't let anything happen to my baby. I'll suffer to pay for my sins." I scrupulously deny myself what had become my main pleasures—candy, ice cream, cookies—to "buy" my baby's safety.

Act II:
The Overhanging Cloud

My child was born, and we moved to Minneapolis. I had two other children before I had been married three years. The oldest child was found to be brain-damaged. I was a "good"

Catholic woman who regularly attended church, did not use birth control, and accepted with stoic grace the blows I had been dealt. But a void in my life widened—and became a gaping hole. I could no longer believe! I blamed myself. My faith in God, my trust of God, was not deep enough. I was not truly given to God. My faith had always been lacking, from even my earliest years. Briefly, I dared get angry with God: "If you're up there, at least make it possible for me to believe in you, since I need to so much." But I backed off quickly, and asked again what flaw in myself made me unable to believe as others did, filled me with doubts and questions. None of my Jesuit training with all its rational argumentation and complicated reasoning succeeded in convincing me of the reality of the spiritual. The hell I was in became deeper and deeper. I thought of casting myself down before the priest, begging him to help me believe, but could not find the courage to do so.

I am twenty-four years old. My husband is reading the newspaper in the living room. The baby in the high chair is screaming. The two toddlers are underfoot in the kitchen, whining. A mess of dirty dishes is stacked up. Something snaps. I put down the baby food I am holding and walk through the living room to the bedroom. I lie down on the bed, promising myself to stare at the ceiling until I go mad, since anything is better than the life I am now living. Eventually, I fall asleep. When I wake the next morning, I am frightened. I push harder to keep going. I do not know how or when my husband finally realized the children were untended the night before. I do not ask him. He does not ask me anything about what happened.

I threw myself into trying to "find" faith again. I taught church school classes and tried to pray. I had another child. I dragged myself through each day and spoke to no one about my pain. At a retreat—a deadly experience for me—the priest humorously acknowledged losing his place in the rosary. I was tremendously impressed with his humble honesty, so proudly was I locked up in my own inability to admit to anyone else my desperate situation with its many felt personal inadequacies. I asked Father Pat for an appointment.

After one false start, in which I could not get myself to talk about what was going on with me, I finally leveled with him and it all came out: my religious past, the empty dryness in which I found myself, my absolute inability to really believe in God—even some of my anger over the unfairness of this when I was trying so hard to believe. When I finished, he told me that I misunderstood faith, that faith was not certainty about the reality of anything, that it could never be simply reasoning to convincing conclusions. He told me my problem was one of love—that I needed to want God badly enough to be willing to "gamble" without any certainty that I would succeed, to stake my entire life on a vision of faith in hope of finding God. I had never been exposed to such an understanding of the religious life, and it terrified me. I had to get away fast.

I am twenty-six years old. I drive—well over the speed limit—down one of the city's main streets until it dead-ends in the country. I sit in the car in the dusk of a late March evening and argue with God. I cry, I scream, I pound the car seat. "It isn't fair that I cannot have the consolation of knowing that it's true if I am supposed to live by it! I am trying so hard to believe—and all I want is to know that what I do isn't in vain. Dammit, all I want is some little sign so that I won't think it's all for nothing." Time passes, and my anger changes to fear and weariness. It is pitch dark outside. "How can I stand to live if God isn't true? God simply has to be true." I shiver in the grip of unbearable thoughts. It is getting very late. I am utterly spent, totally empty. "Okay, God, you win. If this is how it has to be, I'll do it. I want you enough to gamble with my life, so I'll try. I'll give it my all and won't ask for anything except to be sustained. Just keep me going, and let me try to be given to you."

So I went on with my life. I took care of my family and I did my volunteer work. I still could not "believe." However, a small nugget of serenity had replaced the totally dead space inside me. I found I had the energy to do my work, which had before left me utterly exhausted. I was patient, gentle, and more relaxed. I managed to forget about myself as I gave myself to others. I was totally open with Father Pat, now my confessor. I tried to see and serve God in everyone. Then, within a few weeks, I did "see" God.

It is a late spring afternoon. I stop by church to pray—a common custom for me now—on my way home. The intensity of my yearning for God, my longing to be totally given to God, is almost unbearable. Nonverbally, I make my constant offering with all of my being: "Please take me, conform me to your will, use me. I ask only to be sustained." Suddenly, "I" disappear—so do the church, time, everything but God. In an unfathomable darkness, I "see" God; in a silent vacuum, I "hear" God; in a spaceless, timeless, egoless void, I am "in" God. Clock-time does not exist, so I do not know how "long" it lasts; it is an instant of eternity. Finally, slowly, I "come to." It is totally dark outside, and my entire body feels strained and stiff. But I am still "wrapped" in God; I am surrounded by, blanketed in, a globe of warmth, light, and indescribable peace. And I "believe." I believe with a certainty more intense than any other certainty I have ever known in my life.

Thus began several years in which daily I was "lost" to God for long periods. Throughout each day, God's presence was a "tangible" reality for me. People began to come to me. First, the teenagers from my church school classes, then the adults sent me by the priests as problems they could not handle. I talked with the angry, the depressed, the confused, the suicidal, the "sinners." To each of them, something seemed to flow through me as a channel from God; they went away helped, and eventually healed. I was accessible to anyone any hour of the day or night. I had another child. I burned myself out as a candle on the altar before God.

And one priest came to me. He was about my age, being prepared for the missions. He needed a confidante. We talked, we shared. Our spiritual friendship blossomed into emotional intimacy. We found hours each week to spend together. Finally, the love was declared by both of us—but he was a Catholic priest and I a married Catholic woman. We did not touch each other until that fateful evening when we had just learned he was finally to go to the missions. The irresistible impulse, the embrace, the deep kiss—and then simultaneously we both pushed the other away horrified. He begged me to help him, said that if he ever abandoned his vows it would be for someone like me.

I am twenty-eight years old. In turmoil, I go the next morning to one of my favorite churches—the one where each morning I attend a very early Mass. I know that I can seduce Finn from the priesthood if I wish. Everything in me cries out for that close relationship and engages everything in me that also wants to belong to God alone. A titanic struggle wages for hours, as I writhe and groan in despair. I am crucified and torn widely in opposite directions. The tension is unbearable, yet continues—and I continue to bear it. Finally, I droop, I collapse in surrender of my bleeding heart to God. I am instantly filled with a surging, triumphant energy—as if all the hosts of heaven were pouring forth their most glorious alleluias. God is vividly present—not as in the silent darkness of my prayer—but permeating everything, in the midst of the busy traffic on the street, the bright sunshine of the summer day, the blaring stereo my husband is playing, the noisy play of the children. All of my daily life is fully and vividly present—and God is penetrating, radiating from, upholding, encompassing it all. The full intensity of this lasts for days.

Encouraged by another priest, I returned to graduate school the following year. I felt I needed to learn how to do the counseling I was doing, and wanted to study religion. I became very busy with my studies and had another baby the first year. The next year I started working as a graduate student instructor. Some problems with Catholicism were increasingly troubling me. A series of crises of conscience began. I did not feel right sending my children to a Catholic school whose atmosphere (nineteenth-century Irish Catholicism) repelled me, and my first act of disobedience was to send them to public school. Ritual began to look like a "processing through" of people—with care to get the 9:00 bunch out in time so the parking lot would be ready for the 10:30 bunch. I deplored bishops' living in palaces with the poor all around them, and some U.S. clergy encouragement of the war in Southeast Asia. Birth control was another big issue. It seemed to me that, if one judged that having more children was not appropriate, one should take adequate means to prevent it, without seriously distorting the marital relationship. Agonizing at every step of the way, I was slowly working myself away from Catholicism.

I am thirty-one years old. I tell my Catholic gynecologist that I want a prescription for the pill. He asks me if I have my confessor's permission. Angrily, I cry out, "If it is wrong, no one can give me permission. If it is right, I don't need permission." I make an appointment with a friend's gynecologist. The secretary hands me a form to fill out as a new patient. When I come to the place labeled "Religion," I realize that nothing I can fill in will feel accurate. I leave it blank.

I continued my practice of interior prayer, but increasingly found myself in disquieting places with it. Sometimes I felt that I was visiting hell rather than heaven as I had been previously. My spiritual director left the Catholic church shortly after I did, and I had no one to turn to for guidance. My increasing psychological sophistication was also making me wary. I knew that many different things could trigger experiences similar to mine. Was I creating a "perfect relationship" with God to compensate for the lack of a human relationship? Was I immersing myself in some kind of primitive undifferentiated state of consciousness? Was I "tricking" myself in a dangerous or frivolous way? I began asking questions and wanting answers in place of an unself-conscious surrender to God.

Act III:
The Impenetrable Fog

I filled my life with studies, teaching, family life, and research. My husband and I adopted two children of Korean mothers and U.S. servicemen fathers. Life got busier and busier. I almost completely abandoned prayer, yet often felt a nostalgic tug for it. When I tried to pray, the magic no longer occurred; I was sitting in the middle of a desert. I had no way of conceiving of God that "worked." I saw myself as much more impatient, jealous, and self-centered than I had been in the years of the God-cloud. I began to thirst again for the simplicity and purity of that time.

I am thirty-four years old. Some students convince me to hear a yoga teacher speak. I come somewhat reluctantly, yet in a mood of clutching at straws. As he speaks, I hear less what he is saying than I see the beauty of God-givenness shining out of him in every word he utters. Deep inside, something speaks in me and says that he can teach me much. After his talk, I go up to him and tell him I need spiritual guidance. He looks at me intensely, smiles, and says, "Yes, of course." He invites me to a small meditation group and becomes my teacher.

Again, I had a fleeting experience of the timeless-spaceless void from which I emerged bathed in the serenity of a deep peace. I adopted some yogic practices, and was initiated by the teacher. But this time surrender was not easily accomplished. I was full of doubts about what I was doing, and I seemed entrenched in petty selfishness, stubbornness, and caution. Spiritual sweetness was not to be mine. I dreamed of being a pilgrim walking across rocky hills in the heat of noon —barefoot, dressed in a gray robe, carrying a staff. Half a step behind me walked a tall, silent, hooded monk—silently goading me onward. I decided that mine was now the hard path; since I had left Paradise, I must drink the cup of bitterness.

I tried to persevere. I begged for the grace of surrender, I meditated, I joined a circle of other seekers with whom I shared my successes and failures, and I tried various churches —chiefly Quaker and Unitarian-Universalist. I also started my internship in clinical psychology. My marriage worsened. My husband resented my absences from the home and became psychologically abusive. I cowered in fear before him because I knew that he was correct in realizing that I was not really bonded to him and had never been. I felt guilty. Deciding to stay with the marriage did not feel right since everyone was kept churned up by it. Leaving him did not feel right because I had made a commitment to him.

I am thirty-six years old. I consult my yoga master, Panditji, afraid that he will tell me I am in the wrong and to try to give myself more to my husband (as a priest had advised me some years before). I tell him the situation and say that I feel I am at a fork in the road, and it does not feel right to take either side of it. He says gently, "Then sit in the crossroads and learn patience. When it is right for you to act, you will know it."

I sat for several years on this dilemma. My husband became physically abusive and began having affairs. I completed my internship and worked as a psychology instructor and researcher. Several of my children came to me begging me to get a divorce so they could live in peace. Finally, at age thirty-eight, I began the divorce process. Shortly after our separation, my husband had a near-fatal accident which left him an invalid for almost a year. I took him back to try again and nursed him until he could care for himself. Soon things were as bad as ever. A year and a half after our previous separation, we again split.

At a conference, I met another psychologist with whom I had much in common. A spiritual friendship developed between us and flourished in letters over the winter. It deepened into emotional closeness also. In the years of my relationship with Dick, he did much to reconcile me with Christianity. However, he was very conflicted over his intimacy with me while he was still legally tied to a woman with whom he had a marriage in name only. When problems developed in our relationship, they were complicated immensely by his guilt.

I am forty-two years old. Dick and I are attending a professional meeting. He calls his son to wish him Happy Birthday, and also speaks to his estranged wife. He returns from the phone shaken. Later, in my hotel room, a pain begins deep within me, for I finally realize that this relationship will never fully flower. I cry uncontrollably over the loss I am suffering. I look ahead to years of aching aloneness, to never having the solace of a fully intimate relationship. I must face this unfolding vision, must not retreat from it, but must break my way through it. The bleakness deepens. I curl up on the bed into a fetal position, protecting myself as much as I can. My body is shaking and my teeth are chattering. I keep seeing bleak and empty aloneness—as far as I can see. Only the ability to surrender it all to God, to the What-Is, offers any hope. But I cannot do that. I wrestle with myself —let go of it; give it up freely. I reply—no, I need it, I cannot go on without any partner but God. I throw myself onto the floor, prostrate, face down. An attitude of surrender. Give it up, give it up freely. I am crying again, but more softly. I pull myself into a bent-over kneeling position. It is given. Serenity comes. No ecstasy, no exaltation, just serenity. I have surrendered relationship dependence.

In the meantime, I had become successful. I was publishing regularly and earning some professional honors. My children had been growing up, and my household becoming smaller. My spiritual aridity continued. Attempts at regular prayer or meditation were painfully empty, yet I found myself reverting to thoughts of God, the Absolute, the Tao, the Ultimate—I was no longer sure how I might conceive of it —whenever my mind was not otherwise occupied. I occasionally consulted Panditji, and I tried worshiping with Baptists, Methodists, and Catholics. I could worship with—feel "at home" with—just about any group temporarily, but had no "home" of my own.

A colleague suggested that LSD taken in a spiritual setting might open up whatever was blocked. I put him off for some time but finally decided to try it. To find a place where I would feel no fear of legal reprisal required considerable travel, but I undertook it happily. In the small circle of other seekers, I prayed fiercely that my ingestion of this substance be only for the purpose of bringing me closer to God: "Thy will be done." When everyone else started feeling the affects, nothing happened for me. I dropped a second tab. Still nothing. I felt painfully alone as the others later shared their experiences.

I am nearly forty-four years old. I sit on the airplane returning home. The "bruise" that is the sunset—with its layers of hot pink, lavender, greenish purple, gold, orange, and peach, streaked through with greying clouds—reminds me, as it seldom fails to, of the bruises that closing-in darkness (be it emotional, spiritual, or intellectual) regularly inflicts upon the human spirit. Hot, painful tears roll down my cheeks as I am touched in ways the drug seemed unable to touch me—as I have been so many times before touched by sun, moon, ocean, mountain, rainstorm. I remember that Panditji once told me that the pain that a crushed flower or rotted piece of wood causes me is a sign of attachment. Inside the terminal, a blind man tapping by with his cane poignantly reminds me of the painful analogy the blind manifest.

Several years passed and my mother lay dying—my mother who so often had told me that she was praying for me to return to the church. I had been considering this for three years, speaking of it only to my sister. I had not wanted to raise my mother's hopes—only possibly to dash them again. Besides, my return would not mean what she would take it to mean. I had found even more things that distressed me greatly about the Catholic church; its incredible sexism, its patriarchal attitudes, its male symbolism and language, its totalitarian organization, its archaic and personalistic morality (since made worse by almost everything Pope John Paul II says, and better by the U.S. bishops' pastoral teachings on peace and the economy)—to mention a few. A return would be as a critic and reformer, offering this uncomfortable service in exchange for what I hoped to get. What did I want? Although Panditji had been immensely helpful to me and I still continued many yogic practices, I wanted also a tradition of spiritual guidance that resonated more fully with my early emotional conditioning. I hoped to find people with whom I could be in community—although I realized most would not be sensitive to the issues that concerned me. I felt that a solitary road in its demanding no flexibility or compliance had become a hindrance for me. And so my mother died without my talking to her about it.

I am forty-six years old. My mother has been dead a little over a month, and I am on retreat. I feel now is the time to act. One mother has gone from me, and I again embrace another I have so long ago rejected. No bells, no cymbals, no fanfare. I make my confession (as is proper and required) and take the Eucharist (which I had already taken over the years as I saw fit, anyway). I shall try to work within the community. I shall seek a spiritual guide within the tradition. I am at peace with it.

Kevin, a Carmelite priest I had known for some years, agreed to be my spiritual director. I began attending Mass with some regularity—but not with the scrupulosity that would force me to go regardless of circumstances. I again began to meditate and pray regularly, even in the emptiness and darkness. I criticized sexist language and practices, I complained about misplaced moral emphases. The church bond has not been a completely comfortable one. At times I have been convinced it could not last. So far I have kept wandering back.

I have found a new movement within the church—Womanchurch—and become active in developing it. I have also found a community of people in which many, like me, straddle more than one spiritual tradition. We are trying to arrange a life of study and practice together. We want to develop a spirituality that is informed in many traditions and uses what arises from the call of our lives in the contemporary world. I shall almost surely eventually be with these people. I have long believed that my day for a yogic "retreat to the forest," a pulling back from the active and busy professional life in which I am now involved, would come.

I am forty-eight years old. I am on retreat with "my" community—a week of near-silence in a beautiful mountain setting. I sit in appreciation of the haze-veiled mountains. I am steeped in stillness and silence. I walk slowly, in measured steps, to the little chapel at this Catholic retreat house. The tabernacle light—signaling the presence of the consecrated eucharistic host—is a warm, red glow in the dark, little room. I close my eyes and relax into my meditation—a silent, empty, contentless "presence" to the Ultimate. As I later emerge from it, I open my eyes to the tabernacle light's

glow. Suddenly, the eucharistic host "leaps" from the taber-
nacle into my throat to "become" its chakra (one of the seven
major centers of spiritual energy, according to yoga), which
stands for surrendered acceptance of divine grace. The sym-
bols from my two traditions merge into one sign of receptivity
and trust.

Postscript

Thus ends the script. And where am I now? Quite far from
the child and adolescent me with her somewhat fearsome, but
understandable God. Again much different from the ardent
young mystic who next poured herself out in self-abandoning
service to God and others.

I am successful by anyone's standards. I have raised eight
children. I have published three books and have others in
press, in progress, and in mind. I hold a responsible university position and enjoy most of my work. I have good friends
and some spiritual companions. I serve on journal editorial
boards, have programmed major conferences, and held office
in professional societies. I also do psychotherapy and spiritual guidance. I give time, energy, and money to programs
for the community and to various social concerns. I have
concluded that my life now does not call for a committed
relationship to one other person. I am healthy, energetic, and
usually on the sunny side of mood. But all this is not enough.
That tantalizing, enigmatic relationship with God always
beckons.

I know a lot less than I did before. I have no idea of what
God really is except that God is other than anything I have
ever conceived God to be. I guess I could define God as that
unknown Ultimate that I seek. I realize that moral decision-
making is fraught with ambiguity and that most debated
issues have far more complexity than one would generally
guess. Things are at one and the same time immensely more
complicated than before and yet utterly simple. I have no
beliefs, in that there is nothing concerning metaphysical reality about which I have a firm sense of sureness.

I tend to see religious institutions as necessary evils. They can nurture an infant faith but also bind the spirit to constraints that do not fit, that keep one from God. For those who can accept uncritically, they offer a community that supports beliefs and provides encouragement in the hopes offered for the future. And I *do* believe that community is important—and have continually faced the problem of finding an adequate community for the quirks and twists of my own path.

I work within the metaphors of Hindu yoga and Catholic Christianity—and they are simply that: metaphors—ways we grasp at and try to encompass some sense of the spiritual (if there be such outside our own creations). I am reconciled to the loss of the "magic" of my former prayer. So also have I accepted that I need not and probably will not ever feel certainty about the meaningfulness of the endeavor—the God-search—that consumes my life. I seldom envy any more the simple faith of those more confident and less complicated than myself.

I face daily my failures in trying to live according to those values that I want to actualize in my life, that would define a correct stance before God whom I seek. But I am no longer surprised by this display of human limitation. And so I go on seeking a spiritual community, doing my work, loving the adults my children have become, thinking and writing, enjoying mutual care and support with my friends—and waiting, always waiting for God.